A Case Book on the Law of Evidence

NIKI TOBI,
LL. M. (Lagos); Ph.D. (Nigeria), CON;
JUSTICE, COURT OF APPEAL
Professor of Law, Formerly Dean and Deputy vice Chancellar,
University of Maiduguri, Nigeria

FOURTH DIMENSION PUBLISHING CO.

First Published 2002 by
FOURTH DIMENSION PUBLISHING CO., LTD.
16 Fifth Ave, City Layout
P.M.B. 01164
Enugu, Nigeria

ISBN 978-156-4628

Photoset in Nigeria by
Fourth Dimension Publishers, Enugu

CONTENTS

PREFACE

Work on this Book commenced way back in 1983 at the University of Maiduguri. After teaching Course Number LW. 301 (The Law of Evidence) to third year undergraduate classes for five years running, I realised the need to produce this Book to add to the existing literature on this very important area of our adjectival law. I collected some materials between 1983 and 1984 but could not make any substantial progress because of my other writing commitments and general University administration. I therefore had to shelve the idea for a future date. I resuscitated the idea in 1985 when I joined the Bench and struggled to complete the manuscript.

The main idea behind the publication of *A Case Book on the Law of Evidence* is to make it a companion to the leading undergraduate textbook on the subject - Dr. T. Akinola Aguda's, *The Law of Evidence in Nigeria* (1974). Bearing this in mind, I have followed the arrangement adopted by Dr. Aguda in his Book. I did not make any remarkable departures from the arrangement in *The Law of Evidence in Nigeria.*, as it relates to the sub-headings. While *A Case Book on the Law of Evidence* could be used on its own, it will certainly make more impact, if it is used along with its older companion. Each chapter commences with a summary of the provisions of the Evidence Act.

I have virtually reported Nigerian cases as opposed to cases from foreign jurisdictions. This is an intentional act for which I have no apologies. While the point is conceded that there are still very useful English and other foreign decisions illustrating the different sections of our Evidence Act, I do not believe that these are substitutes, particularly when considering the now reasonably established principles of *stare decisis* in our jurisprudence. I am a very strong advocate of the complete indigenisation of our legal system (if I may call it so) and the choice of the case law in this Book merely reflects my pet ideas over the years. I felt that I should try as much as possible to emphasise Nigerian decisions and de-emphasise foreign decisions. While this may not be very successful in some other areas of law where Nigerian case law has not fully grown, it is correct to say that Nigerian decisions proliferate in the Law of Evidence. It will be stupid to claim that I have dealt with all the Nigerian cases on the subject. That is not possible in the light of the production cost of

Books. It is also as a result of that consideration that I have, in a number of cases, given only the brief principles. It is to save cost.

While the main focus of the Book is the undergraduate law student and related disciplines, I believe that the young legal practitioner who is not able to buy the required Books for legal practice will find it useful. I also have the feeling that the generality of the Bench and the Bar will also find the Book handy during the moments of their crowded search for basic authorities on a specific aspect of the law.

My thanks go to Mr. Ben Joseph, a Solicitor and Advocate, who works at the University of Port Harcourt, for arranging to type the manuscript within a very short period. I should also thank Mrs T. O Nwankwo, my colleague in the professer, for finding time of proof reading the manuscript. She did a pleasant job. Finally, I express my gratitude to the publishers for their industry.

Niki Tobi
Justice's Chambers
Court of Appeal, Enugu.

Chapter 1

INTRODUCTION

This work will not deal with a detailed examination of the historical development of the Law of Evidence in Nigeria since that exercise has been adequately undertaken by previous writers on the subject. It is now a notorious fact that the Nigerian Law of Evidence, like most laws of the country, originated from the English Common Law. The first legislation on the subject of Evidence was in 1943. It was known as the Evidence Ordinance No. 27 of 1943. It came into operation in 1945. See *Notice No. 618 in Gazette No. 33 of 1945*. It was based largely on *Stephen's Digest of the Law of Evidence* (12th edition).

Following the attainment of independence in 1960, the Evidence Ordinance was renamed the Evidence Act. Since the Law of Evidence was in the Concurrent Legislative List under the 1960 and 1963 Constitutions, the Regional Governments at the material time also enacted their laws on the subject. These laws closely followed the Federal Act with little or no material changes. This remained the position until the enactment of the 1979 Constitution of the Federation which by Item 23, Part 1 of the Second Schedule to the Constitution, placed Evidence in the Exclusive Legislative List. The Constitution of the Federal Republic of Nigeria, 1989 which did not see the light of day, maintained the same position. See Item 22, Part 1 of the Second Schedule to the Constitution. The 1999 Constitution also places evidence in the Exclusive Legislative List See Item 23, Part 1 of the Second Schedule. This position has made the former regional laws of Evidence moribund, following the doctrine of covering the field. See generally *The Military Governor Ondo State and Another v. Adewunmi* [1988] 3 N.W.L.R. (Pt. 82) 280.

Accordingly, the country now has a single Law of Evidence and not a proliferation of Laws of Evidence by way of enactments as was the position before 1979. The operative law in all the courts is the Evidence Act, Cap. 112, Laws of the Federation of Nigeria 1990 as amended from time to time. In a country operating a uniform police system which use the Evidence Act in its prosecution process, and in a country with a legal system which is not overtly divergent in its aggregate content, the inclusion of Evidence in the Exclusive Legislative List is a most welcome innovation.

As an introduction we will examine in this chapter the Evidence Act as a source of the Nigerian Law of Evidence, the impact of constitutional provisions on the Act and the reception of trial evidence by trial court.

The Evidence Act as source of Nigerian Law of Evidence

Jimo Amoo and Others v. The Queen (1959) 4 F.S.C. 113: (1959) W.R.N.L.R. 199.

The trial court allowed a witness's memory to be refreshed by the reading to him of his deposition at the preliminary investigation, that deposition having been taken some four months after the incidents to which the witness deposed.

HELD

That the deposition could not be brought within section 215 (1) of the Evidence Act.

Referring to section 215(1), Mbanefo, F.J. (as he then was) said at pages 115 to 116:

This provision is clearly in line with the principle enunciated above by Phipson. Where there is conflict between the provisions of the Evidence Ordinance and decision of a Court of England, the courts in this country would be bound to follow the Evidence Ordinance. It may however, be mentioned that in the report of the case of R. *v. Williams 6. Cox's Criminal Cases 343, referred to above, it is not stated how much time between the event about which the witness was speaking and the taking of the deposition. The deposition in that case might very well have been within the rule of contemporaneousness. In this country it must be shown that the statement comes within the provisions of section 215 of the Evidence Ordinance before the witness could be allowed to look at the document to refresh his memory. In this case the deposition was taken five weeks after the event in question and the Assistant Director of Public Prosecutions, Western Region, who appeared before us, conceded that the deposition could not be brought within section 215 of the Evidence Ordinance. We, therefore, agree with appellant's Counsel that the judge acted in error in allowing the 1st prosecution witness's deposition before the Magistrate to be read to him at the trial to refresh his memory.*

R .v. John Agaragariga Itule
[1961] All N.L.R. 462

Brett, Acting C.J.F. (as he then was) delivering the judgment of the Court said at pages 465 to 466:

> *As to whether the part of a confession which tilts in an accused person's favour is evidence of the facts alleged, the position at common law is that 'it is a general rule that the whole of the account which a party gives of a transaction must be taken together; and his admission of a fact disadvantageous to himself shall not be received, without receiving at the same time his contemporaneous assertion of a fact favourable to him, not merely as evidence that made such an assertion, but admissible evidence of the matter thus alleged by him in his discharge'. See* Archbold, *34th edition, paragraph 1127. The matter is not dealt with expressly in sections 27 to 32 of the Evidence Ordinance, and the common law rule therefore applies by virtue of section 5(a)... In applying the common law rule as to confessions we are not holding that every statement admitted under this convention is evidence of the facts contained in it, and our decision in this case only applies to statements which would be admissible at common law as confessions.*

NOTE

Aguda, commenting on the ambit of section 5(a), particularly in the context of the case, correctly stated at page 6 that:

> *No evidence can now be excluded under the common law. This section is not meant to allow the exclusion of evidence otherwise than under the Act, and the rules of the common law governing the exclusion of evidence are no longer applicable here except those that have been incorporated into the Act.*

Admissibility of evidence which is based on relevancy is determined by the provisions of the Evidence Act and section 5(a) is not a reservoir for the determination of admissible or inadmissible evidence by recourse to the English common law. After all, "there is no provision in the Act which allows any evidence to be rejected as inadmissible save as provided in the Act itself." *See R. v. Agwuna* (1949) 12 W.A.C.A. 456 at 458. See also *Onyeanwusi v. Okpukpara* (1953) 14 W.A.C.A. 311.

Right to call and examine witnesses

Danjuma Dan Buhari Rimin Auzinawa v.
Kano Native Authority
(1956) 1 F.S.C. 27.

The appellant was convicted of murder in the Emir of Kano's Court. The main ground of appeal was that the appellant was not given the opportunity to call witnesses to establish his defence of an alibi.

HELD

In cases such as this, an accused should always be asked if he has witnesses.

"In cases such as this the accused should always be asked if he has any witnesses he wishes to call in support of his defence, and it is obviously desirable that care should be taken by the trial court to ensure that the question and answer are recorded - Per Foster Sutton, F.C.J. at page 28.

Malam Sadau of Kunya v. Abudul Kadir of Fagge
(1956) 1 F.S.C. 39.

Judgment was given against the appellant in a civil claim in Chief Alkali's Court at Kano. At the trial the appellant admitted signing a document which the plaintiff/respondent said he had in his possession to support his claim, but stated that he was forced to do so, and he gave the names of his witnesses who could bear out his allegation. The court did not allow the appellant to call his witnesses, but entered judgment against him.

HELD

It is a fundamental principle of natural justice that a defendant and his witnesses should be heard before the case against him is determined and that, the Chief Alkali's Court erred in not allowing the appellant to call his witnesses.

In the same way, the Chief Alkali was wrong in assuming that the evidence of the appellant's witnesses, whom he had not heard, would be of no value to the appellant. How could he prejudge the value of the evidence of the witnesses when he had neither seen nor heard them? It is a fundamental principle of the administration of natural justice that a defendant and his witnesses should be heard before the case against him is determined, and it is, in my view, a denial of justice to refuse to hear a defendant's witnesses - Per Jibowu, F.J. at page 41.

Kano Native Authority v. Raphael N. Obiora
(1959) 4 F.S.C. 226.

The respondent was convicted in the Grade 'A' Native Court of the Emir of Kano for stealing. The main complaint on appeal was that the respondent was not given an opportunity to put forward his defence or call witnesses.

HELD

1) Natural justice requires that an accused person must be given the opportunity to put forward his defence fully and freely, and to ask the court to hear any witnesses that might help him.
2) As a rule, where it is shown that the accused was duly allowed to state his defence, and that the Native Court in fact heard the evidence of any witnesses who might be able to assist the court in arriving at the truth, and of whose existence it knew or should have known, whether from information supplied by the accused or otherwise, there are no grounds for holding that there has been a denial of natural justice.

Namo Tsaku and Others v. The State [1986] 1 N.W.L.R. (Pt. 17) 516.

The appellants were convicted of various offences by the High Court of Plateau State, sitting at Lafia. During the trial, counsel for the appellants sought to recall two prosecution witnesses for further cross-examination, but the court refused on the ground that there was no useful purpose for the further cross-examination and that the appellant's counsel was merely trying to prolong the trial unnecessarily.

HELD

1) An accused person can, when making his defence, call as his own witness, a witness who had already testified for the prosecution.
2) Every person who is tried for a criminal offence must be given full opportunity to present his case and to call witnesses in his defence. Any failure on the part of a trial court to give an accused person that full opportunity is a breach of natural justice.
3) The rights of persons accused of criminal offences are protected by the Constitution. If full opportunity is not given to call defence witnesses and there is reason to suppose that a defence witness would have given material evidence for the defence, there is a failure of justice. But there is no failure of justice if there is no reason to suppose that the defence witness could have given material evidence for the defence.

NOTE

The Court of Appeal cited with approval the decision of Bate, S.P.J. in *M. Ngubolo v. The State* 1973 N.N.L.R. 20 at 22 where the learned trial Judge called in aid the decision of the Federal Supreme Court in *Kano N.A.v. Raphael Obiora, supra.* In *Fagge* the Federal Supreme Court held that the Chief Alkali was wrong in assuming that a piece of evidence he was yet to hear would be of no value. But in this case, the Court of Appeal, relying on *Ngubolo* seems to hold the contrary view. It is the view of the

Court of Appeal that there is no failure of justice if there is no reason to suppose that the defence witness could have given material evidence for the defence. It is submitted that in a criminal matter, the accused should be given all the opportunity to defend himself. Accordingly, it should not lie in the mouth of the trial court to come to the conclusion that the witness the accused person intends to call will be of no use to his case.

See further *Jalo Guri and Another v. Hadeija Native Authority* (1959) 4 F.S.C.44; *Otufade and Others v. The State* [1968] N.M.L.R. 261; *Yanor and Another v. The State* [1965] 1 All N.L.R. 193. It is important to note also that most of the above cases were decided on the provisions of the 1963 Constitution and section 33(6) (d) of the 1979 Constitution which are similar to section 36(6) (d) of the 1999 Constitution. The subsection provides:

> *Every person who is charged with a criminal offence shall be entitled to examine in person or by his legal practitioner the witnesses called by the prosecution before any court and to obtain the attendance and carry out the examination of witnesses to testify on his behalf before the court on the same conditions as those applying to the witnesses called by the prosecution.*

Interpretation of Evidence of Witnesses

Buraima Ajayi and Others v. Zaria Native Authority 1964 N.N.L.R. 61

The proceedings in the Native Court were in Hausa, which the appellants neither spoke nor understood. They were Yoruba speakers by birth and understood English, but not perfectly. The proceedings were interpreted by five different interpreters at successive stages. Two interpreted into English and one into Yoruba. It did not appear what language the others interpreted into.

HELD

1) It was essential to be satisfied that the appellants had a fair opportunity to defend themselves, and in particular that they were accorded in full the right conferred by section 21 (5) (e) of the Constitution of the Federation, which requires that there shall be adequate interpretation to the accused person of anything said in a language that he does not understand, and equally that there shall be adequate interpretation to the court of anything said by the accused person in a language that the court does not understand.

2) On the High Court's finding that the ability of the interpreters to interpret satisfactorily might in at least two instances be questioned, the appellants had discharged the burden of showing that a failure of justice had been occasioned.

The Queen v. Imadegbor Egbuabor [1962] 1 All N.L.R. 287

The appellant was charged with murder and was represented by counsel at the trial in the High court. During the trial, evidence had been given in English by certain witnesses. The appellant did not understand English. The Record of the proceedings in the High Court did not indicate whether the evidence of those witnesses who spoke in English was interpreted to the appellant or not.

HELD

1) The right of an accused to have without payment the assistance of an interpreter if he cannot understand the language used at the trial of the offence conferred by section 21(5) (e) of the Constitution of the Federation, 1960, cannot be invoked, on appeal by an appellant who was represented by counsel at the trial, as a ground for setting aside a conviction, unless he claimed the right at the proper time and was denied it.

2) Where an accused had not expressly asked for the assistance of an interpreter, and the correct practice with regard to the conduct of proceedings in a language not understood by the accused had not been followed by the trial court, the Federal Supreme Court will, on appeal, treat the matter as a question of practice, and will consider whether any substantial miscarriage of justice had resulted from the failure of the trial court to follow the correct procedure. See also *Zaria Native Authority v. Bukari* 1964 N.N.L.R. 25; *Locknan and Another v. The State* (1972) 5 S.C. 22.

NOTE

Section 21(5)(e) of the 1960 Constitution which was interpreted in *Ajayi* is similar to section 22(5)(e) of the 1963 Constitution, section 33(6)(e) of the 1979 Constitution and section 36(6)(e) of the 1999 Constitution.

Trial Court and Reception of Trial Evidence

Ibrahim Mai Abinkumi v. M. Kasimu
1962 N.N.L.R. 26.

A case part-heard in the Kwara Native Court was transferred to the Provincial Court. The Judges of the Provincial Court, besides hearing witnesses, read the Kwara Native Court's record of the evidence of a witness who did not appear before the Provincial Court. The Provincial Court was influenced in its judgment by the evidence which the Judges read.

HELD

The Provincial Court should in its judgment only have considered oral evidence of witnesses who appeared before it.

In *Ikonyi v. Ofune* [1985] 2 N.W.L.R. (Pt. 5) 1, it was held that it is not the function of a trial Judge, by his own exercise of ingenuity to supply the evidence or carry out the mathematics of arriving at an answer which only evidence tested under cross-examination could supply. In *Incar Nigeria Limited and Another v. Adegboye* [1985] 2 N.W.L.R. (Pt. 8) 453, it was held that in evaluating the evidence adduced by parties before him, a trial Judge need only put such evidence on an imaginary scale of justice before deciding to prefer the evidence of one party to that of the other. He does not need to write it down in his judgment that he has put the evidence on such imaginary scale. In *Ogungbemi v. Asamu* [1986] 3 N.W.L.R. (Pt. 27) 161, it was held that the evidence of an expert ought to be assessed and properly evaluated by the trial Judge. Where there are competing pieces of evidence of who did a particular act, the trial Judge ought to evaluate the evidence of both sides on the matter before arriving at his finding. In *Olubode v. Salami* [1985] 2 N.W.L.R. (Pt. 7) 282, It was held that when there is conflicting evidence as to physical facts, the trial Judge may use his own observation to resolve the conflict.

In *Salamatu v. Biba* 1975 N.N.L.R. 176, it was held that every decision by a court should be based on evidence properly admitted before that court in open session or on such information as the court is permitted to use without its being proved by evidence. No court may use its private information acquired by its research outside the hearing in open court. See also *Udofe v. Agusiua* (1973) 1 S.C. 119. In *Okoko v. The State* [1964] 1 All N.L.R. 423, it was held that it is the duty of the court not to speculate on any evidence before it. It must rely on the evidence before it and no more. See also *Seismegraph Ltd. v. Ogbeni* (1976) 4 S.C. 85. In *Arum v. The State* [1974] 4 E.C.S.L.R. 368, it was held that the duty of appraising evidence given at a trial was pre-eminently that of the trial court which saw and heard the witnesses; it was the right of that court to ascribe values to such evidence and the Court of Appeal would not disturb conclusion on the fact as long as the judgment of the trial court was supported by the evidence rightly accepted by that court. See also *Ogundulu and Others v. Phillips and Others* [1973] 1 N.M.L.R. 267; *Egri v. Uperi* [1973] 11 S.C. 299; *Nwosu v. The State* [1986] 4 N.W.L.R. (Pt. 35) 348.

Chapter 2

RELEVANCY OF FACTS

Sections 3 to 12 of the Evidence Act.

The Law of Evidence is essentially based on admissibility. Admissibility itself is predicated or anchored on relevancy. Evidence is said to be relevant when it is material to the facts in issue and therefore admissible by the trial court. As a general rule, once a piece n of evidence is relevant to the facts in issue, it is prima facie admissible. Admissibility is a rule of evidence based on relevancy. Relevancy, on the other hand, is more of a rule of logic than a rule of evidence although its applicability is dependent on the Evidence Act itself and not on rules of logic as such.

The Act defines fact in issue as any fact from which either by itself or in connection with other facts the existence, non-existence, nature or extent of any right, liability or disability asserted or denied in any suit or proceeding necessarily follows (S. 3). Evidence may be given in any suit or proceeding of the existence or non-existence of every fact in issue and of such other facts as are declared to be relevant in accordance with the Act. However, the Courts will exclude evidence which though relevant is remote to be material in the case. Similarly, a person cannot give evidence of a fact which he is disentitled to prove by any provision of the law for the time being in force (S. 6).

Facts which, though not in issue, are so connected with a fact in issue as to form part of the same transaction, are relevant, whether they occurred at the same time and place or at different times and places (S. 7). The impression is generally created that this provision creates the English common law doctrine of *res gestae.* This is not correct. Section 7 has a wider operational scope than the doctrine. The element of contemporaneity in the English doctrine is restrictive in the context of section 7, as the section, in its wider context, also includes the admissibility of facts which occurred "at different times and places". While facts which occur at the same time and place could be said to be contemporaneous, facts which occur at different times and places cannot be so said. Section 7 provides for both situations. It is submitted that the doctrine is generally applicable under section 5(a), and here it is only for the purposes of admissibility of evidence.

Facts which are the occasion, cause or effect, immediate or otherwise, of relevant facts or facts in issue, or which constitute the state of things under which they happened, or which afforded an opportunity for their occurrence or transaction, are relevant (S. 8). Any fact is relevant which shows or constitutes a motive or preparation for any fact in issue or relevant fact. Similarly, the conduct of any party, or of any agent to any party, to any proceedings, in reference to such suit or proceedings, or in reference to any fact in issue therein or relevant thereto, and to the conduct of any person an offence against whom is the subject of any proceeding, is relevant, if such conduct influences or is influenced by any fact in issue or relevant fact, and whether it was previous or subsequent thereto (S. 9 (1) and (2).)

Generally, facts necessary to explain or introduce a fact in issue or relevant fact are relevant in so far as they are necessary for that purpose (S. 10). Similarly, things said or done by conspirators in reference to common intention are relevant facts but not statements made by individual conspirators. (S. 11). Facts not otherwise relevant are relevant (a) if they are inconsistent with any fact in issue or relevant fact; (b) if by themselves or in connection with other facts they make the existence or non-existence of any fact in issue or relevant fact probable or improbable (S. 12).

Relevance and Admissibility

Musa Sadau and Another v. The State [1968] N.M.L.R. 208

The appellants were convicted in the High Court, Kaduna on various charges. The case against the 1st appellant was that he had procured the 2nd accused to print for him a quantity of vehicle licensing forms which he sold for money. He was known as a licence agent and would collect money from vehicle owners and issue forged licences to them. In the early hours of April 21, 1964, his house was searched and a large quantity of vehicle licences and forms and similar papers were recovered. His statements to the police were ruled inadmissible at the trial. In his evidence before the court he denied having in his possession any of the items recovered in his house. He said his sole occupation was that of a bicycle repairer. He stated that all the goods recovered were all contained in a bag carried into the house by the police officer who searched his house and planted them there. In his judgment, the Judge disbelieved this story and convicted him on the evidence of the prosecution witnesses.

On appeal, learned counsel for the appellant contended that as section 78(1) of the Criminal Procedure Code was not complied with during the search of the appellant's house as no neighbours were present, the search was illegal and the properties removed therefrom should not have been received in evidence. The learned Director of Public Prosecutions submitted that section 78(1) of the Criminal Procedure Code did not make the presence of witnesses mandatory during a search.

HELD

1) Where a fact is relevant it could not be excluded at law except by virtue of a specific statutory provision or rule of law.

2) There is no general rule of law in civil as well as in criminal cases that evidence which is relevant is excluded merely by the way in which it has been obtained.

Coker, J.S.C., delivering the judgment of the Supreme Court, said at page 212:

> *We think the argument in this case bears solely on whether or not the properties recovered during the search of the applicant's premises were rightly admitted in evidence. Admissibility is a rule of evidence and it is based on relevancy. Sections 6 - 18 of the Evidence Act provide for the admission in evidence of the variety of facts and other matters described therein and the circumstances under which they are admissible in evidence. It was submitted by the learned Director of Public Prosecutions that admissibility in evidence is based on relevancy and it has not been argued before us that where a fact is relevant it could be excluded at law except by virtue of a specific statutory provision or rule of law.... There is no general rule of law in civil as well as in criminal cases that evidence which is relevant is excluded merely by the way in which it has been obtained. This is subject in criminal cases to the discretion of a trial judge to set the essentials of justice above technical rule if the strict application of the latter would operate unfairly against the accused.*

See also *Igbinovia v. The State* (1981) 2 S.C. 5; *Milla v. The State* [1985] 3 N.W.L.R. (Pt. 11) 190; *Aiyeola v. The State* (1956-84) 10 S.C.N.D. 26; *Nwanyanwu v. The State* (1956-84) 10 S.C.N.D. 28; *The Queen v. Thomas* (1958) 3 F.S.C. 8; *The Queen v. Haske* [1961] All N.L.R. 330; *Nwabiala v. Inspector-General of Police* (1960) 5 F.S.C. 243; Yassin v. Barclays Bank [1968] All N.L.R. 171; *Korgba v. The State* [1968] All N.L.R. 97; *Alade v. Olukade* (1976) 2 S.C. 183.

NOTE

The admissibility of illegally obtained evidence is a perennially vexed problem in the Law of Evidence the world over. The position is more helpless because the Evidence Act does not specifically provide for the admissibility or otherwise of illegally obtained evidence. The question is whether the courts should admit or exclude relevant evidence which was obtained illegally. The American approach, which vindicates their age long doctrine of the exclusion of the "fruits of the poisoned tree", is against admissibility of such evidence. See *Olmstead v. United States* (1928) 277 U.S. 438. Another reason for the exclusion is that it is consistent with the 4th Amendment. See *Mapp v. Ohio* (1961) 367 U.S. 656; *Weeks v. United States*, 232 U.S. 383 (1914). The Scottish approach seems to emphasise the discretionary power of the trial court in the whole affair. See *Lawrie v. Muir* (1950) S.C. (J) 19. While the Australian approach, like the Scottish approach, places emphasis on the need for a cautious judicial discretion in the matter, leans in favour of the individual. See *R. v. Ireland* (1970) C.L.R. 321 at 335. The English approach is not quite easy to comprehend as the case law tries to draw a dichotomy between admissibility of facts discovered in consequence of inadmissible confessions (See *R. v. Warickshall* (1783) I Leach 263; *R. v. Voish* [1918] 1 K.B. 531) and the admissibility of evidence procured in consequence of illegal searches and other unlawful acts (*see Elias v. Pasmore* [1934] 2 K.B. 164; *Kuruma v.* R. [1955] A.C. 531; *King v.* R. [1996] 1 A.C. 304. And what is more, there are conflicting decisions, particularly in respect of the first category. On the admissibility of evidence procured in consequence of illegal search, the English authority of the Kenya case *of Kuruma v. R, supra* is the *locus classicus.* The Judicial Committee of the Privy Council held that in so far as the evidence is relevant, the method of obtaining it was not relevant for the purposes of admitting the evidence. The Supreme Court in *Sadau* adopted the views of the Privy Council in *Kuruma.* The facts of *Kuruma* are quite different from those of *Sadau* and there was therefore really no need to follow *Kuruma.*

What should be the position? Cross, who seems to be in favour of the admissibility of illegally obtained evidence, and therefore towing *Kuruma,* said in his book; *Cross on Evidence*, Butterworths (5th edition) at page 328:

> *In spite of the great weight of opinion to the contrary, too much importance may be attached to the rejection of illegally obtained evidence as an incentive to good behaviour on the part of the police.*

> *Bad behaviour, it is felt, is prompted by the hope that it will not be brought to the notice of the Court, not by the belief that evidence discovered in consequence of it will be received in any event.*

With respect, the motive of the police in procuring evidence through illegal means is prompted by one basic reason. By their conduct the police equally have in mind a possible conviction of the accused if the illegally obtained evidence is admitted. And as long as the position is as in *Sadau*, the police will be very much encouraged to procure evidence through illegal means if they choose to, since in any case, such evidence will be admissible in law for purposes of conviction. In order to police, police indiscretion in the whole matter and the further fact that it will cause miscarriage of justice or grave injustice to the accused if not checked, there should be a clear provision in the Evidence Act to the effect that illegally obtained evidence shall not be admissible in court of law. As long as the courts do not admit confessional statements caused by inducement, threat or promise from a person in authority, it is equally important to legislate against other illegally procured evidence.

Admissible evidence under the Evidence Act is evidence which is relevant and it should be borne in mind that what is not relevant is not admissible: *Agunbiade v. Sasegbon* [1968] N.M.L.R. 223. See also *Are and Another v. Ipaye and others* [1986] 3 N.W.L.R. (Pt. 29) 416; *Williams v. Williams* (1974) 10 S.C. 237; *Barclays Bank v. Abubakar* (1977) 10 S.C. 13. The admissibility of a document has nothing to do with the weight to be attached to it by the trial court. Once a document passes the test of relevancy, it is admissible at the stage of hearing. The court at that stage is not at all concerned with the weight to be attached to the document because that issue does not arise until the entire evidence is completed. It is after the admissibility that the court will determine the evidential or probative value to be placed on the document: *Ayeni v. Dada* (1978) 3.S.C. 35.

Facts which are Relevant

Samuel N. Thomas v. Commissioner of Police (1949) 12 W.A.C.A. 490

The appellant was issued with books of "tote" tickets for sale to the public at a race meeting. It was proved that the appellant had removed a few tickets from the bottom of each of some of the books, instead of from the top downwards serially. Evidence was given that, on a former occasion on which tickets had been entrusted to the appellant for sale, some had been found to have been removed from the bottom of the books.

HELD

This evidence was both relevant and admissible.

It was part of the appellant's defence that the manager's servants could have taken the missing tickets and, as his counsel said in his address to the Magistrate 'evidence has been led that the manager's gardener and steward had access to the box...' All the missing tickets of 4th September had been taken from the books issued to the appellant, and it was unlikely that any servant (or other person) with access to all the books would by chance have helped himself to tickets only from books afterwards issued to the appellant; and evidence that the same had been the case also on the former occasion virtually ruled out this defence. The evidence was thus relevant and admissible - Per Ames, J. at page 491.

Godwin Nwankwere v. Joseph Adewunmi [1966] 1 All N.L.R 129

The defendant, a Vehicle Inspection Officer in the police, ordered the plaintiff's lorry off the road and impounded the certificate of its road worthiness. After certain repairs had been carried out, he declared it roadworthy but neither returned the old certificate nor issued a fresh one. The plaintiff's evidence was that the defendant was extorting money and wanted more. He sued for damages for loss of earning caused by the defendant's refusal to issue a certificate. The defendant submitted that the case fell within section 137(1) of the Evidence Act because of the allegation that he wanted money to return the certificate.

HELD

1) No question arose under section 137(1) of the Evidence Act, for the evidence that the defendant refused to return the certificate so as to extract money showed a motive for his refusal, but, as the plaintiff could have succeeded in his claim without proving any motive, the alleged motive was not a fact in issue or directly in issue.

2) The above implies that a fact directly in issue is a fact which the plaintiff must prove in order to succeed in his claim.

Oloyede Akingbade v. Oyeyipo Elemosho
F.S.C. 353/62 decided on 9/4/64.

The plaintiff sued the defendant for a declaration of title to a piece of land which was a plot of land out of many other plots on a layout. In order to establish the identity of the land in dispute, the plaintiff tendered deeds of conveyance with plans attached in respect of other plots of land on the same layout which were executed in favour of other purchasers by the person who sold the land to the plaintiff. The trial Judge rejected these conveyances as being irrelevant. On appeal, the Supreme Court held that the conveyances were relevant under section 12 of the Evidence Act. See *Aguda*, at page 27.

Balogun v. Police
(1953) N.L.R. 148

Appellant and two other persons were convicted of conspiracy to steal and stealing 300 bags of cement. The 2nd and 3rd co-defendants made statements incriminating the appellant in his absence. It was argued for the appellant that the evidence did not establish a conspiracy between him and his co-defendants to steal the second load of cement, and that what the 2nd and 3rd co-defendants had said in appellant's absence could not be used against him.

HELD

> Although the statement made by the 2nd and 3rd co-defendants in the absence of the appellant could not be used as evidence against the appellant of his being a party to a conspiracy, there was other evidence which showed that the appellant had only one note for 300 bags from the U.A.C. so that he had no valid reason to come back for more cement. His coming back for more cement was *prima facie* evidence of a conspiracy between him and his co-defendants who had already approached the U.A.C clerks with suggestion to let the appellant have more cement.

NOTE

The direct implication of the decision is that the statements made in the circumstances by the two co-accused persons against the appellant in his absence were not relevant facts and therefore inadmissible in evidence against the appellant. But the Court was able to hold that the conduct of the appellant by returning a second time for more cement was relevant evidence on the charge of conspiracy. The appeal was accordingly dismissed. The Court was involved in the interpretation of section 11 of the Act. *NA Enahoro v. The Queen* [1965] 1 All N.L.R. 125, the Supreme Court also had cause to interpret the section. The Court held that the evidence of the 4th prosecution witness, Dr. Sanya Onabamiro, clearly showed that there was a *prima facie* case of conspiracy between the appellant and others. Idigbe, J.S.C. said at page 134:

> *Learned Counsel for the appellant, however, conceded that it was not open to the prosecution to lay any or all of the conspiracies charged in the Information as overt acts to the first count. That being so, we see no substance in counsel's submission since it is our view that, if in the course of a trial the case for the prosecution suggests that a conspiracy existed between the accused and persons unknown and there is evidence which the Court accepts as prima facie ground for believing in the existence of such a conspiracy, the provisions of section 11 of the Evidence Act, Cap. 62, will apply.*

In *Bayo and Others v. Inspector-General of Police* [1971] N.M.L.R. 184, it was held that to be guilty of conspiracy, it is not necessary that the appellant should be present when money was received by the 1st and 3rd accused, since evidence shows that he had earlier acted his own part of the conspiracy. This is the position of section 11 of the Evidence Act. And in *Oyediran v. The Republic* [1967] N.M.L.R. 122, it was held that once conspiracy is proved to exist, evidence admissible against one conspirator is also admissible against the other or others.

R. v. Griliopoulous and Others (1953) 20 N.L.R. 114

Accused persons were charged with receiving stolen tin from one Maigadi Maiango, and evidence was given besides to show that they received on the same day and a week earlier stolen tin from others.

HELD

> Evidence of other instances of receiving cannot be used to prove the act of receiving charged. That act must be proved *aliunde* and if it is so proved, the other instances serve to show that the receiving was accompanied by guilty knowledge that the goods received were stolen.

Peter Ozunde v. Inspector-General of Police [1965] 1 All N.L.R. 102

Someone was assaulted and those accused of it were bailed out by U., who testified that the defendant (a corporal) asked for money to spoil the case; that he (U) went with money, in the company of M. and O., to the defendant's house; that he (U) went in alone and handed the money to the defendant; and the evidence of M (as also of O) was that when U came out, he told M and O that he had given the money to the corporal.

HELD

> What the one told the others on coming out of the house, that he had given the money, was damaging hearsay, and section 8 of the Evidence Act was no warrant for admitting it in evidence.

Res Gestae

Brownson Udo v. The Queen
[1964] 1 All N.L.R. 21

The defendant's wife died as a result of a fracture and dislocation of her neck. She told someone, in the defendant's presence, that he had "put his hands between her legs, carried her up, and knocked her to the ground headlong" because she had permitted someone to cut sticks whom her husband (the defendant) suspected to be her lover. The defendant said nothing but the next day when she described the assault to another, he said his wife abused him.

HELD

> The evidence of the deceased's statement was not part of the res gestae, but it was admissible as evidence of accusations made in the defendant's presence in circumstances reasonably calling for comment by him.

R. v. Bang Weyeku
(1943) 9 W.A.C.A 195

On a charge of murder the principal evidence against the accused was that the deceased shortly after he had been stabbed said "Bang has shot me". Accused was not present. There was no evidence that deceased believed himself in danger of death. There was other evidence to connect the accused with the crime, but it was by no means conclusive. The trial Judge admitted the evidence of deceased's statement and it was primarily on that evidence that the accused was convicted.

HELD

The evidence of the deceased's statement was inadmissible, whether as a dying declaration or as part of the *res gestae* and it was impossible to say that without this evidence the trial Judge must inevitably have come to the same conclusion as he did. The appeal was allowed.

Oruakpor Okokor v. The State
[1967] N.M.L.R. 189

The appellant was convicted by the High Court of murder and sentenced to death. The case of the prosecution was that the accused dealt machete blows on the deceased and two of the prosecution witnesses heard the deceased shout "Ovuomarienor has killed me! Ovuomarienor has dealt machete blows on me !!". The deceased later died as a result of the machete wounds. The learned trial Judge in his judgment said:

> *It was clear from the words used by the deceased that he believed himself to be in danger of approaching death. The serious nature of the wound as given by the doctor, the surrounding circumstances and the fact that the deceased died soon after support this. I hold that they form part of the* res gestae...

HELD

The statement was admissible in evidence as part of the *res gestae* and the learned trial Judge rightly received the statement in evidence on that basis.

Sunday Akpan v. The State
[1967] N.M.L.R. 185

The appellant was convicted of murder in the Calabar High Court. The only eye witness, a boy of twelve years testified that when he went to bed he later heard his mother shout "Sunday has killed me!", and when he went out, he saw the appellant cutting his mother with a machete.

HELD

The statement of the deceased (as narrated by the boy) "Sunday has killed me!" was admissible as part of the *res gestae.* But the Supreme Court allowed the appeal on the ground that the learned trial Judge did not warn himself of the risk or danger of convicting the appellant on the uncorroborated evidence of a child of twelve years.

Olubi Oyename v. Oyedele (1957) L.L.R. 37

Immediately after a collision had occurred between the plaintiff's and defendant's motor vehicles, the defendant's driver told the plaintiff that his brakes had failed, and that he had to choose between falling into the river or colliding with the plaintiff's car. Subsequently, the driver made a statement to the police in which he admitted negligence and eventually pleaded guilty to a charge of driving with inefficient brakes. At the trial the defendant did not see fit to call either the driver or the engineer whom he alleged had repaired his vehicle only the day before the accident.

HELD

The spontaneous words of the defendant's driver were sufficiently contemporaneous with the collision to form part of the *res gestae* and were admissible against the defendant.

In *Salawu v. The State* [1971] N.M.L.R. 249, it was held that the cry "*Sule a pa mi*" (meaning, "Sule is killing me") heard by several witnesses following which the deceased was found in a pool of blood is *res gestae* and properly admissible in evidence. In *Anekwe v. The State* (1976) 9-10 S.C. 255, it was held that a statement made by a dying person may not qualify as a dying declaration but may form part of the *res gestae*. See also *Nwadialor v. Onyia* [1971] 1 U.I.L.R. 524. In order to form part of the *res gestae*, it is necessary that a statement should not only establish a fact, but should also go further to prove the circumstances surrounding that fact: *Vorgbo v. The State* (1972) 5 S.C. 1.

Facts Relevant in Special Circumstances

The Commissioner of Lands v. Kadiri Adagun (1937) 3 W.A.C.A. 206

The learned trial Judge made use of traditional evidence that the respondent derived his title to the land in question from one Ori, the founder of the Olorogun family, of which the respondent was the head. No objection was taken to this evidence at the trial, but counsel for the appellants at the Court of Appeal urged the court to exercise its discretion in favour of the appellants by virtue of Order 6, Rule 28 of the Supreme Court Rules.

Delivering the judgment of the Court, Graham Paul, J. said at page 206:

> *I see no reason why the discretion should be so exercised. Apart from that, in my view the evidence was not misconceived. It is the undoubted practice in this country to accept as admissible in cases as to title to family land evidence of the tradition of the family ownership. Literacy among the people of this country does not go back very far, and the oral tradition is generally the only evidence available as to ownership of land other than the memory of living witnesses.*

See also *Lajide Akuru v. Ibadan-In-Council* (1954) 14 W.A.C.A. 523; *Idundun v. Okumagba* (1976) 9-10 S.C. 227; *Omeregie and Others v. Idugiemwanye* [1985] 2 N.W.L.R. (Pt. 5) 41; *Mogaji and Others v. Caodbury Fry (Export) Ltd.* [1985] 2 N.W.L.R. (Pt. 7) 393; *Alhaji Bala v. Mrs. Bankole* [1986] 3 N.W.L.R. (Pt. 27) 141; *Ayanwale and Others v. Atanda and Others* [1988] 1 N.W.L.R. (Pt. 68) 22.

Nathan Okechukwu and Others v. Frederick Okafor and Others [1961] All N.L.R. 685

The appellants brought an action against the respondents seeking for (a) a declaration of title to certain lands at Oko, (b) damages for trespass to the said lands; and (c) an injunction to restrain the respondents from further acts of trespass to the lands. There was evidence that the appellants laid possession of lands adjoining the lands in dispute.

HELD

1) By virtue of section 45 of the Evidence Act, acts of possession and enjoyment of land may be evidence of ownership not only of the particular piece of land with reference to which the acts are done, but also of other lands so situated or connected therewith, by locality or similarity, that what is true as to one piece of land is likely to be true of the other piece of land.

2) The appellant acts of possession and enjoyment of the lands adjoining the disputed lands claimed and possessed under the same grant as that under which the appellants claim the lands in dispute, together with the erection by them of boundary pillars, constitute sufficient evidence to support their claim of title to the disputed vacant and unenclosed lands under that grant.

In *Akingbada v. Elemosho* [1964] 1 All N.L.R. 154, it was held that in an action for declaration of title to land, a party can lead evidence of relevant facts on the identification of the land in dispute under sections 7, 10 and 12(b) of the Evidence Act.

Odutade v. Police
(1952) 20 N.L.R. 81

Appellant was charged with others with stealing and with receiving, and by himself of being a rogue and vagabond. Evidence of convictions over ten years old was given. He was acquitted on the vagrancy charge but convicted of receiving. One ground of appeal was that the convictions were inadmissible as evidence of guilty knowledge. For the police it was argued that the convictions were put in for the vagrancy charge. At the trial no application was made to try the vagrancy charge separately.

HELD

> The charge of being a rogue and vagabond, which was preposterous ought not to have been joined with the unrelated charge of stealing or receiving to prejudice the appellant; and although he did not object to the misjoinder, the trial had been unfair on that account and the conviction would be quashed.

On relevancy of facts generally, see further *Candide-Johnson v. Edigin* [1990] 1 N.W.L.R. (Pt. 129) 659, *Otti v. State* [1991] 8 N.W.L.R. (Pt. 207) 103; *Hausa v.The State* [1992] 1 N.W.L.R. (Pt. 219) 600; *Umaru v. Oduogbo* [1993] 6 N.W.L.R. (Pt. 298) 217. *Owhoeri v. Ikanone* [1994] 1 N.W.L.R. (Pt. 322) 605.

Chapter 3

ADMISSIONS AND CONFESSIONS

Sections 19 to 32 of the Evidence Act.

An admission is a statement, oral or documentary, which suggests any inference as to any fact in issue or relevant fact, and which is made by any of the persons, and in the circumstances contained in the Act (S. 19). Admissions could be made by a suitor in a representative character, a party interested in the subject-matter and a person from whom the parties to the suit have derived their interest in the subject-matter of the suit (S. 20). While section 24 deals with when oral admissions as to contents of documents are relevant, section 25 provides for instances when admissions in civil cases are relevant. Admissions are not conclusive proof of the matters admitted, but they may operate as estoppels (S. 26). See also sections 21 to 23.

A confession is an admission made at any time by a person charged with a crime, stating or suggesting the inference that he committed that crime (S. 27(1)). Confessions, if voluntary, are deemed to be relevant facts as against the persons who make them only (S. 27(2)). Where more persons than one are charged jointly with a criminal offence and a confession made by one of such persons in the presence of one or more of the other persons so charged is given in evidence, the court shall not take such statement into consideration as against any of such other persons in whose presence it was made unless he adopted the said statement by words or conduct (S. 27(3)).

By section 28, a confession caused by inducement, threat or promise from a person in authority is irrelevant in a criminal proceedings. But a confession made after the impression caused by any such inducement, threat or promise has been fully removed is relevant (S. 30). A confession otherwise relevant cannot become irrelevant because of a promise of secrecy or any of the circumstances mentioned in section 31 (S. 31). Facts discovered in consequence of information given by an accused are admissible in evidence (S. 29). Similarly, evidence in other proceedings amounting to a confession is admissible (S. 32).

The provisions of sections 30 and 31 are not easy to reconcile with the position of the accused in the interrogation room. Apart from the fact that it is extremely difficult to lead evidence to prove the provisions of section 30, it is not easy to establish the yardstick or criterion to determine the impact of the provisions on the accused since it is largely subjective. Similarly, section 31 gives rise to a number of problems. How can a confession be otherwise relevant if it is obtained under any of the circumstances enumerated under the section? It is submitted that a confession obtained through any of the procedures enumerated under the section should not be admissible because admissibility will be in conflict with the intendment and intention of section 28.

The procedure for obtaining confessions is as contained in the Judges Rules of England 1964 which are applicable to the Southern States and the Criminal Procedure (Statement to police Officers) Rules, 1960 which are applicable to the Northern States. Before a confessional statement is obtained from the accused, the Police administer the words of caution. We will not go into the debate here whether the caution is in any way helpful to the accused in the interrogation room. But this much is clear that from the generality of police practice, the caution is of little use to the accused in the investigation process as it relates to confessions. The caution, instead of making the accused to be cautious in the interrogation room, exposes him to police techniques and police brutality, with the result that he 'volunteers' a confession. In order to ameliorate the ordeal of the accused in the interrogation room, the only viable solution is to place a constitutional embargo on the admissibility of confessions in courts of law. This is the way India managed to solve the problem. Unless such a pragmatic solution is adopted, the dilemma of the accused arising from the enforcement of the criminal process as it affects the admissibility of confessions at the trial will remain with us.

Admissions

Adeyemi Ogunnaike v. Taiwo Ojayemi [1987] 1 N.W.L.R. (Pt. 53) 761

The plaintiff brought an action in the Grade 'B' Customary Court Sagamu for a declaration of title to a parcel of land and N200 damages for trespass. Judgment was given to the plaintiff. The judgment was reversed on appeal by the appellate Judge on the alleged ground that there were certain admissions made by the plaintiff at the trial about the title of the Ijokun Community, admissions which if considered would have titled the case in favour of the defendant. The learned appellate Judge allowed the appeal and dismissed the claims of the plaintiff. The judgment of the learned appellate Judge was set aside by the Court of Appeal.

Dismissing the appeal of the defendant the Supreme Court

HELD

1) An admission s ia statement, oral or written (expressed or implied) which is made by a party to civil proceeding and which statement is adverse to his case. It is admissible as evidence against the maker as the truth of the fact asserted in the statement.

2) In the instant case, there is no portion of the plaintiff's evidence that one can regard as an admission and thus the learned appellate Judge misdirected himself by treating as admissions statements which do not constitute admissions. See also *Seismograph Services (Nigeria) Ltd. v. Eyuafe* (1976) 9 and 10 S.C. 135.

Standard Consolidated Dredging and Construction Company Limited and Another v. Katonescret Nigeria Ltd.[1986] 5 N.W.L.R. (Pt. 44) 791

The plaintiff had brought an action to recover some money allegedly owed it by the defendants before the High Court of Lagos State. Judgment was entered in favour of the plaintiff by default of appearance. The defendants brought an application to set aside the judgment. In the course of the hearing of the application, the trial Judge asked the plaintiff's counsel how much was owed by the defendants, whereupon counsel said N80,000.00. The trial Judge thus gave another judgment setting aside his earlier judgment, but upon the condition that the defendants pay the sum of N80,000.00 within fourteen days. On appeal it was HELD that the value of an admission depends very much upon the circumstance under which the admission was made. Where as in the instant case an admission was alleged to have been made by a party or his counsel during the course of a hearing, the value of such admission must depend upon the explanatory facts in the case, the tenor of the case of the person alleged to have made the admission, and the trend of the argument in the course of which the admission was made. See also *African Continental Seaways v. Nigerian Dredging Roads and General Works Ltd* [1974] 1 F.R.C.R. 227.

Chief Akinbiyi v. Raliatu Anike (1959) W.R.N.L.R. 16.

The appellant sued to recover a sum alleged to have been paid by him on behalf of the respondent who counterclaimed for the return of goods wrongly detained. The Magistrate dismissed the appellant's claim and entered judgment for the respondent on her counterclaim for the return of the goods or their value. In support of her claim the respondent had tendered in evidence list of the goods which she alleged the appellant had detained, which contained also the value of the goods. This list was admitted in evidence by the Magistrate without objection by the appellant. The admissibility of the list was contested on appeal.

HELD

Counsel for the appellant having taken no objection to the admissibility of the list at the trial the appellant could not be heard to raise such objection on appeal.

Modupe Oloko v. Simeon Olatunde Oloko and Another (1961) W.N.L.R. 101

In a cross-petition for divorce on the ground of adultery it was proved that the cross-petitioner lived in a different town from his wife whose petition for divorce on the ground of cruelty the court had dismissed and that he was in the habit of visiting her at intervals of about one week, the morning of the alleged adultery having fallen on a week-end when such a visit was probable. The evidence adduced in support of the allegation was *inter alia* to the effect that when he visited his wife in the morning in question in the company of a witness the cross-petitioner had found the door unlocked, seen her running out of the bed-room half-dressed and met the co-respondent lying on the bed; that when the allegation was made by the cross-petitioner in the presence of a witness it was not denied by the petitioner and the co-respondent and also that another witness's questions put to the co-respondent had remained unanswered.

HELD

The fact that the allegation when made by the cross-petitioner was not denied by the petitioner and the co-respondent could not be accepted as admissions made by them and that the failure of the co-respondent to answer questions put to him was not by itself of much significance. Irwin, J. said at page 103:

The cross-petitioner's sixth witness, Igiebor, a police constable, said that the allegations made by the cross-petitioner in his presence were not denied by the petitioner and the co-respondent. I am not, however, prepared to accept his evidence that admissions were in fact made by them. I regard the cross-petitioner's fourth witness, Amole, as comparatively disinterested, but I do not consider the fact that his questions to the co-respondent remained unanswered by itself to be of much significance.

See also *Oguma Associated ltd. v. Esiso* [1985] H.C.N.L.R. 1415

John Wilberforce Bamibo v. S.C.O.A. (1941) 7 W.A.C.A. 150

This was a claim to damages for injury caused to the appellant's house by vibration during building operations of the respondents. Experts were called in to examine the house and an undertaking was given to repair any damage after the building had been completed. The experts were not available at the trial, at which the appellant called two other expert witnesses and the respondents one. The trial Judge gave judgment to the respondents, relying on a letter put in as a promise in writing in somewhat vague terms to make good any damage to plaintiff's premises caused by their operations.

HELD

There was ample evidence on which the court below could reach the conclusion it did that the appellant had failed to prove damages, that there was no suggestion that a cause of action arose on the alleged admission of liability and undertaking to repair which were evidence but not proof of the claim; further that it may be shown that an admission was made under an erroneous view of the party's own liability.

Persons who make Admissions

Nigerian National Supply Company Ltd. v. Alhaji Hamajoda Sabana and Company Limited and others [1988] 2 N.W.L.R. (Pt. 74) 23.

In an action for ownership of 23,000 metric tons of Thailand Rice shipped abroad the vessel M.V. Eastern Maid, counsel for the appellant in answer to a question whether he will give an undertaking that nothing will happen to the consignment of rice before the next date of adjournment, said "Yes". Counsel had then not received instructions on the issue. The learned trial Judge made an order that the rice be released by the appellant to the Nigerian Merchant Bank Ltd. for ultimate disposal to the persons from whom money has been received for the purchase of the rice. The appeal to the Court of Appeal was dismissed. It was argued at the Supreme Court that the undertaking of appellant's counsel could not bind the appellant because he had not received instructions when he made same.

HELD

1) An admission by counsel to a party is to a certain extent like that of any other agent, and cannot have any more binding effect than if it was made by the party itself. Where such an admission is made from facts not within the personal knowledge of the party who makes the admission, it rests, indeed, on a very shaky wicket.
2) The admission of counsel of acts beyond his knowledge and of which he had confessed he had taken no instructions cannot be given such a sacrosanct effect, as against the affidavit evidence of the four managers of the appellant who were in the best position to know the true facts.
3) Where a solicitor in interlocutory proceedings make an admission of facts which his client considers to be incorrect, his client can, before the opposite party acts on it, withdraw the admission.
4) A client is not bound by an admission made by counsel in the course of interlocutory proceedings, unless the circumstances are such as to give rise to estoppel, for example, if the other party had acted to his detriment on the faith of it.
5) In the instant case, since counsel to the appellant had on 9th May, 1986 informed the court that he had not received any instructions from the appellant, the undertaking subsequently given by the counsel, was given without authority and therefore not binding on the appellant. It cannot be taken to be within his apparent authority as counsel who appears for a party in a case, for he had received no instructions in the matter.

In a dissenting judgment, Uwais, J.S.C. (ad he then was) cited with approval the following passage from *Halsbury's Laws of England, 4th Edition* volume 3, at paragraph 1184.

> *The statement of counsel, if made on the trial of an action or in the course of any interlocutory proceeding in the presence of the client or his solicitor or someone authorised to represent the solicitor, and not repudiated at the time, bind the client and may be used as evidence against him.*

The learned justice (as he then was) also relied on the English case of *Holt v. Jesse* (1876) 3 Ch. D. 177.

NOTE

The dissenting judgment appears more appealing. If the client is physically in court, nothing should stop him from telling his counsel what he thinks is the correct factual position. Where he decides to keep quiet, then both counsel and the court should assume that the representation made by counsel on behalf of the client is correct. After all, a party who has briefed counsel is expected to take the sweetness and bitterness of the professional conduct of that counsel *cum onere*. But it will however be a different case, if in the circumstances of the case, the party was not at all in court.

Siesmograph Services (Nigeria) Ltd. v. Chief Keke Ogbenegweke Eyuafu (1976) 9 and 10 S.C. 135.

The respondent brought an action for compensation in respect of alleged damages done to roads which he claimed and described in a letter to the appellants as "my private roads". In a reply, the appellants used the expression "your roads". The trial Judge held that by the use of the expression, "your roads", the appellants had conceded that the respondent owned the roads.

HELD

> The expression *prima facie* was intended to be more of a description of the roads as set down in the respondent's letter than an admission of title.

Proof and Relevance of Admissions

The value of an admission depends upon the circumstances under which it was made. It is for the court to consider the evidence of such circumstances as are available and decide the issue thereon after giving due weight to such evidence. Admissions by a party are not estoppels or conclusive against the party whom they are tendered. Such persons are entitled to give evidence to explain away such admissions: *Nigerian National Supply Company Ltd. v. Alhaji Hamajoda Sabana and Company Limited and Others, supra.* See also *NII Abossey Okai II v. NII Ayikai* II (1946) 12 W.A.C.A. 31; *Iga v. Amakiri* (1976) 11 S.C. 1 at 11. An admission made at any time by a person charged with a crime suggesting the inference that he committed the offence is a relevant fact against the maker and if made voluntarily is admissible in evidence: *Onungwa v. The State* (1976) 2 S.C. 169. See also *The Queen v. Igboekweze* (1956-84) 10 S.C.D.N. 44. For an admission to be binding, it must have been made by the person against whom the admission is being enforced or by someone acting on his behalf: *Ikabala and others v. Ojosipe* [1988] 4 N.W.L.R. (Pt. 86) 119. Facts admitted need no further proof and any dispute on the facts so admitted should be disregarded by the court: *Nwankwere v. Ugorji* (1956-84) 10 S.C.N.D. 38.

Nature of Confessions

R. v. Asuquo Etim Inyang
(1931) 10 N.L.R. 33

The accused was resident in Calabar, and went through a form of legal marriage in the United Free Church there. Some eighteen months later proceedings were taken against him in the Police Magistrate's Court to enforce a maintenance order made against him by the West London Magistrate in respect of a marriage which the accused had contracted in England seven years previously. Before the Calabar Police Magistrate, counsel for the accused admitted the facts, and the accused himself merely gave evidence as to his financial circumstances and prayed that the rate of maintenance ordered by the West London Magistrate should be reduced. In criminal proceedings on bigamy the prosecution relied upon two marriage certificates and on the admissions made before the Calabar Police Magistrate.

HELD

The admissions made before the Calabar Magistrate could not be treated as confession for the purposes of a criminal charge.

Raimi Adebisi Afolabi v. Commissioner of Police [1961] All N.L.R. 654

The appellant, a storekeeper, was convicted by the Chief Magistrate Ibadan on twelve counts of stealing specific items, the property of his employers. The Manager in his evidence said that the appellant told him that he had been busy with his election campaigns and had taken a certain of the stock and sold them to assist in his expenses. The accused did not say how much he used".

HELD

A confession must be direct and positive so far as the charges are concerned. In this case the alleged confession was neither direct nor positive as to the items contained in the charges.

R. v. Akpan Udo Essien (1939) 5 W.A.C.A. 70

The appellant was charged for murder. The trial Judge erroneously found the statement of the appellant on arrest as a voluntary statement and a "complete confession".

HELD

The statement was not a complete confession but a confession of implication in the crime. But since there existed other conclusive evidence of guilt, the court dismissed the appeal. The court said at page 72:

> *In our opinion the statement of the appellant cannot properly be termed a complete confession of the charge of murder, and if that statement had been incorporated in the judgment it would have amounted to a misdirection upon the facts.*

A statement will not qualify as a confessional statement if such a statement does not admit the guilt of the offence charged: *Milla v. The State* [1985] 3 N.W.L.R. (Pt. 11) 90. What constitutes a confession is a matter of fact and not of law: *Enweluku v. The State* [1970] 1 All N.L.R. 55. A confession does not become inadmissible merely because the accused person denies having made it and in this respect a confession contained in a statement made to the police by a person under arrest is not to be treated differently from any other occasion. The fact that the appellant took the earliest opportunity to deny having made the statement may lend weight to his denial, but it is not in itself a reason for ignoring the statement: *R. v. Itule* [1961] All N.L.R. 462. A statement could amount to a confession even if made before the accused was charged with the offence: *R. v. Ebong* (1947) 12 W.A.C.A. 139.

See further *Saidu v. State* (1982) 4 S.C. 41; *Obosi v. The State* [1965] N.M.L.R. 119; *The State v. Enabosi* [1966] 2 All N.L.R. 116; *Otufale and Others v. The State* [1968] N.M.L.R. 261; *Uche and Another v. R.* [1964] 1 All N.L.R. 195; *R. v. Jonah and Others* (1934) 2 W.A.C.A. 120; *Njovens and Others v. The State* (1973) 5 S.C. 17; *Omisade and Others v. The Queen* [1964] 1 All N.L.R. 233; *Shittu v. The State* [1970] 1 All N.L.R. 288; *Kanu and Another v. The State* (1952) 14 W.A.C.A 30.

"Voluntary" in the Definition of Confession, Inducement and Threats.

Samuel Ojegele v. The State [1988] 1 N.W.L.R. (Pt. 71) 414

The appellants were charged with the murder of a hunch-backed man with a view to get rich quick. Each appellant volunteered a confessional statement to P.W.9, a police officer who then took them to P.W.12, a Senior Police Officer before whom their statements were read and interpreted to them by P.W.13. P.W.12 then endorsed the statements while P.W.13 signed as interpreter. After conducting a trial within trial, the statements were admitted. The Court of Appeal confirmed the decision of the trial court.

Dismissing the appeal, the Supreme Court held as follows:

1) An extra-judicial statement of an accused person amounting to a confession is relevant only when it is admitted or else proved to be voluntary.
2) If an extra-judicial statement of an accused person amounting to a confession was not made freely and voluntarily it cannot even be admitted in evidence and if an accused person admits making this statement, but alleges that he was induced by any threat or promise by a person in authority to make the said statement in order to gain an advantage or avoid an evil of a temporal nature, then the first duty of the Court is to decide whether or not the statement was voluntary.
3) Where any doubt exists as to the voluntary nature of any given statement amounting to a confession, the onus is on the prosecution to prove positively and affirmatively beyond reasonable doubt that the statement is voluntary.

See also *R. v. Onabanjo* (1936) 3 W.A.C.A 43; *Achabua v. The State* (1976) 12 S.C. 63; *R. v. Sapele* (1957) 2 F.S.C. 24; *Nwigbeke and Others v. The Queen* (1959) 4 F.S.C. 101; *Owie v. The State* [1985] 1 N.W.L.R. (Pt. 3) 470; *Ogbodu v. The State* [1986] 5 N.W.L.R. (Pt. 41) 294; *Auta v. The State*

[1975] 1 All N.L.R. (Pt. 1) 165; *Adekanbi v. Attorney-General of Western Nigeria* (1966) 1 All N.L.R. 47; *Dawa v. The State* (1980) 8-11 S.C. 236.

In *The Queen v. Nimiel Viapbong* 1961 N.N.L.R. 47 a police sergeant in cautioning the accused had said to him: "You should bear in mind that any statement you make shall be written down by me and taken before the court so that it may be your evidence" or "so that it may be evidence for you". It was held that the caution was clearly an inducement to speak. In the opinion of the court, the inducement sufficient to render a confession irrelevant and inadmissible in evidence is an inducement to make a statement; it need not be an inducement to confess the truth, nor need it be an inducement calculated to make the confession untrue.

In *R. v. Nyinya Kwaghbo* 1962 N.N.L.R. 4, after the accused had been apprehended he made a statement to a police constable. The statement was tendered in evidence at the trial as a confession. In his evidence at the trial the constable said he "obtained" the statement from the accused who had "agreed" to make it. It was shown that the prescribed caution had been administered. It was held that there were strong indications that the accused had been induced to make the statement, and there was no satisfactory evidence that it was voluntary. See also *Madu Fatumani v. R.* (1950) 13 W.A.C.A. 39.

R. v. Baba Haske
[1961] All N.L.R. 330

The accused was charged with murder. When the body of the deceased was found there were circumstances giving cause for suspecting the appellant. The Head Chief summoned the villagers and said to them: "all of you will be in the case and will be gaoled if you do not tell the truth". He told the accused that he would inform the police of the circumstances of suspicion against him and he added: "I hear that you followed this man with a gun; if you shot him please let me know".

HELD

The confession following the dialogue between the Head Chief and the accused was a threat which made the confession inadmissible.

See further *Ebhomien and Others v. The Queen* [1963] 1 All N.L.R. 365; *R. v. Bodom* (1935) 2 W.A.C.A. 390; *The State v. Oladele and Others* [1969] N.M.L.R. 210; *Akinrolabu v. The State* [1971] N.M.L.R. 25; *Udofia v. The*

State (1956-84) 10 S.C.N.D. 42; *Onuoha v. The State* [1988] 3 N.W.L.R. (Pt. 83) 460.

Person in Authority

A person in authority means, generally speaking, any one who has authority or control over the accused or over the proceedings or the prosecution against him. And the reason that it is a rule of law that confessions made as a result of inducements held out by persons in authority are inadmissible is clearly this, that the authority that the accused knows such person to possess may well be supposed in the majority of instances both to animate his hopes of favour on the one hand and on the other to inspire him with awe: *Igbinovia v. The State* (1981) 2 S.C. 5. A Village Head or a Village Chief is a person in authority: *Madu Fatumani v. R, supra; Nweke v. The Queen (1959)* 4 F.S.C. 225; R. *v. Baba Haske, supra; Chingi v. The Queen* (1956-84) 10 S.C. N.D. 55.

Confessions of Other Offences in Addition to Those Charged

In R. *v. Eraruwomi Otedia* (1959) W.R.N.L.R. 43 the accused person was charged with murder. His statement to the police was tendered in evidence. The statement contained confessions of other and similar offences. It was held that only that portion of the statement of the accused which dealt with the charge should be tendered. But in R. *v. Esologba and Others* (1943) 17 N.L.R. 24, the West African Court of Appeal reached a different decision. The accused were charged with Shopbreaking, and the Crown put in evidence voluntary statements made by them to the police and taken down in writing. When the statement of the first accused was being read it was found that it contained in a second paragraph a confession of another but similar fact. The court held that in the circumstances the whole statement should be rejected and expunged from the record.

In the light of the clear provisions of section 47 of the Evidence Act, it does not appear that the decision is correct, unless it is shown that the portion of the statement does not form part of the longer statement.

Application of the Judges Rules in Nigeria

The so-called Judges Rules which lay down *inter alia* that persons in custody should not be questioned without the usual caution being first administered, are rules of caution laid down by the Judges in England as the procedure to be followed in that highly civilized country. They should be followed, *mutatis mutandis*, so far as is possible and practicable in this country: *R. v. William Opara* (1943) 9 W.A.C.A. 70. The police should not interrogate prisoners with reference to any charge against any one of them, or invite form one defendant a statement against a co-defendant; and they should not obtain evidence by confronting prisoners with one another: *Jonny Evbuomwan and Others v. Commissioner Police* (1961) W.N.L.R. 257. When a person charged is an illiterate, the statement may be read over or interpreted to him apart by some person other than a police man. Anything said to such a reader by the person charged when the statement is read shall not be admissible in evidence against him, but if, after the statement has been so read he shall be desirous of making a statement to the police in reply, such statement shall be taken only after the usual caution has been administered: *R. v. Afose and Others* (1934) 2 W.A.C.A. 118 at 119. Statements obtained from prisoners contrary to the Judges Rules are not *ipso facto* inadmissible, in so far as they were made voluntarily: *R. v. Jackson Akpan Umo and Others* (1944) 10 W.A.C.A. 254. The practice of a superior police officer counter signing a confessional statement is a prudent one but failure to comply with it should not expose the statement to unnecessary suspicion. See *Nwangbo v. Nwigboke and Others* (1959) 4 F.S.C. 26; *R. v. Nwangbo Igwe* (1960) 5 F.S.C. 55; *Oke v. The Republic* [1967] N.M.L.R. 69; *Udofia v. The State* (1979) 1 F.C.A. 40.

On the Rules, see further *R. v. Ajani and Others* (1936) 3 W.A.C.A. 3; *Ugama v. The Queen* (1959) 4 F.S.C. 218; *Saidu v. The State* (1982) 4 S.C. 41; *Samuel Ojegele v. The State, supra.*

Effect of Confession

If a person makes a free and voluntary confession which is direct and positive, and if properly proved he may be convicted on the confession alone without any further evidence, unless the offence is one of such that corroboration is required by law: *Samuel Ojegele v. The State, supra.* See also *Queen v. Obasa* [1962] 1 All N.L.R. 651; *Achabua v. The State* (1976) 12 S.C. 63; *R. v. Erumesi* (1959) W.R.N.L.R. 258; *R. v. Omakoro* (1941) 7 W.A.C.A.

176; *Wonaka v. Sokoto N.A* (1956) 1 F.S.C. 29. The evidential value of a confession if true is great indeed. It is very much soght after by police investigators and prosecutors. It lightens the burden of the prosecution by dispensing with the need to call a host of witnesses in cases where there are no or very few eye witnesses. A confession can support a conviction if proved to e made and true: *Saidu v. The State, supra; Yesufu v. The State* (1976) 6 S.C. 167. If a confession is relevant and is free and voluntary, it is admissible in evidence and when admitted, the weight to be attached depends on its probative value and pure truth in content: *Igbinovia v. The State* (1981) 2 S.C. 5. A confessional statemfnet consititute a cogent proof of an act of the accused: *Ofoha v. The State* (1976) 1 S.C. 55. See also *Sanusi v. The State* (1956-84) 10 S.C.N.D. 45; *Bos v. Khawam* (1956-84) 10 S.C.ND. 54; *Kure v. The Queen* (1956-84) 10 S.C.N.D. 49. There is no evidence stronger than a person's own confession: *Ufot v. The State* (1956-84) 10 S.C.N.D. 52.

Fact Discovered in Consequence of Information Given by an Accused.

Musa Sadau and Another v. The State (1968) N.M.L.R. 208

Coker, J.S.C cited with approval at page 212, the following passage of the Privy Council in *Kuruma v. The Queen* (1955) A.C. 197:

> *In their Lordships' opinion the test to be applied in considering whether it is relevant to the matters in issue. If it is, it is admissible and the court is not concerned with how the evidence was obtained. While this proposition may not have been stated in so many words in any English case there are decisions which support it, and in their Lordships' opinion it is plainly right in principle... There can be no difference in principle for this purpose between a civil and criminal case. No doubt in a criminal case a judge always has a discretion to disallow evidence if the strict rules of admissibility would operate unfairly against an accused.*

For the fact of the case, see Chapter 2, supra.

On admission and confessions generally, see further: *Diri v. African Newspapers (Nig.) Ltd.* [1990] 3 N.W.L.R. (Pt. 139) 1392; *Umeojiako v. Ezenamuo* (1990) 1 N.W.L.R. (Pt. 126) 253; *Gwani v. Ebule* [1990] 5 N.W.L.R. (Pt. 149) 201, *Pas (Nig.) Lt. v. New Nigeria Salt Co. Ltd* [1990] 6 N.W.L.R. (Pt. 159) 764; *Ejidike v. Akunyi* [1990] 5 N.W.L.R. (Pt. 152) 564; *Aromolaram v. Oladde* [1990] 7 N.W.L.R. (Pt. 162) 359; *Akpan v. State* [1990] 1 N.W.L.R. (Pt. 124) 92; *Agholor v. A.G. Bendel* (1990) 6 N.W.L.R. (Pt. 155)

141; *Ogugu v. State* [1990] 2 N.W.L.R. (Pt.1340 539; *Adeyemi v. State* [1991] 6 N.W.L.R. (Pt. 195) 1; *Udo v. Okupa* [1991] 5 N.W..R. (Pt. 191) 365; *Faponle v. U. I. T.H.B.M.* [1991] 4 N.W.L.R. (Pt. 183) 43, *Sam v. State* (1991) 2 N.W.L.R. (Pt. 176) 699; *Bature v. State* [1991] 5 N.W.L.R. (Pt. 194) 697; *Gbadamasi v. State* [1991] 6 N.W.L.R. (Pt. 196) 182; *Ejinima v. State* [1991] 6 N.W.L.R. (Pt. 200) 627; *Ekpenyong v. State* [1991] N.W.L.R. (Pt. 200) 683; *Mohammed v. State* [1991] 5 N.W.L.R. (Pt. 192) 438; *Omotayo v. N.R.C.* [1992] 7 N.W.L.R. (Pt. 254) 471; *Honika Sawmill Ltd v. Hoff* (1992) 4 N.W.L.R. (Pt. 238) 673; *Durugo v. State* [1992] 7 N.W.L.R. (Pt.225) 525; *Abasi v. State* (1992)1 N.W.L.R. (Pt. 260) 383; *Ezewusim v. Okoro* [1993] 5 N.W.L.R. (Pt. 294) 478; *Onwuanumkpe v. Onwuanumkpe* [1993] 8 N.W.L.R. (Pt. 310) 186; *Ogunjobi v. State* [1993] 8 N.W.L.R. (Pt. 313) 602; In Re: *Osakwe* [1994] 2 N.W.L.R. (Pt. 326) 273; *Balogun v. A G., Federation* [1994] 5 N.W.L.R. (Pt. 345) 442; *Kasa v. State* [1994] 5 N.W.L.R. (Pt. 344) 269.

Chapter 4

STATEMENT BY PERSONS WHO CANNOT BE CALLED AS WITNESSES

Sections 33 to 37 of the Evidence Act.

This chapter relates to the English common law rule of hearsay, an expression or term not contained in the Evidence Act.

> *Evidence of a statement made to a witness by a person who is not himself called as a witness may or may not be hearsay. It is hearsay and inadmissible when the object of the evidence is to establish the truth of what is contained in the statement. It is not hearsay and is admissible when it is proposed to establish by the evidence, not the truth of the statement, but the fact that it was made:*

Subramaniam v. Public Prosecutor [1956] 1 W.L.R. 965 at 969. See also *N.C.H.C. Ltd. v. Owoyele* [1988] 4 N.W.L.R. (Pt. 90) 588. There are exceptions to the rule against hearsay.

Statements, written or verbal, of relevant facts made by a person who is dead are themselves relevant facts in the following cases:

a) when the statement is made by a person as to the cause of his death or as to any of the circumstances of the transaction which resulted in his death, in cases in which the cause of that person's death comes into question;
b) when the statement was made by such person in the ordinary course of business;
c) when the statement is against the pecuniary or proprietary interest of the person making it;
d) when the statement gives the opinion of any such person, as to the existence of any public right or custom or matter of public or general interest;
e) subject to certain conditions, when the statement relates to the existence of any relationship by blood, marriage or adoption, the person making the statement had special means of knowledge;
f) the declarations of a deceased testator as to his testamentary intentions, and as to the contents of his will (S. 33).

Evidence given by a witness in a judicial proceeding, or before any person authorised by law to take it, is relevant for the purpose of proving, in a subsequent proceeding, or in a later stage of the same judicial proceeding, the truth of the facts which it states, when the witness is dead or cannot be found, or is incapable of giving evidence, or is kept out of the way by the adverse party, or when his presence cannot be obtained without an amount of delay or expense which, in the circumstances of the case, the court considers unreasonable (S. 34(1)). See also the proviso and S. 34(2) and (3). A statement in accordance with the provisions of sections 290, 291 or 319 of the Criminal Procedure Act or section 244 of the Criminal Procedure Code, may afterwards be used in evidence in the trial of any person accused of an offence to which the same relates, if the person who made the statement is dead or the court is satisfied that for any sufficient cause his attendance cannot be procured (S. 35). Section 36 provides for the admission of written statements of investigating police officer who cannot attend the court in certain cases. Finally any statement made by an accused person at a preliminary investigation or at a coroner's inquest may be given in evidence (S. 37).

The Rule Against Hearsay

Armels Transport Ltd. v. Madam Atinuke Martins [1970] 1 All N.L.R. 27.

The plaintiff claimed N6,447 damages for the negligent driving by the defendants' driver of an omnibus which collided with the plaintiff's tipper on the Lagos/Ikorodu Road. A sketch plan, Exhibit 'J' was admitted in evidence. P.W.6, the police constable who took the sketch plan said under cross-examination: "the people in the bus showed me the point of impact. I do not know their names and they did not sign the sketch". The learned trial Judge relied on this evidence.

HELD

The point shown on the plan as the point of impact not being within the personal knowledge of the policeman and not being admissible by virtue of section 90 of the Evidence Act was inadmissible, being hearsay evidence.

Lewis, J.S.C., said at page 31:

We must first of all indicate that the evidential value of exhibit J, the sketch plan, was very limited. The plan was not agreed by the parties and could only therefore be produced by the witness to support his evidence of what he actually said at the spot and had recorded at the time... John Ogunleye who was the 8th P.W. was never asked any question about showing 6th P.W. the point of impact and it was not shown that the persons who informed the 6th P.W. of where the point of impact was could not be found and called as witnesses so that the plan could not be admitted as a whole.... The measurements on the sketch plan made by the 6th P.W. of what he himself saw and found were admissible.... but the point marked as the point of impact on which the learned trial judge relied was not admissible.

A. J. Adeka and another v. M.A. Vaatia [1987] 1 N.W.L.R. [Pt. 48] 134.

The plaintiff/respondent claimed against the defendant/appellant at the trial court the sum of N54,300.00 as special damages for breach of a building contract between the plaintiff and the defendant. The learned trial Judge *inter alia* made the following findings:

P.W. 3..... testified that ... the plaintiff informed him that he was to build some 3-bedroom quarters with their boys' quarters and he was to be paid 80% of each valuation..... The witness impressed me as a witness of truth and I believe him. D.W. 4.... said the plaintiff told him that he was to receive 80% of monies paid to the defendants while the defendants would keep 20%.... I therefore find as a fact that the agreement between the plaintiff and the defendants was that the plaintiff would be paid 80% of the money due on each valuation certificate and the defendant would keep 20% thereof.

HELD

Hearsay evidence is inadmissible and cannot form the basis of any judgment given by any court and it is immaterial whether the evidence was objected to or not at the trial court.

A most cursory examination of the evidence of P.W.3 and D.W.4 relied upon by the learned trial Judge in this regard will show that the evidence was hearsay evidence. It is clear that both P.W.3 and D.W.4 were only repeating to the court what the plaintiff told either of them as to the terms of payment in the building contract between the plaintiff and the defendants. Neither of them was talking of his personal knowledge on the point in question" - Per Agbaje, J.C.A. (as he then was) at page 145.

Management Enterprises Ltd. and Another v. Jonathan Otusanya [1987] 2 N.W.L.R. (Pt. 55) 179

The plaintiff brought an action claiming N16,000.00 as damages in respect of a motor accident in which the plaintiff received serious injuries and the 2nd defendant died. In his testimony, the plaintiff said *inter alia*:

"I made inquiries about Insurance papers and I was told that the vehicles were not covered by any Insurance policy."

HELD

The evidence of the plaintiff was hearsay and therefore inadmissible.

In *Tyosar v. The State* (1979) 3 C.A. 386, it was held that where a police investigator narrates to court what a third party told him in the course of his investigation and the third party is not called to give evidence such testimony would amount to hearsay and therefore inadmissible if the testimony seeks to prove the veracity of what the third party told the police investigator. See *also R. v. Fumeh* (1944) 10 W.A.C.A. 148; *Abowaba v. Adeshima* (1946) 12 W.A.C.A. 18; *The Queen v. Electoral Commissioner, Western Region and Another* (1957) W.R.N.L.R. 135; *Koki v. Kano Native Authority* 1968 N.N.L.R. 58; *Ogulechi v. The State* (1956-84) 10 S.C.N.D. 6.

Dying Declarations

R. v. John Ogbuewu(1949) 12 W.A.C.A. 483

The deceased made a statement to a police constable on the day he had the wound. This was on his hospital bed. He was weak and appeared to be in pain and the constable asked him if he could speak and make a statement, which he said he could. The constable then said to him: "Do you think you are going to die?" to which the deceased replied: "I don't know whether I was going to die." The deceased then made a statement as to the cause of his injuries which were the cause of his death three days later.

HELD

For a dying declaration to be admissible in evidence, there must be proof that the deceased, when making it, believed himself to be in danger of approaching death.

Garba and Another v. The Queen (1959) 4 F.S.C. 162

After suffering an attack which ultimately caused his death, the victim told the first person who found him injured that he was going to die, that he had been beaten and that one Momo had instigated that beating. The evidence as to the deceased's statement of impending death was extracted by a leading question. No objection to the form of the question was taken until it had been put and answered. After the deceased had been taken home and given water, he made a further statement as to how he received his injuries, in the presence of two persons. According to them the deceased then said nothing about his expectation of death. In spite of the objection to this evidence, the trial Judge admitted it. He said: "That is a sufficient belief in impending death to support further declarations made the same evening."

HELD

> That is too wide an expression because of the possibility that the expectation of death might have been, owing to his being at home and among friends, removed from the mind of the deceased, and therefore the evidence of the later declaration was wrongly admitted.

R. v. Daniel Bubowariowe Bebetebe (1938) 4 W.A.C.A. 67.

The deceased was struck by the appellant with a machete. She was then admitted at the Degema Hospital on 14th May, 1937. On 15th May, 1937, a Justice of the Peace, with an interpreter visited the deceased at the hospital and took from her a "dying declaration". In this, after giving her name she said "I am wounded and likely to die." The appellant though in custody at the material time the statement was made, was not present. The trial court admitted the statement as a dying declaration.

HELD

> The dying declaration was properly admitted.

The court said at page 68:

> *It is to be noted that these provisions (referring to section 51 of the Criminal Procedure Ordinance (Cap. 20) are very materially different from the law in England, where before a dying declaration is admissible it has to be shown that it was made in a settled hopeless expectation of immediate death. Here the requirements are far less and we are of the opinion that the woman's own statement "I am wounded and likely to die" is sufficient to comply with the section and shows that she believed herself to be in danger of approaching death.*

See also R. *v. Harry and Others* (1938) 4 W.A.C.A. 37; *Sunday Akpan v. The State* [1967] N.M.L.R. 185; *Oruakpor Okoror v. The State* [1967] N.M.L.R. 189; *Dan-Almajiri v. The State* (1956-84) 10 S.C.N.D. 2;

Okoronkwo v. The Queen (1956-84) 10 S.C.N.D. 21; Ndiono v. The Queen (1956-84) 10 S.C.N.D. 22 2; *Vorgho v. The State* [1972] 1 All N.L.R. (pt. 2) 1; *Akinfe v. The State* [1988] 3 N.W.L.R. (pt. 85) 729.

NOTE

The rationale behind the principle of law that dying declaration is an exception to the hearsay rule was given by Eyre, C.B. *in R. v. Woodcock* (1789) 1 Leach 500 at 503. The basis for the exception is that nobody *in extrimis* would choose to depart this world with a lie on his lips. He would certainly choose to tell the truth if even for the first and the last time. The principle of law is contained in section 33 of the Evidence Act. There is one material difference between section 33 and the English law. The position under the English law is that the court can infer from the nature of the wounds sustained by the deceased that he was "in fear of death" when he made the declaration. See *The Sussex Peerage case* (1844) 11 C and F. 85 at 112. The position is different in Nigerian Law. Before a dying declaration is admitted by the court, there must be a positive evidence that the deceased was "in fear of death". This point was clearly made by the Supreme Court in *Oruakpor Okoror v. The State, supra*. In other words, in order to constitute a dying declaration in Nigerian law, the deceased must believe himself to be in danger of approaching death at the time of making the declaration.

Declarations Made in the Course of Business

R. v. Taoridi Lawani
1959 L.L.R. 97.

At the trial of the accused for manslaughter the prosecutor sought to tender in evidence a Police 'Accident Report' book in which entries were made by a police constable since dead both from and outside his personal knowledge.

HELD

That the entries in the 'Accident Report' book within the knowledge of the deceased constable are admissible under section 33(b) of the Evidence Act on the ground that they were made in the course of his professional duty.

Relevancy of Certain Evidence Given in a previous Judicial Proceeding

The Queen v. Adiaha Nwa Ikpe (1960) 5 F.S.C. 180

Two witnesses were absent at the trial: one was dead and in regard to the other, who was on leave abroad, the evidence was that he might perhaps be back about the end of July. Their depositions were tendered through the registrar of the High Court and accepted in evidence.

HELD

> The Judge was justified in accepting both depositions in the circumstances; and although it is desirable that evidence identifying the depositions should be given, there was no miscarriage of justice in accepting them as authentic as they came from the custody of the registrar. See also *Alade v. Aborishade* (1960) 5 F.S.C. 167.

The Queen v. Enebieni Ijoma [1961] All N.L.R. 518.

The accused was charged on an information containing nine counts of forging and uttering a certificate and testimonial and thus procuring himself to be registered as a medical practitioner under the Medical Practitioners and Dentists Act, Cap. 116. He was also charged with possession of poison for an illegal purpose contrary to section 59 of the Pharmacy Act, Cap. 152. The prosecution applied for the depositions of three witnesses, who gave evidence at the preliminary investigation in the Magistrate's Court, to be admitted in evidence under the provisions of section 34 of the Evidence Act. The witnesses were resident in the United Kingdom and had to be brought to this country at great expense to the Federal Government to give evidence at the preliminary inquiry. It was argued for the accused that the said depositions were inadmissible.

HELD

> The court has a discretion to admit or refuse to admit the deposition of a witness under section 34 of the Evidence Act.
>
> *The court undoubtedly has a discretion whether it will admit evidence envisaged by section 34 of the Evidence Ordinance. The Director of Public Prosecutions has rightly pointed out it must be shown that the court took into consideration facts which it should not have. It does not necessarily follow*

that, because another court has refused the admission of a deposition under certain circumstances that I should do the same" - Per Dickson J. at page 528.

See also *Odu v. The State* [1965] N.ML.R. 129; *Mozie v. Mbebie and Another* [1966] N.M.L.R. 167; *Doka and Others v. The State* (1968) N.M.L.R. 487; *Korgba v. The State* [1968] N.M.L.R. 344; *Philips and Another v. The State* [1968] N.M.L.R. 409; *Ajao and Other v. Owoseni and Others* [1986] 5 N.W.L.R. (Pt. 43) 578; *Majekodunmi v. The Queen* (1952) 14 W.A.C.A. 64; *Babalola and Another v. The State* [1970] 1 All N.L.R. 44.

Omidokun Owonyin v. Omotosho [1961] All N.L.R. 304.

This was an action for title to land. The plaintiff claimed a declaration that the land belonged to his family. With the consent of the plaintiff the defendant put in evidence the proceedings in a case he had against one Onitabo.

HELD

The proceedings in *Omotosho v. Onitabo* (the case between the respondent/defendant and a stranger) was not legal evidence and could not have been relied upon.

Bairamian, F.J. said at page 308:

In the judgment under appeal Omotosho v. Onitabo *begins to be used in the review of the evidence for the plaintiff; both there and later the entire proceedings are used as if they were legal evidence, which, with respect, was a mistake. Evidence given by a witness in another case may be used to impeach his credit if, in the later he says something different, but what he said in the earlier case does not become evidence in the later case. And a judgment given in another case can, in appropriate cases, be put in later suit, to prevent the re-opening of the same question. One hopes that the indiscriminate introduction of other proceedings into a trial will be discontinued.*

George Obi Ikenye and Another v. Akpala Ofune and Others [1985] 2 N.W.L.R. (Pt. 5) 1

The plaintiffs brought a representative action for themselves and on behalf of the people of Ekpechor Community at Ogwuashi-Uku High Court, Bendel State for a declaration of title to a parcel of land at Ekpochor, damages for trespass and an injunction restraining the defendants from committing further trespass on the land. There had been previous litigations between the communities over land disputes. A copy of the record of proceedings in one of the previous suits was admitted in evidence as *Exhibit 2* without objection.

HELD

1) It was wrong for the trial Judge to consider the evidence of the plaintiff in *Exhibit 2* when the plaintiff was not called as witness before the trial Judge.
2) Where a piece of evidence is inadmissible by virtue of non-compliance with the provisions of section 34 (1) of the Evidence Act, the fact that there was no objection to its admissibility is irrelevant; it remains inadmissible.
3) The provision in section 34(1) is an exception to the hearsay rule; and being such an exception, there are constraints on the admissibility of such evidence as truth of what it says and these constraints are mentioned in the proviso to the section.

See further *Lawal v. Dawodu and Another* (1972) 8-9 S.C. 83; *Nahman v. Odutola* (1953) 14 W.A.C.A. 381; *The Queen v. Iziogu* [1963] 1 All N.L.R. 99; *Umoren v. The Queen* [1963] 1 All N.L.R. 369; *Ayanwale and Others v. Atanda and Another* [1988] 1 N.W.L.R. (Pt. 68) 22; *Folarin v. Durojaiye* [1988] 1 N.W.L.R. (pt. 70) 351.

On the chapter generally, see further: *Ogba v. State* [1990] 3 N.W.L.R. (Pt. 139) 505; *Folami v. Cole* [1990] 2 N.W.L.R. (Pt. 133) 445; *Olekaibe v. State* [1990] 1 N.W.L.R. (Pt.129) 632; *Judicial Service Committee v. Omo* [1990] 6 N.W.L.R. (Pt. 157) 407; *Achara v. A.G. Bendel State* [1990] 7 N.W.L.R. (pt. 160) 92; *Utteh v. State* [1990] 3 N.W.L.R. (Pt. 138) 301; *Daniels v. State* [1991] 8 N.W.L.R. (Pt. 212) 715 *Ojiako v. The State* [1991] 2 N.W.L.R. (pt. 175) 578; *Akpan v. State* [1992] 6 N.W.L.R (Pt. 248) 439, *Utteh v. State* [1992] 2 N.W.L.R. (Pt. 223) 257; *Glorylux Ass. Ind. v. N.P.F.M.B.* [1993] 7 N.W.L.R. (Pt. 305) 341; *Oladejo v. State* [1994] 6 N.W.L.R. (Pt. 348) 101.

Chapter 5

STATEMENTS MADE IN SPECIAL CIRCUMSTANCES

Sections 38 to 44 of the Evidence Act.

Entries in books of account, regularly kept in the course of business, are relevant whenever they refer to a matter into which the court has to inquire, but such statements shall not alone be sufficient evidence to charge any person with liability (S. 38). Any entry in any public or other official bank, register or record, stating a fact in issue or relevant fact and made by a public servant in the discharge of his official duty, or by any other person in performance of a duty specially enjoined by the law of the country in which such book, register or record is kept, is itself a relevant fact (S. 39). Statements of facts in issue or relevant facts made in published maps or charts generally offered for public sale, or in maps or plans made under the authority of Government, as to matters usually represented or stated in such maps, charters or plans, are themselves relevant facts (S. 40).

While section 41 provides for relevancy of statement as to fact of public nature contained in certain Acts and notifications, section 42 provides that certificates of specified officers will be sufficient evidence in all criminal cases. The specified officers include Government chemists, a Government pathologist, entomologist, the Accountant-General, the Governor, the Deputy Governor or the General Manager of the Central Bank of Nigeria. But see Evidence (Amendment) Decree No. 17 of 1988. By section 43, a copy of such certificate intended to be produced at the proceedings must be sent to the adverse party at least ten clear days before the day appointed for the hearing. The court shall, in the absence of evidence to the contrary, presume the genuiness of the signature contained in such certificate and that the person signing it held the office which he professed at the time when he signed it (S. 44). The presumption is rebuttable.

Entries in Books of Account.

Oguma Associated Companies (Nig.) Ltd. v. International Bank for West Africa Ltd. [1988] 1 N.W.L.R. (Pt. 73) 658.

The plaintiff bank sued the defendant company for a sum of N1,155,695,46 being balance of money had and received by the defendant for their use at their own request by way of loan, overdraft, accomodation and or facilities. At the trial the bank called four witnesses and tendered without any objection the certified statements of account it forwarded to the defendant company and were admitted as Exhibit G. The learned trial Judge in his judgment on his own volition reopened the issue of admissibility of the certified statements of account, held them to be inadmissible and expunged them from the record, holding that they did not comply with section 96 of the Evidence Act.

HELD

1) Copies of entries in a bankers book are admissible in evidence under certain conditions provided by sections 96 (1)(h) and 96 (2)(e) 2(e) of the Evidence Act. They are not inadmissible in evidence in any event in law

2) Exhibit G, the statement of account is not inadmissible in any event in law and that it is evidence subject to certain conditions and it has been admitted without any objection to its admissibility, any further objection to its admissibility is deemed to have been waived and the court could not properly reopen the admissibility of the document.

Esso West Africa Inc. v. T. Oyegbola [1969] N.M.L.R. 194.

In the Ikeja High Court, the plaintiff claimed against the defendants balance of amount due and owing for petroleum products sold and delivered to them. The Accountant of the plaintiffs testified that he kept the defendant's accounts and that at the end of every month he made out Statements of Accounts which he sent to the defendant by post or through the sales representatives in charge of his area. He sought to tender the ledger copies of the Statements of Accounts but an objection was raised. The learned trial Judge upheld the objection on the ground that no evidence was led as to the whereabout of the originals and that

the ledger copies sought to be tendered did not constitute the type of Books of Account contemplated
by law as those were "unusually bound and the pages are not easily replaced". The plaintiff's claim was dismissed.

HELD

1) Section 37 of the Evidence Act does not require the production of "Books of Account" but makes "entries" in such books relevant for purposes of admissibility
2) The Ledger cards were wrongly rejected by the trial Judge. They should have been admitted.
(3) Section 37 of the Evidence Act deals only with admissibility and leaves the issue of weight to be attached to the entries admitted thereunder to the Court.

In *Yesufu v. African Continental Bank* (1976) 4 S.C. 1, it was held that for the purpose of sections 96 (1) (h) and 37 of the Evidence Act, 'bankers books' and 'books of account' include ledger cards.

See further *Yassin v. Barclays Bank* [1968] 1 All N.L.R. 171; *New Nigerian Bank Ltd. v. Legemah* [1986] 2 N.W.L.R. (pt. 25) 785; *Alade v. Obikade* (1976) 2 S.C. 183; *Duriminiya v. Commissioner of Police* 1961 N.R.N.L.R. 70.

Entry in Public Records

R. v. Taoridi Lawani
1959 L.L.R. 97

For the facts, See chapter 4, supra.

HELD

That a Police 'Accident Report' book is not a public or other official book within the meaning of section 38 of the Evidence Act.

Bellamy, J. on the interpretation of section 38 said at page 98:

"As to the first condition, the question arises, is Police Book A/67 a 'public or other official book, register or record' within the section? It cannot possibly be said to be a 'register' or 'record'. Is it a 'public or other official book?' I have no hesitation in answering that question in the negative. Public documents are defined in section 108 of the Evidence Ordinance. The relevant words are 'documents forming the acts or records of the acts, of public offcers'. In my view, the kind of 'acts which section 108 has in view is indicated in section 112 of the Evidence Ordinance. In my opinion, it does not cover the inquiries which a police officer may make, whether under the Criminal Procedure Ordinance or otherwise which may or may not result in action. Therefore I rule that the entries are not admissible on this ground".

Mewi Onyeanwusi and Another v. Stephen Mbaochu and Others. (1953) 14 W.A.C.A. 311.

In cross-action relating to a piece of land, an entry in the minute book of a meeting of the Native Authority responsible for the land including the piece in dispute was admitted. The trial Judge admitted the entry under section 38 of the Evidence Act.

HELD:

The entry was admissible under section 38 of the Evidence Act.

Foster Sutton, P. said at page 312:

The learned trial Judge admitted the entry under section 38 of the Evidence Ordinance, but when discussing the question of its admissibility or otherwise he said: 'To reject such evidence would be to exclude a type of evidence which is admitted in the Native Courts'. I agree that it is admissible under the Evidence Act, but am unable to agree that the fact that evidence is admissible in proceedings before Native Courts makes it admissible in proceedings before the Supreme Court.

NOTE

The learned Justice of the Court of Appeal was right in pointing out that the mere fact that a document is admissible in Native Courts does not mean that it is also admissible in the High Court, the then Supreme Court. While that point is very well taken, particularly in the context of the "guiding principle", one would have expected the learned Justice to state the reason why the particular entry was admissible under the section. While he was not obliged to give the reason under normal circumstances, the facts of the case were such that he ought to have done so. It is only logical to think that since the learned Justice rejected the reason given by the learned trial Judge for admitting the document, he ought to have stated the correct reason. It would appear that the entry is admissible under section 38 because it is an entry in a public or official book and most probably by an official of the Native Authority in the performance of his official duties.

Chief Ayeni (Odofin in Ikoro) and others v. His Highness Joseph Dada (the Olojaoke of Okemesi and others (1978) 3 S.C. 35

The plaintiffs' claim in the High Court of Akure was for declaration of title to land, forfeiture of rights as customary tenants, recovery of possession, damages for trespass and injunction. The case of the plaintiffs was based on traditional evidence and various acts of ownership. Part of the evidence in support of the acts of ownership consisted of intelligence reports prepared by former administrative officers who served in the area in the course of their official duties. The reports were produced in Court from the custody of Director of National Archives.

HELD:

The Intelligence Reports were properly admitted in evidence in view of the provisions of sections 6 and 38 of the Evidence Act.

Maps, Charts and Plans.

In *Ndubokwu v. Chukwuma* (1956-84) 10 S.C.N.D. 17, the Supreme Court held that the mere fact that a map or plan is produced from the custody of a Government Department as part of its records is not sufficient evidence of its having been prepared under the authority of the Government.

Certificates of Certain Government Officers

In *The State v. Omoraka* [1971] 1 U.I.L.R. 26, it was held that a ballistician was not one of the class of persons covered by the provisions of section 41(1) of the Evidence Act which deals with certificates of certain specified Government Officers. Accordingly, his report, which would have assisted the Court in determining whether the gun-shot was accidental or intentional, could not be admitted in evidence. In *Huston Okpara (Alias Austin Okpara) v. Federal Republic of Nigeria* (1977) 4 S.C. 531, the appellant was convicted of having in his possession some counterfeit American Bank Notes knowing same to be counterfeit contrary to section 5(1)(b) of the Counterfeit Currency (Special Provisions) Decree, 1974. The only evidence purporting to show the notes to be counterfeit was a letter written by the Central Bank of Nigeria in which the Bank conveyed the opinion of the Department of Trade of the United States of America to the effect that the notes were forged. It was held that since the letter from the Central Bank was hearsay evidence, it was inadmissible for the purposes of proof within the meaning of section 41 of the Evidence Act. In *Chiokwu and Others. v. The State* (1979) 1 F.C.A 159, it was held that the modification in section 41 of the Evidence Law of Eastern Nigeria is intended to make a certificate issued by the Officers mentioned in that section admissible if such a certificate is issued by any other offficer known by any other title in the service of the State.

NOTE

In view of the fact that evidence is now in the Exclusive Legislative List, the amendment is no longer the law. But it was quite a meaningful amendment because changing circumstances of governmental machinery may necessitate slight or even major changes of official nomenclature. And in these times of frequent changes of government with corresponding changes of government machineries and institutions, the amendment is justifiable. The point should be made that the Evidence (Amendment) Decree, No. 17 of 1988 has amended the section, that is section 41 of the Evidence Act.

By the amendment, the category of specified officers is extended to include "any other chemist so specified by the Government Chemist of the Federation or of the State, any pathologist or entomologist specified by the Director of Medical Laboratories of the Federation or of the State or any Accountant specified by the Accountant-General of the Federation or of the State". The above apart, notwithstanding the provisions of subsection (1) of section 41"any cetificate issued and produced by any officer in charge of any laboratory established by the appropriate authority may be taken as sufficient evidence of facts stated therein." (New S. 41(2). "Appropriate Authority" by the amendment means the Inspector-General of Police, the Director of Customs and Excise or the Minister of Health. (New S. 41(3). The repealed section 41(2) vested the power to give notice in the gazette of officers eligible to sign certificates to the Federal Minister of Health. The amendment is a welcome change.

Peter Ogbera v. The State
[1985] 3 N.W.L.R. (Pt.11) 120

The appellent was chargedwith murder but was convicted of manslaughter. At the trial, the prosecution tendered the report of the post mortem examination which was performed by one Dr. S.A. Bankole, Chief Consultant Pathologist who was part time Government pathologist. He certified the cause of death to be "Internal Haemorrhage" from gun wound. He was however not called as a witness as he was said to have left the service and his whereabouts were unknown.

HELD:

Section 41 of the Evidence Act allowed the tendering of the medical report without calling the maker to come to court although the court under the proviso to the section has the power on the application of a party to the proceedings or on its own motion to direct that any such officer shall be summoned to give evidence before it. The medical report was held admissible. See also *Idirisu v. The State* [1967] N.M.L.R. 12.

Chapter 6

JUDGMENTS OF COURTS OF LAW

Sections 49 to 56 of the Evidence Act.

The existence of any judgment, order or decree which by law prevents any court from taking cognizance of a suit or hold a trial, is a relevant fact when the question is whether such court ought to take cognizance of such suit or to hold such trial (S. 49). By section 50(1), a final judgment, order or decree of a competent court in the exercise of probate, matrimonial, admiralty or insolvency jurisdiction which confers upon or takes away from any person any legal character, or which declares any person to be entitled to any such character, or to be entitled to any specific thing, not as against any specified person but absolutely, is relevant when the existence of any such legal character, or the title of any such person to any such thing, is relevant. See also S. 50(2). Judgments, orders or decrees other than those mentioned in section 50 are relevant if they relate to matters of a public nature relevant to the inquiry; but such judgments, orders or decrees are not conclusive proof of that which they state (S. 51).

Judgments, orders or decrees other than those mentioned in sections 50, 51 and 52 of the Act are irrelevant unless the existence of such judgment, order or decree is a fact in issue, or is relevant under some other provisions of the Act or any other Act (S. 52). Any party to a suit or other proceeding may show that any judgment, order or decree which is relevant under sections 49, 50 or 51 and which has been proved by the adverse party, was delivered by a court without jurisdiction, or was obtained by fraud or collusion (S. 53). Every judgment is conclusive proof, as against parties and privies, of facts directly in issue in the case, actually decided by the court, and appearing from the judgment itself to be the ground on which it was based; unless evidence was admitted in the action in which the judgment was delivered which is excluded in the action in which that judgment is intended to be proved (S. 54).

Section 55 provides for effect of judgment not pleaded as estoppel. By the section if a judgment is not pleaded by way of estoppel it is as between parties and privies deemed to be a relevant fact, whenever any matter, which was, or might have been, decided in the action in which it was given, is in issue in any subsequent proceeding (S. 55(1)). Such a judgment is conclusive proof of the facts which it decides or might have decided, if the party who gives evidence of it had no opportunity of pleading it as an estoppel (S. 55(2)). When any action is brought against any person for anything done to him in a judicial capacity, the judgment delivered and the proceedings antecedent thereto, are conclusive proof of the facts therein stated, whether they are or are not necessary to give the defendant jurisdiction, if, assuming them to be true, they show that he had jurisdiction (S. 56).

Previous Judgment: When Relevant

A.G. Ijale v. A.G. Leventis and Co. Ltd
[1965] 1 All N.L.R. 176.

The company employed the appellant as a produce-buying agent on salary and commission and gave him advances to buy produce with. The first suit was brought by the company with a claim for an amount for money had and received for their use. He pleaded that there could only be finality in computation when the upgraded produce had been graded and he was credited with its value. The Privy Council in its judgment said that "it became necessary to know the state of the final account between the parties" and credited him with less for produce than the Supreme Court had done and increased the amount awarded to the company. There was also a second suit. Part of the claim in that suit brought by the company related to four lorries given to the agent. The referee allowed him credits which he accepted. The third suit which was the basis of the appeal was brought by the agent claiming

1) a sum as balance of commission short paid,
2) a sum as balance of salary due,
3) a sum as value of lorries returned,
4) a sum as value of graded cocoa not accounted for by the company, and
5) a sum for labour and grading expenses.

HELD

On the pleadings the balance of indebtedness between the parties on the produce transactions was directly in issue in the first suit; the judgment in it was conclusive proof of what that balance was, and having regard to section 53 of the Evidence Act, the claims numbered (1), (2) (4) and (5) could not be made.

Peter O. Ezeani and Others v. Nneli Ezene and others (1935) 2 W.A.C.A. 342.

The plaintiffs claimed in the High Court of the Onitsha Judicial Division a certain amount as special damages being value of their properties alleged to have been wilfully destroyed and looted by defendants. The claim was dismissed and the plaintiffs appealed on the ground that the learned trial Judge refused to receive in evidence the certified copy of criminal proceedings in which the defendants were convicted in respect of the same acts on which proceedings were grounded.

HELD

The learned trial Judge was in error in not receiving in evidence the certified copy of the criminal proceedings.

Kingdom C.J. referring to the English cases of Re Crippen (1911)p. p. 108 and Mash v. Darley [1914] 1 K.B.1 said at page 343:

> *Accepting this as a correct statement of the present law, it follows that the document should have been admitted in the court below and admitted to prove not only the fact of the conviction but as presumptive proof of the commission by the defendants of the acts for which the convictions were had. This being so this court has, in my opinion, no option but to send the case back to the court below for re-trial.*

Chief Dugbo and others v. Chief M. Kporoaro [1958] W.N.L.R. 73

Persons interested in the subject matter of an action for a declaration of title but not made parties thereto applied for joinder as defendants. Joinder was refused, court suggesting that they bring a separate action. They did so and the two actions were consolidated. In the first suit certain earlier judgments were pleaded but the paragraph in the statement of claim so pleading was struck out. In the second suit these judgments were pleaded by way of defence. The trial Judge took the judgments into account in deciding both actions. He also took into account one of these judgments the copy of which admitted in evidence had not been certified.

As a result, he entered judgment for the plaintiffs in the first case and for the defendants in the second. The unsuccessful parties appealed to the Federal Supreme Court.

HELD

Where judgments are not pleaded as an estoppel they may be admissible in evidence although not pleaded if they are matters of evidence and relevant to the issue .

See further *Alade v. Aborishade* (1960) 5 F.S.C. 167; *Agunbiade v. Sasegbon* [1968] N.M.L.R. 223; *Okunoren v. United Africa Co. Ltd.* (1951) 20 N.L.R. 25; *Chiwendu v. Mbamali* (1980) 3-4 S.C. 31.

Inspector-General of Police v. Marke
1957 N.R.N.L.R. 97; (1957) 2 F.S.C. 5.

The accused was tried in a Magistrate's Court for the offence of stealing. After most of the evidence had been led, the prosecution applied for an adjournment in order to call a further witness. The application was refused, whereupon the prosecution closed its case. The Magistrate then ruled that a *prima facie* case has not been made out against the accused sufficiently the require him to make a defence. He accordingly discharged him under section 286 of the Criminal Procedure Act. Subsequently the accused was again charged before another Magistrate with the same offence. He pleaded *autrefois acquit* and his plea was upheld.

De Lestang, F.J. said at pages 99 and 101:

> *We will now proceed to examine the relevant sections of the Criminal Procedure Ordinance. The first section requiring consideration is section 181. In so far as it is material in this appeal, this section provides that a person who has once been tried by a court of competent jurisdiction for an offence and acquitted, shall not, while such acquittal remains in force, be liable to be tried again for the same offence. This is really an explanation of what the plea of* autrefois acquit *is... Applying this construction to the present case, it is plain that the discharge of the accused was on the merits and that accordingly the Magistrate was right to uphold the accused's plea, and that the High Court was also right in upholding the Magistrate's decision.*

The State v. Ede and Others
[1964] 8 E.N.L.R. 60

At the previous proceedings the State Counse for the prosecution after the prosecution's evidence, discontinued the proceedings and the High Court discharged the accused persons. Thereafter another indictment was preferred against the accused persons on charges based on the same facts. At the trial the defence counsel submitted that the discharge of the accused persons was a bar to subsequent criminal proceedings against them for the same offence.

HELD

A discharge after all the evidence of the prosecution has been led is a bar to subsequent proceedings on the same set of facts.

See also *Nwali v. Inspector-General of Police*, 1 E.R.N.L.R. 1. See generally *Edu v. Commissioner of Police* (1952) 14 W.A.C.A. 163; *Ogeyi and Others v. Inspector-General of Police* 1957 N.R.N.L.R. 140.

Previous Judgment: When Irrelevant

Bello Adeleke v. Benjamin Adewusi
[1961] 1 All N.L.R. 37

In an action for a declaration of title to a piece of land and an injunction against trespass, the plaintiff put in evidence the entire proceedings of a 1954 case but it was only a page of the judgment that was referred to in the address of his counsel.

Taylor, F.J. said *per incuriam* at pages 39 and 40:

> *The proceedings were tendered in bulk without any reference being made to any particular portion of same at the time they were tendered. During the address of counsel for the appellant there was only one reference to them and that was in respect of one page in the judgment of the High Court. I would draw attention to S. 34 and SS. 48 to 55 of the Evidence Ordinance as showing the conditions under which statements, evidence, proceedings and judgments in previous matters and suits are admissible in subsequent suits in the hope that in future this all too frequent practice of tendering parts of proceedings which are of no possible evidential value and in some cases are utterly irrelevant and inadmissible will cease. At the hearing of this appeal with the exception of a few passages in the judgment of the High Court contained in exhibit "C", no further use was made of this 164 page exhibit. This must and will reflect itself in the costs to be awarded in this appeal.*

Gabriel Agu v. Nwakama Atuagwu
(1955) 21 N.L.R. 83

The appellant began by complaining to the police who prosecuted the respondent for theft, but he was acquitted. The appellant then sued the respondent for damages in connection with the goods he had lost, and the civil action was heard before the Magistrate who had heard the criminal prosecution. At the beginning of his cross-examination, the appellant was asked whether there had been an unsuccessful prosecution in which he had given evidence and he said, Yes; and then at the request of counsel for the respondent and in spite of an objection by counsel for the appellant, the Magistrate admitted the whole record of the criminal proceedings in evidence. The hearing continued and in the end the Magistrate dismissed the claim.

HELD

The record of the criminal proceedings should not have been admitted in evidence.

Dan Boyi Gyel Zang v. Commissioner of Police 1960 N.R.N.L.R. 86.

The appellant, the holder of a mining lease, was convicted on a charge laid under section 3(2) of the Minerals Act which makes it an offence to mine on any lands in Nigeria except as is provided in the Act. To prove the charge, the prosecution sought to prove that labourers employed by the appellant had committed an offence against section 14(2) of the Act which prohibits mining on certain lands and after offering proof of that, invoked section 104 of the Act, which provides that upon proof that an offence against the Act has been committed by a person employed by the holder of the mining lease, such holder shall be held liable for the offence and to the penalty provided therefore, unless he proves that the offence was committed without his knowledge or consent and that he had taken all reasonable means to prevent the commission of the offence.

HELD

The fact that the workman had been convicted was not admissible evidence that they had committed the offence. It was evidence that another court considered that they had committed it, and the opinion of that other court, like all opinions, except expert opinion, was irrelevant.

See also *A.T.M.N. Ltd. v. Chief Inspector of Mines* (1950) 19 N.L.R. 69.

R. v. Lasisi Jinadu (1948) 12 W.A.C.A. 368

The appellant, a lance corporal in the police was tried and acquitted by the police in orderly room proceedings of the offence against Regulation 17(2) of the Police Regulations, made under the Police Ordinance, 1942.

At the trial in the Magistrate's Court for charges of compelling action by assault contrary to section 367 of the Criminal Code assault occasioning harm contrary to section 355 of the same code, the appellant raised the point that he had been previously acquitted of similar charges by the police.

HELD

> Proceedings against a police officer in a Police Orderly Room for an offence against discipline are not proceedings in a court having jurisdiction to hear and determine a criminal charge and therefore the special plea of *autrefois acquit* or *autrefois convict* cannot be raised upon a criminal prosecution of the police officer for an offence against the Criminal Code arising out of the same facts.

See also *Inspector-General of Police v. Johnson* 1959 L.L.R. 55; *Ababio v. The Republic* (1967) 1 G.L.R. 347; *Onuoha v. The State* [1988] 3 N.W.L.R. (Pt. 83) 460.

Chapter 7

OPINION OF THIRD PERSONS

Sections 57 to 66 of Evidence Act.

As a general principle of law, opinion evidence of a witness is irrelevant and therefore inadmissible. This general principle is contained in section 66 of the Evidence Act. The section provides thus:

> *The fact that any person is of opinion that a fact in issue, or relevant to the issue, does or does not exist is irrelevant to the existence of such fact except as provided in sections 57 to 65 of this Act.*

The exceptions to the general rule are contained in sections 57 to 65 of the Act. These will be briefly examined here.

When the court has to form an opinion upon a point of foreign law, native law or custom, or of science or art, or as to identity of handwriting or finger impression, the opinions upon that point of persons specially skilled in such foreign law, native law or custom, or science or art, or in question as to identity of handwriting or finger impressions, are relevant facts. Such persons are called experts (S. 57). Sections 58, 59, 61 and 62 which further provide for opinions as to foreign law, native law and custom, handwriting and general custom or right respectively, expatiate the main provision of section 57.

Facts, not otherwise relevant, are relevant if they support or are inconsistent with the opinions of experts, when such opinions are relevant (S. 60). When the court has to form an opinion as to

(a) the usages and tenets of any body of men or family; or

(b) the constitution and government of any religious or charitable foundation; or

(c) the meaning of words or terms used in particular districts or by particular classes of people, the opinions of persons having special means of knowledge thereon are relevant facts (S. 63). When the court has to form an opinion as to the relationship of one person to another, the opinion, expressed by conduct, as to the existence of such relationship, of any person who, as a member of the family or otherwise, has special means of knowledge on the subject ; is a relevant fact. However, such opinion will not be sufficient to prove a marriage in proceedings for a divorce or in petition for damages against an adulterer or in a prosecution for bigmany (S. 64). Whenever the opinion of any living person is relevant, the grounds on which such opinion is based are also relevant (S. 65).

Opinions of Experts: Competence of Experts

Michael John Aouad and Another v. Inspector-General of Police (1954) 14 W.A.C.A. 449

The appellants were convicted by a Magistrate of an offence under section 427 of the Criminal Code relating to certain ore, on the nature of which a person holding office as an Inspector of Mines under the Minerals Act was called by a prosecution as an expert and gave evidence of the office he held and the tests he had made to ascertain the nature of the ore, but was not cross-examined on those tests or his qualifications. In the appeal from the Magistrate to the Supreme Court the question of his being an "expert" was raised for the first time and decided against the appellants, who further appealed.

HELD:

The nature and duties of the witness's public office and the technical or scientific tests he made, which were not challenged, constituted *prima facie* evidence of his qualification to be admitted as an expert witness.

Seismograph Service Ltd.v. Benedict Etudjere Onokpasa [1972] 1 All N.L.R. (Pt. 1) 343

The plaintiff claimed a sum of money being special and general damages for damage caused by the defendant to the plaintiff's eight college buildings; because of a seismic operation the defendant carried out near the buildings. In order to determine the crucial point as to the cause of the damage to the plaintiff's building both parties called technical evidence on the seismic operations.

HELD:

The correct test of the relevance of the witness's opinion as that of an expert is whether he is specially skilled in the particular field in question; and if, applying that test, the only expert opinions before the court are those of one party's witnesses the trial Judge, unless for good reasons otherwise, should accept them. "It is, therefore, clear that the only expert evidence that the learned trial Judge had before him was that of defendant's experts; these show that the defendant was responsible for the damage caused to buildings. Ground 2 (a) of appeal is therefore upheld" - Per Sowemimo, J.S.C. (as he then was) at page 355.

Seismograph Service (Nig) Ltd. v. Robinson Kwavbe Ogbeni [1976] 1 N.M.L.R. 290

The plaintiff claimed a sum of money being special and general damages for nuisance caused by defendants in the course of carrying out an oil exploratory exercise of exploding oil testing chemicals. The plaintiff alleged that the vibration damaged his house. He called no expert evidence but the defence called an expert who testified that the exercise could not have damaged the building. The learned trial Judge held that expert evidence was not absolutely necessary to establish that damage to the house was traceable to seismic operations.

HELD:

(1) Following *Seismograph Service Limited v. Onakpase* (Supra) it is not correct to say that the evidence of an expert is not absolutely necessary to prove damage alleged to be caused by vibrations radiating from seismic operations taking place within a reasonable distance from the property damaged; these being phenomena beyond the knowledge of the unscientific and untrained in siesmology and civil engineering, expert evidence is essential.

(2) The need for experts or persons specially trained or qualified in the particular discipline to assist the court by testifying on causation arising from certain phenomena studied by them is acknowledged in subsections (1) and (2) of section 56 of the Evidence Act. See also *Seismograph Service (Nig.) Limited v. Akperuovo* (1974) 6 S.C 119 at 128.

Lawrence Fasugba v Inspector-General of Police [1964] 2 All N.L.R. 15

The appellant was convicted mainly on the strength of the evidence of the police handwriting analyst whom the Magistrate treated as an expert. There was no evidence that the expert witness had ever been concerned with comparison of handwriting nor any attempt made to show that the witness was sufficiently qualified to be treated as an expert. The appellant contended that the expert evidence was wrongly admitted.

HELD:

There was not enough evidene from the record to warrant treatment of the witness as an expert. "I do not think there was enough material before the Magistrate - judging from the record - to warrant treatment of the witness as an expert and the reception of his opinion as relevant evidence. As this opinion was the crucial evidence on which the Magistrate relied, the appeal must be allowed". Per Onyeamar, Ag. C.J. (as he then was) at page 16.

In Ajani v. The Comptroller of Customs (1954) 14 W.A.C.A. 37, the Judicial Committee of the Privy Council said that "a principle which emerges from them (referring to the decided cases) considered together is that not only the general nature, but also the precise character of the question upon which expert evidence is required, have to be taken into account when deciding whether the qualifications of a person entitle him to be regarded as a competent expert".

In R.v. Onitiri (1946) 12 W.A.C.A. 58, it was held that there is no objection to a police officer giving expert evidence for the prosecution on a charge of foregery in order to prove the falsity of the document, provided that the trial court is satisfied that he is sufficiently qualified to do so.

See further *Adeseye v. Taiwo* (1956) 1 F.S.C. 84; *Alonge v. I GP* (1959) 4 F.S.C. 203; *Wambai and Another v. Kano Native Authority* [1965] N.M.L.R. 15; *Commissioner of Police v. Ogechukwu* [1974] 4 E.C.S.L.R. 147; *The Queen v. Wilcox* [1961] All N.L.R. 631; *Okojie and Others v. Commissioner of Police* [1961] W.N.L.R. 91

Opinion as to Foreign Law Joseph

Adeniji Ogunro v. Christian Ajoke Ogedeagbe (1960) 5 F.S.C. 137

The deceased owned land in Lagos and in Ghana, and the applicants took out summons for directions on who were entitled to his estate and for an order of distribution. Counsel for the other side contended that the court had no jurisdiction to deal with the property in Ghana; he was given time to produce evidence on the Ghana law of succession. The court below made an order, that one item of property be given to one and another item to another, including the land in Ghana, on the basis of the law of Nigeria. The respondents to the action appealed as appellants.

HELD:

It was the duty of the appellants to prove that the law of Ghana was different; they did not produce evidence; so the trial Judge was bound to apply the law of Nigeria.

Said Ajani v. The Comptroller of Customs (1952) 14 W.A.C.A. 34

The appellant had number of Franc Notes in a suitcase in an aeroplane at the Kano airport on his way to Rome. The suitcase and notes were seized and the Comptroller of Customs brought an action for penalties against the appellant as defendant for attempting to export the notes. A witness, the Manager of Barclays Bank Kano who claimed that he had thirty-two years experience of banking business, twenty-four years being in Nigeria, testified that to the best of his knowledge the notes were French Colonial Franc Notes and that they were legal tender in French West Africa on the material date.

HELD:

The witness had by virtue of his banking experience in Nigeria pecular means of knowledge on the subject, and as the Manager of a branch of an authorised dealer in foreign currency had important and responsible public duties in relation to such currency and was bound to make himself acquainted with the subject; his evidence was rightly admitted and was sufficient to establish that the notes were legal tender in French West Africa.

Opinions of Men of Science or Art

Okojie and Others v. Commissioner of Police (1961) W.N.L.R. 91

The appellants who were all officers of a Customary court were charged before a Benin Magistrate's Court for assault occasioning harm. They were convicted. At the trial, a dispenser was called who deposed that complainant was brought to his dispensary for treatment but in his judgement the trial Magistrate said that he was disregarding this evidence in so far as it purported to show that it came from an expert.

HELD:

The trial Magistrate was right in exercising caution in disregarding the evidence of the dispenser in so far as it was meant to be the evidence of an expert witness. See also Yau *Tittidabele v. Sokoto Native Authority*(1964) 1 Nigerian Law Journal, 123.

Customary Law

Liadi Giwa v. Bisiriyu Erinmilokun [1961] All N.L.R. 294

The action was commenced by the plaintiff for himself and all other members of the Aromire Chieftaincy Family claiming a declaration of title under native law and custom to certain lands in LAgos, and for an order of possession against the respondent. An issue arose as to whether the grant made to Saba was absolute under native law and custom.

HELD:

In the absence of any reported case establishing the position of warrant chiefs as regards grants by land-owning chiefs, of which case the trial judge would be bound to take notice, the trial Judge was perfectly justified, on the evidence before him, in saying that the appellant family had not discharged the onus placed upon them.

Taylor, F.J. said at page 296:

It is a well established principle of law that native law and custom is a matter of evidence to be decided on the facts presented before the court in each particular case, unless it is of such notoriety and has been so frequently followed by the courts that judicial notice ought to

be taken of it without evidence required in proof.

Pastor S.G. Adegboyega and Others v. Peter Otasowie Igbinosun and Others [1969] N.M.L.R. 9

The plaintiffs in the Benin High Court laid claim to a piece of land which they averred belonged to them as registered trustees of the Apostolic Church Benin. They averred that the land, upon which the church stands had been acquired by them in accordance with Bini customary law and that it was later conveyed to them by His Highness Akuenzua II, Oba of Benin, the trustee of all land in Benin. The defendants denied the plaintiffs story. There was no evidence led as to Benin customary law but the trial Judge relied on *Uwagboe v. Eubumwan* (1959) 4 F.S.C. 91 and held that all Benin land was vested in the Oba of Benin as legal owner and that all grantees obtained only possessory title.

HELD:

(1) It is settled law that except, where a rule of customary law has received judicial recognition, such rule is treated for the purpose of proof as a matter of fact.

(2) Since no evidence of Benin customary law on the grant of lands was in fact led, the plaintiffs did not prove the grant they stated they originally received from Oba Eweka II or the subsequent formal one which they purported to receive from Oba Akenzua II "in accordance with Bini native law and custom" as alleged in their work.

(3) The judge erred when he purported to treat as a matter of judicial notice a fact which according to the pleadings, the plaintiffs must prove.

Asani Fijabi v. Odunola (1955-56) W.N.L.R. 133

The appellant claimed against the respondent in an Ibadan Native Court a debt. Judgement was given to the appellant. The respondent appealed to the Judicial Native Committee of Appeal, Ibadan. The appeal was allowed on a proposition of a rule of customary law which was not referred to by any of the witnesses in the court of first instance nor by the only witness called in the Court of Appeal. A further appeal was made to the High Court.

HELD:

The Judicial Native Court of Appeal was wrong in deciding the case on a point of customary law upon which evidence was never led.

NOTE

It does not appear that the decision of Taylor, J. is correct. It is not consistent with decisions which came before and after. For purposes of proof, the courts have drawn a dichotomy between native or customary courts presided over by non-legal practitioners and those presided over by legal practitioners. On the authority of *Edokpolor v. Idehen* (1961) W.N.L.R. 11 and *Ehigie v. Ehigie* [1961] All N.L.R. 842, customary law will be regarded as a fact to be proved in a customary court presided over by a legal practitioner even when they are natives of the areas. The point must be made that a contrary decision was taken in *Ehioghae and Another v. Ehioghae* (1964) N.M.L.R. 30 to the effect that it is not obligatory on Presidents of Customary Courts who are natives of the area of juridiction of the court familiar with their own custom to require proof of that custom. While the decision or *Ehioghae* is preferred to those of *Idehen* and *Ehigie*, the decision of Taylor, J. in *Odunola* is still indefensible as it is against the correct decision of the West Africa Court of Appeal in *Ababio*

II v. Nsemfo (1947) 12 W.A.C.A. 127 in which the court held that the proof by evidence of a native custom is not necessary before a Native Court whose members are familiar with that custom. See also *Odufuye v. Fatoke* (1977) 4 S.C. 11 Cf. *Chiga v. Umaru* [1986] 3 N.W.L.R. (Pt. 29) 460, where the Court of Apeal held that the presumption that Area Courts knew native law and custom in their areas of jurisdiction does not apply to Upper Area Court which because of its wide jurisdiction, cannot be expected to be conversant with all the native laws and customs of the diverse tribes within its jurisdiction. See also *Pam v. Gyang,* 1969 N.N.L.R. 99.

On proof of customary law, see further *Ayoola and Others v. Folawujo and others* (1942) 8 W.A.C.A. 39; *Oshodi v. Aremu* (1952) 14 W.A.C.A. 83; *Adedibu v. Adewoyin and Another* (1951) 13 W.A.C.A. 191; *In the Estate of Alayo* (1946) 18 N.L.R. 89; *Waziri v. Ugye and others* 1977 N.N.L.R. 129.

General Custom or Right

The Queen: Ex Parte Chief Lewis Ekenga v Chief Ideliaguahan Ozogula II [1962] 11 N.L.R. 265

The respondent who was an aspirant to the stool of his deceased father alleged an Igbo custom on the part of the appellant to perform certain ceremonies to enable him take over the father's stool. The appellant refused. The proceedings were brought to compel the appellant to perform the ceremonies. Evidence was led to the effect that without the performance of the ceremonies, there could be no succession to a sub-chieftaincy under the customary law of the town. The Head Chief, in his evidence gave a different version of the Native Law and Custom, which according to him, was applicable in the circumstances. He did not, however, call any witness to corroborate his version.

HELD

Native law and custom must be strictly proved, and, although its proof does not depend on the number of witnesses called, the uncorroborated evidence of the person who asserts it is not sufficient.

Olubunmi Cole and Another v. P.A. Akinyele and Others (1960) 5 F.S.C. 841

Deceased was married to a wife under the Marriage Ordinance. He also had two children by another woman - one born during his wife's lifetime, and another born shortly after her death; and he acknowledged both as his children. They sued for a declaration that the y were his legitimate children and entitled to share in his estate, he having died intestate. They relied on the Yoruba custom accepted by the courts in *Alake v. Pratt (1955) 15* W.A.C.A. 20.

On the issue of proof of the alleged Yoruba custom, *Brett, F.J.* said at page 86:

> *No attempt was made to call any evidence as to any rule of native law and custom which might apply to their case, but the court was invited to take judicial notice, under S.14 (2) of the Evidence Ordinance, of the rule under the native law and custom of the Yoruba people which was held proved by Jibowu, J. and the West African Court of Appeal in Alake v. Pratt (1955) 15 W.A.C.A. 20 to the efffect that if paternity of children is acknowledged by a man during his lifetime they are to be regarded as legitimate and entitled to share in his estate with his children born of a marriage contracted under the Marriage Ordinance... I would accept the decision in Alake v. Pratt as one of sufficient authority to enable the courts to take judicial notice of the rule of Yoruba law and custom which was there held proved, but there can be no warrant for extending it, without evidence, beyond the circumstances in which it has been held to apply.*

In Larinde v. Afiko and Another (1940) 6 W.A.C.A. 108, it was held that a particular custom to be proved by calling witnesses and a decision of one case in 1892 does not make it notorious by frequent proof. In *Santos v. Ikosi Industries Limited and Another* (1942) 8 W.A.C.A. 29, the court refused to follow an earlier decision in *Henshaw v. Henshaw (1927)* 8 N.L.R. 77 on the ground that the decision which was based on native law and custom at Calabar was not necessarily applicable in Epe. In *Buraimo v. Gbamgboye* (1940) 15 N.L.R. 139, it was held that it is unnecessary to bring evidence to prove particular customs which have been so frequently before the courts as to be well established and notorious. See also Giwa v. Erinmilokun, supra.

NOTE

The law is not settled as to the level of notoriety of a custom to enable the court take judicial notice in future cases. In *Larinde v. Afikpo, supra* the West African Court of Appeal refused to accept a single decision as sufficient to satisfy the notoriety test, but in *Cole v. Akinyele, supra*, the Federal Supreme Court accepted a single previous decision on Yoruba customary law of legitimacy. In *Qnisiow v. Fagbenro* (1954) 21 N.L.R. 3, De Comarmond, S.P.J. accepted three previous decisions of Yoruba customar land law. Finally, *in Kareem and Others v. Ogunde and others* [1972] 1 All N.L.R. 73, the Supreme Court took judicial notice of a Yoruba customary law where children are entitled to succeed to the property of a deceased who died intestate in Lagos. He relied on three provious decisions in *Lewis v. Bankole* (1908) 1 N.L.R. 81; *Miller Brothers v. Ayeni* (1924) 5 N.L.R. 42 and *Caulcrick v. Harding* (1926) 7 N.L.R. 48.

While it is difficult to know the yardstick or rationale used by the courts, this much is clear that the whole procedure is largely speculative, depending upon the whims and caprices of the court at the material time and the extent of notoriety as sensed by the court. Perhaps a more scientific way of approaching the fluid position is to distinguish between decisions of the Supreme Court, the highest court of the land, and those of other courts below it. A single authoritative decision of the Supreme Court should satisfy the notoriety test, within the meaning of section 14(2) of the Evidence Act. And in this respect, the custom involved must form the ratio decided of the case and not a mere obiter. (*Cf. Ifediorah and Others v. Ume and Others* [1988] 2 N.W.L.R. (Pt. 74) 5). Decisions of other courts which practice the doctrine of precedent or *stare decisis* could satisfy the notoriety test by more than one pronouncement on the custom. A rule of the thumb is not possible; not even a rule of the hand. Each case has to be determined in the light of the circumstances. For example there is nothing wrong for a single decision of the Court of Appeal to satisfy the notoriety test if it is given by a full court and the issue was not a subject of appeal.See further *Apoeslo v. Awodiya* [1964] 1 All N.L.R. 48; *Toriola v. Williams* (1982) 7 S.C. 27; *Shaibu v. Bakare* (1956-84) 10 S.C.N.D. 108; *Odunsi v. Ojora* [1961]1 All N.L.R. 283; *Erokwu v. Bosah* [1966] 1 All N.L.R. 166; *Taiwo v. Dosunmu* [1965] 1 All N.L.R. 399; *Nelson v. Nelson* (1932) 1 W.A.C.A. 215; *Solomon v. Botchway* (1943) 9 W.A.C.A. 127; *Archibong v. Archibong* (1947) 18 N.L.R. 117; *Kosoko v. Kosoko* (1937) 13 N.L.R. 13; *Owoo v. Owoo* (1945) 11 W.A.C.A. 81.

Opinions of Non-Experts as to Handwriting

Salami Lawal v. The Commissioner of Police (1960) W.N.L.R. 72

The appellant was convicted in a Magistrate's Court for stealing various sums of money. At the trial, the Magistrate accepted the evidence of a witness who was not an expert but who stated he was conversant with the appellant's signature as they had worked together, as proof that the appellant had made certain signatures in dispute. In addition to the acceptance by the Magistrate of the evidence of the witness referred to above, the Magistrate himself compared the disputed signatures with others admitted by the appellant to be his own and came to the conclusion that the disputed signatures were made by the appellant.

HELD:

(1) The trial Magistrate being a judge of fact and law was within his right in making the comparison referred to and acting upon the conclusion of fact.

(2) The trial Magistrate was right in law in accepting the evidence of the witness referred to above.

Kester, Ag J. said at page 74:

> *It is for the purpose of ascertaining the means and extent of the witness being acquainted with a party's handwriting that the tests in section 60(2) of the Evidence Ordinance are to be applied by the opponent. It is not necessary for the witness to state them in his evidence in chief to prove that he was acquainted with the writing. The learned trial Magistrate did not therefore err in law in accepting the evidence of the fourth prosecution witness on that point. Apart from the evidence about handwriting the learned trial Magistrate believed and accepted the evidence of the fifth prosecution witness that it was the appellant who made the disputed signature. This is a finding of fact which this court cannot, on the whole evidence before the Magistrate disturb.*

The Queen v. Michael Adedapo Omisade and Others [1964] N.M.L.R. 67

The appellants along with others, all numbering thirty-one were charged with treasonable felony and conspiracy to commit a felony and to effect an unlawful purpose. To prove that one of the appellants paid a visit to the Naval Base in furtherance of the alleged conspiracy the prosecution produced the Visitors' Book of the Institution. A police handwriting expert also gave evidence which would appear to favour the defence that the signature in the book alleged to be that of the particular appellant was in fact not his. The trial Judge discarded the evidence of the expert and resolved the matter himself by comparing the signature in the Visitors' Book with other writing of the accused and found as a fact that it was the accused who made the signature.

HELD:

The learned trial Judge was wrong in completely discarding the evidence of a police handwriting expert, confused though it was, and resolving the matter himself by comparing the signature in the Visitors' Book of the Naval Base with other writings of the appellant (7th accused).

Joseph Zakiah v. Board of Customs and Excise [1966] N.M.L.R. 293

The appellant was charged with the offence of "knowingly and with intent to defraud the Government of Nigeria of the customs duty" payable on certain goods contrary to section 145 (a) of the Customs and Management Act, 1958. The first prosecution witness and the owner of certain premises entered into a tenancy agreement with the appellant. The trial Judge on close examination found that the signature on the agreement and the statement signed by the appellant were identical. He found the appellant guilty.

HELD:

It is good law that a court is entitled to examine disputed writings and form ts own opinion. There could be no doubt at all on a comparison of the two documents that there was a striking similarity. Moreover, the trial Magistrate bearing in mind the positive evidence of identification of the appellant by the landlord and the witness to the tenancy agreement as the person who signed Exhibit "A" as J.A. could have come to no other conclusion than he did on this point.

In *Odulaja v. Inspector-General of Police* (1955-56) W.R.N.L.R. 3, it was held that a court can properly reject the evidence of an expert under section 56(1) of the Evidence Act and accept that of a witness who was familiar with the writing of the accused under section 60 of the Act.

See generally R.v. Onitiri (1946) 12 W.A.C.A. 58.

Opinions as to Identity

Sunday Omega v. The State
[1964] 1 All N.L.R. 379

The appellant was convicted in the High Court of Jos on three counts of robbery and brigandage contrary to sections 298 and 301 of the Penal Code. He was tried along with three others and he was the first accused. The second and fourth accused were discharged and acquitted and discharged, whilst like the appellant the third accused was convicted on some of the counts.

On the issue of identification parade, Coker, J.S.C. said at page 381:

> *With regard to (ii) (this was the identification parade) we observe that although answers were elicited from the 5th prosecution witness in the course of his cross-examination to the effect that he was at some time during the investigation of the case shown the photographs of the accused persons and the knife seized from him, the witness was not examined as to what stage of the investigaton he was shown these photographs, for unless it was clear that the photographs were shown to the witness in order to enable him to identify the suspects at a subsequent identification parade, we cannot see how the propriety of the identifiction parade in the circumstances of the present case can be impungned. The learned trial Judge adverted to this point in his judgment and observed that it was not clear whether this (i.e the showing of the photographs) was before or after the identification parade and that the police officer who conducted the parade was not questioned on the point. We do not think there is any substance in this point.*

Samuel Bozin v. The State
[1985] 2 N.W.L.R. (Pt. 8) 465

The appellant was charged with armed robbery punishable with death under section 1(2) (a) of the Robbery and Firearms (Special Provisions) Act, No. 47 of 1970. Each of the witnesses who testified for the prosecution said that he knew the appellant before the night of the robberies. They knew him by name; they knew that he lived at No. 5 Eboh Road Close, Warri. An identification parade was conducted by the police whereupon the appellant was identified as one of the robbers. On the identification parade, the 2nd P.W. testified inter alia:

> *... the policemen... came in a beetle car and asked if we knew Samuel Bozin and we replied "yes". They asked if we could identify him if we saw him? We replied, "yes".. When we got to the Police Station the policemen asked us "Is this the man?" We answered "yes".*

HELD:

(1) The identification of a suspected person must be very carefully conducted and it is very wrong to point out the suspected person and ask "Is that the man". The

usual and proper way is to place the suspected person with sufficient number of others and to have the identifying witness pick out the accused without any assistance. This is what is called an identification parade.

(2) It is highly improper to invite witnesses to identify the accused not mixed up with other people. A parade with only one accused on parade is definitely not an identification parade known to the law.

(3) The identification parade conducted in this case fell far short of the requirement of the law. It was not proof beyond reasonable doubt. See also *Ajibode v. The State* [1987] 1 N.W.L.R. (Pt. 48) 205; *Isaku and Others v. The State* [1986] 1 N.W.L.R. (Pt. 17) 516.

Opinions as to Age

Sunday Modupe v. The State [1988] 4 N.W.L.R.(Pt. 87) 130

The appellant along with eight others were charged in the Owo High Court, Ondo State, with the murder of one Dapo Awobayokun on 20th December, 1983. He and two others were convicted of the offence and sentenced to death. His appeal to the Court of Appeal was dismissed. It was argued that the death sentence passed on the appellant who was under seventeen years at the time of the commission of the offence was in violation of sections 208 and 368 (3) of the Criminal Procedure Act.

HELD:

(1) Where a trial Judge is in doubt as to age, when as in this case evidence of the proper age is material, he is obliged and obligated by the provisions of section 208 of the Criminal Procedure Act not to estimate, in vacuo the age of the accused, but to make due inquiry as to the age of that person and for the purpose may take such evidence as may be forthcoming at the time or at the time to which the inquiry may be adjourned.

(2) If the trial court believes that the accused put his age rather low, he is at liberty to adjourn the case and call a medical witness to testify to the age of the accused.

(3) Where the Judge calls for medical evidence, he will be perfectly within his right to compare the evidence of the accused as to his age with the evidence of the doctor and could pick and choose which he believes.

Oputa, J.S.C. said at page 137:

To reject the positive assertion by the appellant that he was born on the 3rd of November, 1967 without any contrary evidence at all - either in cross-examination or in rebuttal seems to be much more than a trial court is allowed to do. To base such a rejection on the subjective estimation of the

> *trial Judge looks quite arbitrary, nay dangerous. It looks as though the trial Judge converted himself into a witness, gave evidence of the age of the appellant, and then proferred his own evidence of age to that of the appellant.*

See also Oladimeji v. The Queen [1964] 1 All N.L.R. 131; R.v. Bangaza (1960) 5 F.S.C. 1; R.v. Jonal and Others (1934) 2 W.A.C.A. 120.

On expert opinion, see further: *Shell Petroleum v. Otoko* [1990] 6 N.W.L.R. (Pt. 159) 693; *Bello v. Ringim* [1991] 7 N.W.L.R. (Pt. 206) 668; *M.I.A. and Sons Ltd. v. F.H.A.* [1991] 8 N.W.L.R. (Pt. 209) 295; *J.E. Elukpo and Sons Ltd. v. F.H.A.* [1991]3 N.W.L.R. (Pt. 179) 322; *Aina v. Jinadu* [1992] 4 N.W.L.R. (Pt. 233) 91; *Otti v. Otti* [1992] 7 N.W.L.R. (Pt. 252) 187; *Zimit v. Mahmoud* [1993] 1 N.W.L.R. (pt. 267) 71; *Azu v. State* [1993] 6 N.W.L.R. (Pt. 299) 303; *Uchegbu v. State* [1993] 8 N.W.L.R. (Pt. 309) 89; *A.S.T.S. v. Atoloye* [1993] 6 N.W.L.R. (Pt. 298) 233.

Chapter 8

EVIDENCE OF CHARACTER

Sections 67 to 72 of the Evidence Act.

In civil cases the fact that the character of any person concerned is such as to render probable or improbable any conduct imputed to him is irrelevant, except in so far as such character appears from facts otherwise relevant (S. 67). The general rule of law is that the prosecution cannot lead evidence of the accused person's bad character or that he committed another offence or misconducted himself on any occasion at the trial. The law requires the prosecution to prove its case beyond reasonable doubt on the facts before the court and not rely on the previous bad conduct of the accused person. However, the Act contains some exceptions to this general rule.

In criminal proceedings, the fact that the person accused is of a good character is relevant (S.68). Although section 69(1) provides that the bad character of an accused person is irrelevant, section 69(2) contains exceptions. By the subsection, the fact that an accused person is of bad character is relevant when the bad character of the accused person has given evidence of his good character. An accused person may be asked questions to show that he is of bad character in the circumstances mentioned in paragraph (d) of the proviso to section 160 (S.69(3)). Whenever evidence of bad character is relevant, evidence of a previous conviction is also relevant (S. 69(4)).

In civil cases the fact that the character of any person is such as to affect the amount of damages which he ought to receive, is relevant (S. 70). In actions for libel and slander in which the defendant does not by his defence assert the truth of the statement complained of, the defendant is not entitled on the trial to give evidence in chief with a view to mitigation of damages, as to the circumstances under which the libel or slander was published, or as to the character of the plaintiff, without the leave of the judge, unless seven days at least before the trial he furnishes particulars to the plaintiff of the matters as to which he intends to give evidence (S. 71). The word "character" in the above context means reputation as distinguished from disposition, and except as mentioned above, evidence may be given only of general reputation, and not particular acts by which reputation or disposition is shown (S. 72).

The General Rule

Wahabi Alao Lawal v.The State [1966] N.M.L.R. 343

The appellant was convicted on a charge of murder in the High Court of Lagos. He appealed to the Supreme Court. There was evidence on which a jury properly would have been justified in convicting the appellant for murder, but; by a grave error of judgement the prosection called evidence showing that the appellant was a man of bad character, given to acts of voilence and cross-examined the appellant to the same effect, although none of the circumstances in which such evidence or such question are admissible were present.

HELD:

So far as its prejudicial effect is concerned there is no distinction between calling evidence of bad character and asking questions in cross-examination of an accused person tend to show his bad character.

In *Haruna and Another v. Police* [1967] N.M.L.R. 145, where a witness said "I know the accused's financial background. He is financially sound. Since I have known the accused, I don't remember him getting involved in any trouble". The court held that it was character evidence within section 71 of the Evidence Act.

Evidence of Character: Civil Cases

M.A. Oyewole v. J. Kelani (1948) 12 W.A.C.A. 327

Plaintiff instituted an action claiming damages done to his motor-car by the reckless driving of defendant's lorry by defendant's driver. Upon the action coming on for hearing, counsel for the plaintiff sought to put in evidence the proceedings in criminal action against defendant's driver, heard in the Magistrate's Court and in which defendant was convicted in respect of the said collision between plaintiff's car and defendant's lorry. There was an objection.

HELD:

Evidence of conviction of a person for a motoring offence arising out of an accident which is later on the subject of civil proceedings to which that person is a party, is inadmissible at the civil trial.

Criminal Cases: Accused's Good Character

Muhammadu Haruna and Another v Police [1967] N.M.L.R. 145

The first appellant was convicted of robbery and the second appellant was convicted of abetment of the robbery and of voluntary causing hurt of the complainant. The second appellant called two witnesses as witnesses to character. One of them was the Manager of a Bank (but he did not say in his evidence whether or not the accused was a customer in his bank) who said "I know the accused's financial background. He is financially sound. Since I have known the accused I don't remember him getting involved in any trouble". In his judgment, the learned trial Chief Magistrate said"

> *I have completely disregarded the evidence of his two character witnesses which for the purpose of considering the guilt of the second accused in respect of the offence charged is completely irrelevant.*

HELD:

The evidence of a witness to character, the Manager of a Bank where the accused was not a customer, was character evidence within section 71 of the Evidence Law of Northern Nigeria and admissible under section 67.

Hurley, C.J. said at page 148:

> *However, character evidence which is not logically relevant having regard to the nature of the offence can have weight even though it is relevant in law and therefore admissible. Such, for example, would be evidence of a reputation for honesty on a charge of violence, or evidence that the accused was of a pacific character on a charge involving dishonesty. But the charges against the 2nd appellant involved both violence and dishonesty. It seems to us therefore, having regard to the evidence which the character witnesses gave, that the learned Acting Chief Magistrate must have had section 71 of the Evidence Law in mind.*

Criminal Cases: Accused's Bad Character

Odutade v. Police
(1952) 20 N.L.R. 81

Appellant was charged with others with stealing and with receiving, and by himself of being a rogue and vagabond. Evidence of convictions over ten years old was given. He was acquitted on the vagrancy charge but convicted of receiving. One ground of appeal was that the convictions were inadmissible as evidence of guilty knowledge.

HELD:

> The charge of being a rogue and vagabond which was preposterous, ought not to have been joined with the unrelated charge of stealing or receiving to prejudice the appellant; and although he did not object to the misjoinder, the trial had been unfair on tha account and the conviction would be quashed.

De Commarmand, S.P.J. said at pages 81 and 82:

> *I would observe that there is no indication in the record to the effect that the previous convictions were to be used against the appellant only to establish the charge of his being a rogue and vagabond. The learned Magistrate did not expressely say that he disregarded that evidence when dealing with the charge of receiving stolen property... It is usually difficult to say with cetainty that a certain piece of evidence has not affected a decision. The task is slightly easier when the decision is that of a Judge or Magistrate sitting without a jury... In the present case, whether or not the learned Magistrate was careful to disregard the previous convictions when deciding the charge of receiving stolen property, I feel that I cannot overlook the fact that the appellant did not have a fair trial.*

James Popoola v. Commissioner of Police
[1964] N.M.L.R. 1

The appellant was convicted by a Magistrate's Court of the offence of burglary, stealing, and unlawful wounding, contrary to sections 351, 331 and 281 respectively of the Criminal Code of Western Nigeria. At the trial, counsel for the appellant asked the complainant, testifying for the prosecution, some questions, answers to which were: "Yes, I know accused's house; I know there were 22 rooms in the house. It is a very large house. Yes, he is richer than I. I am not surprised that the accused in spite of having a 22-room house should come and steal from me, if stealing is his profession". The Magistrate ruled that by the questions and answers the appellant had put his character in issue and that evidence of his bad character was therefore admissible. When the appellant gave evidence he was asked and he answered a number of questions tending to show that he was a man of bad character. Defence counsel objected to only some of the questions.

HELD:

By the questions and answers the appellant could not be held to have put his character in issue and therefore the evidence of character later elicited from the appellant was wrongly admitted even though most of it was not objected to by counsel for the appellant.

In *Maizako and another v. Superintendent-General of Police* [1960] W.N.L.R. 188, the first appellant in his evidence made allegations against the police to the effect that they had yielded to threats by one of the prosecution's withnesses to prefer a false charge against him and the other appellants and that the prosecution's witnesses were not speaking the truth. Questions were then put to the appellant on his previous conviction on some offences. Despite the court's warning that he had no duty to answer the questions, he did so in the affirmative, saying that he used to be a dangerous burglar. On appeal, it was held that since the appellant in his cross-examination of the prosecution's witnesses cast imputations on the character of some of them, the evidence of his previous conviction was rightly admitted. In R.v. Gide (1935) 2 W.A.C.A. 334, the first witness for the prosecution when giving evidence in chief was asked: "What is accused's occupation" and replied, "stealing". It was held that was at once evidence of accused's bad character and therefore inadmissible.

Some Similar Facts

R.v. Effiong Edet Itah (1943) 9 W.A.C.A. 35

The appellant was employed by the Campagnie Francaise de L'Afrique Occidentale as a Sales Clerk. He was authorised to give "dashes" of goods to regular customers and in support prepared vouchers which were verified by the Agent and debited at the end of each month to the shop expenses. The appellant did give "dashes" and accounted for them in this way, but concurrently in returns which he rendered periodically to the Agent he made entries making it appear that a larger number of goods had been sold than had in fact been sold, and showing a similar balance of stock in hand than was truly there or should have been. Deficiencies thus concealed were discovered at an audit and take of stock. The appellant was charged with fraudulent false accounting contrary to section 438 (b) of the Criminal Code. The defence of the appellant that the missing goods had been "dashed" to customers, denying falsity of the entries, was disbelieved by the trial court.

HELD:

> The decision of the trial Judge that the entries were false and unauthorised and had been consistently repeated, while the established method of accounting for "dashes" had not been followed, with the consequence that shortages of stock had been concealed, thus resulting in fraud, was supported by ample evidence before him.

The Queen v. Olubunmi Thomas (1958) 3 F.S.C. 8

The appellant was tried in the High Court in 1957 and convicted for forgery. On appeal his conviction was questioned by the Federal Supreme Court, and a retrial ordered. One of the reasons for quashing the conviction was that inadmissible evidence given by Mrs. Ademiluyi had been admitted. The court took the view that the evidence was highly prejudicial to the appellant. He was retried and convicted. On appeal again to the Federal Supreme Court, one of the grounds was that at the retrial, Mrs. Ademiluyi's evidence was wrongly admitted again and acted upon by the learned trial Judge.

HELD:

> Since the learned trial Judge relied on Mrs. Ademiluyi's evidence, it must have prejudiced the appellant.

In *R.v. Adeniji and Others* (1937) 3 W.A.C.A. 185, it was held that evidence of previous uttering of counterfeit coins by appellant was admissible on a charge of being in possession of moulds in order to prove guilty knowlege. In R.v. Agwuna (1949) 12 W.A.C.A. 456, Blackall, P. said at page 461:

> *The only kind of previous conviction which a court is entitled to take into account when assessing sentence is one in which conviction took place before the commission of the offence for which the accused is instantly charged and convicted, the principle being that a man who already had a conviction for a similar offence before he commited the second one does not deserve to be treated with leniency.*

The Integraton of Section 159 (d) of the Act

Audu Maizako and another v. Superintendent-General of Police (1960) W.N.L.R. 188

During the trial of the appellants before the Grade A Customary Court at Oyo for assault occasioning harm, the prosecution put questions to the first appellant to show that he had been previously convicted of some offences. In spite of the court's warning that he need not answer the questions, he nevertheless answered and admitted that he used to be a dangerous burglar. The appellants were thereafter convicted and sentenced to a term of two years imprisonment with hard labour each.

HELD:

(1) That since the first appellant in his cross-examination of the witnesses had cast imputations on the character of some of the prosecution witnesses, the evidence of his previous convictions was properly accepted and his appeal against his conviction failed.

(2) That having regard to the previous character of the first appellant the sentence passed on him was not excessive; but that as the second appellant had no previous conviction the sentence passed on him was excessive and would be reduced to one of one year imprisonment with hard labour.

Cyril Anyanwu v. The Queen [1963] 1 All N.L.R. 273

The appellant was tried with another for conspiracy, fraudulent false accounting and stealing. He admitted negligence but not fraud. The co-defendant, who admitted inflating vouchers, said he did so in obedience to his superior, the appellant; he had done it too, he said, under the appellant's predecessor, who had been convicted for it. The trial Judge would not allow cross-examination of the co-defendant on his previous convictions; they related to similar frauds.

HELD:

(1) An accused person who has given evidence against any other person charged with the same offence makes himself liable to cross-examination as to his character and convictions, and the other accused person may so cross-examine him as of right.

(2) If the Judge disallows such cross-examination and it appears, as in this case, that the other accused person thereby lost a chance, albeit slight, which was fairly open to him of being acquitted, the case is one of substantial miscarriage of justice.

Chapter 9

MEANS OF PROOF

Sections 76, 77 131 to 133 of the Evidence Act.

The most common way of proof in a court is by oral evidence. This is given statutory recognition in section 76 of the Act. By the section, all facts except the contents of documents may be proved by oral evidence. Oral evidence must, in all cases whatever, be direct in the sense that if it refers to a fact which could be seen, it must be the evidence of a witness who says he saw that fact. If it refers to a fact which could be heard, it must be the evidence of a witness who says he heard that fact. If it refers to a fact which could be perceived by any other sense or in any other manner, it must be the evidence of a witness who says he perceived that fact by that sense or in that manner. If it refers to an opinion or to the grounds on which that opinion is held, it must be the evidence of the person who holds that opinion on those grounds (S.77). See also the provisos to the section.

There are however certain exceptions to the rule that all facts must be proved by oral evidence. Section 76 itself is so cautiously worded thus anticipating the exceptions to the general rule. Part VI of the Act provides for the exclusion or oral evidence by documentary evidence. As a general rule, oral evidence is excluded in respect of terms of judgments, contracts, grants, other dispositions of property (S.132) and the interpretation of documents,(S.133). The general rule applies only to parties to documents, and their representatives in interest, and only to cases in which some civil right or civil liability is dependent upon the terms of a document in question. Any person other than a party to a document or his representative in interest may, notwithstanding the existence of any document, prove any fact which he is otherwise entitled to prove. Any party to any document or any representative in interest of any such party may prove any such fact for any purpose other than that of varying or altering any right or liability depending upon the terms of the document. The provision will not affect the construction of wills (S.134)

View: Visit to Locus In Quo

R.v Albert Dogbe (1947) 12 W.A.C.A. 184

The wife of the appellant gave evidence for the prosecution. There was nothing to show if she was his wife by Christian marriage or native custom. The appellant was charged for murder. In the course of the trial the court decided to inspect the *locus in quo.* This inspection was carried out and when the court assembled the learned presiding judge made the following note on the record:

> *Court and Jurymen and defendant and counsel and witnesses and Assistant Superintendent of Police visited Afloa and the scene of the alleged shooting on the 11th April, 1947. The following notes were made by court on the scene and have been read in court to Jurymen.*

One of the grounds of appeal complained about the notes of evidence taken at the *locus in quo.*

HELD:

Where an inspection to the *locus in quo* is carried out, each of the witnesses need at the view to point out material places and things and measure distances etc. should, on the re-assembly of the court, be put into the witness box and state on oath what part he took at the inspection and what he did. He can then be cross-examined by the appropriate party in the usual way.

Lucie-smith, C.J. said at page 185:

> *The practice, and to our mind an excellent practice, in several colonies and we believe in England, is for the court accompained by the accused and his Advocate together with the Advocate for the crown and such witnesses for the prosecution and the defence as may be deemed material to proceed to the locus.*

See also *Yeku v. Inspector-General of Police* 1959 L.L.R.138.

Agbafuna Ejidike and Others v. Christopher Obiora (1951) 13 W.A.C.A. 270

Counsel for the appellant argued that the trial Judge had erred in law in holding an inspection after the close of the evidence of the *locus in quo.* It appeared from the judgment that the trial judge had referred therein to certain facts of which there was no evidence on record. The court considered the purpose of such visits and added that the judge should be careful to avoid placing himself in the position of a witnesses and arriving at conclusion based upon the record.

HELD:

Although the Judge may have erred in referring in his judgment to certain facts observed by him on the inspection, of which there was no evidence on record, and had drawn certain conclusions therefrom, the court was not satisfied that these conclusions materially affected his decision, or that if he had made such observations he would have come to a different conclusion.

Verity. Ag. P. (as he then was) said at page 274:

To this I would do no more than add that in all cases in which a visit is paid by the court to the locus in quo in a civil action the judge should be careful to avoid placing himself in the position of a witnesses and arriving at conclusion based upon his personal observation of which there is no evidence upon the record. When there is conflicting evidence as to physical facts, I have no doubt that he may use his own observation to resolve the conflict, but I do not think it is open to him to substitute the result of his own observation for the sworn testimony nor to reach conclusions upon something he has observed in the absence of any testimony on oath to the existence of the facts he has observed. Should he do so he would, in my view, be usurping the position of the witnesses....

See also *Awoyegbe and Another V. Chief Ogbeide* [1988] 1 N.W.L.R. (Pt. 73) 695: *Evoyoma and others v. Daregba and Others* [1968] N.M.L.R. 389.

Ayisatu Adunfe and others v. Inspector-General of Police (1957) 2 F.S.C. 21

During the trial at Ilesha of 125 accused persons on a charge of riot contrary to section 71 of the Criminal Code, the magistrate adjourned the case and proceeded to view the *locus* at Oshogbo in the absence of the accused.

HELD:

It was irregular for the magistrate to inspect the scene of the crime in the absence of the accused person although it might be difficult to convey 125 accused persons to view the *locus.*

Chief Aaron Nwizuk and Others v. Chief Warribo Eyeyok (1953) 14 WACA 345

In after the evidence, the judge went to inspect the land in dispute- some islands in the case- in the presence of two plaintiffs representing the plaintiffs and a defendant representing the defendant. There the defendant admitted that some of the evidence given for his side was untrue and the two plaintiffs admitted that evidence given for them regarding some of the islands was false. In the judgment dismissing the plaintiffs' claim to the islands the Judge gave an account of his inspection and mentioned the said admissions. The plaintiffs appealed arguing that it was a mistake of law to take into account statements made at the inspection; that the Judge ought to have recalled those concerned for future examination; and also that there ought to have been a separate note of the inspection made at the first opportunity.

HELD:

(1) The court did not cease to be a court when on inspection and the statements were as much oral admissions by a party in court as if they had been made in a court room, and could be taken into account as such.

(2) The absence of a record of the inspection is not fatal; statements by the Judge in a solemn judgment must be taken as a correct account of what occurred and therefore final.

In *Awoyegba and Another v. Chief Ogbeide, supra*, the Supreme Court cited the above decision in *Nwizuk* with approval. In that case, the respondents sued the appellants for a declaration of title to a disputed land situate in Ward 17H Benin-City, damages for trespass and an injunction. At the close of case for the defence, the defence counsel moved the court to visit the *locus in quo*. After the visit, the trial Judge did not make a record of what he saw nor did he state whether anybody gave evidence on the site and what were there-at said. The trial Judge did not state whether any prominent features were shown to him or whether any of the names which had been mentioned in court were pointed out to him. He adjourned the case for address and thereafter for judgment.

Craig, J.S.C. said at pages 709 and 710:

The import of the words underlined is that the court does not cease to be a court merely because it is sitting in some other place other than its normal habitat. This means that any material statement made in the course of the visit must be recorded and the opposing party given the opportunity of testing that statement, if need be, by cross- examination. In the case of Chief A. Nwizuke v. Waribo Enoyok and Anor. (1953) 14 W.A.C.A 345 ;it was held that the absence of a record of the inspection is not necessarily fatal to the case and that statements by the judge in a solemn judgment should be accepted as a correct account of what occurred. See also, Musa Naji v. Mallam S. Shafi (1956) N.M.L.R. 33. In the instant case however, the statement made by the trial Judge in his 'solemn' judgment was not a correct account of what occurred, because no witness had given that evidence. In effect what the trial Judge had done was to treat his view of the locus as "findings" in the case. In this respect, I am of the view that he erred in law and the Court of Appeal was right to uphold the appeal before it on this ground.

Adeleke Arutu v. The Queen
(1959) 4 F.S.C. 66

In March 1958 one Adesoke Adelabu who was a prominent leader in Ibadan, of a political party known as the N.C.N.C. died as a result of a motor car accident. Some of his followers, probably misguided, for some reasons, gathered together in different centres, and either deliberately or spontaneously started to attack houses of and persons of members of the rival political party known as the Action Groups and killed the deceased. After the case for the defence was closed and counsel addressed the court, the learned trial Judge reserved judgment. Three days later, that is, on the 9th August, 1958, the learned trial Judge, in his record, made a note of an inspection carried out by him that day. According to the note, the appellant, his counsel, crown counsel and witnesses in the case were present at the inspection. The note described the village and the houses in it, showing the position in which the 3rd and 4th witnesses for the crown, were described by the Judge as eye-witnesses for the crown, were hiding. The two men (3rd and 4th witnesses for the crown), the note continued, then demonstrated to the Judge where they were hiding on the two different occasions, the direction to which the deceased ran, where he was caught and where he was finally dragged to. No more proceedings appeared to have been taken after the inspection and notes taken of the demonstration by the 3rd and 4th witnesses for the crown and what they said at the inspection.

HELD:

Where an inspection of a *locus in quo* takes place, the rules and procedure applicable must be carefully observed.

Ademola, C.J.F. said at pages 67 and 68:

Counsel for the appellant has attacked this judgment mainly on two grounds. The first concerns the inspection carried out by the Judge and his notes thereon. We find it difficult to accept that the learned trial Judge meant the inspection to be part of the proceeding in this case. There is no record of any evidence taken at the inspection except the Judge's own private notes which he made part of the record. It can, therefore, be assumed from this that he did not intend to regard the inspection as part of the evidence in the case. We are not saying that an inspection of the Iocus could not be made after judgment had been reserved in a case.... But where in a case of this nature, the inspection raises matters which are prejudicial to an accused person, he or his counsel has every right to put questions to the witnesses who have made statements and demonstrated to the Judge at the scene of the crime. In fact, an inspection at which a witness demonstrates is part of the evidence and should be treated as such. See The Queen v. Karmat (1956).A.C. 256. The procedure to be carried out at an inspection was clearly set out by the West African Court of Appeal in R. v. Togbe 12 W.A.C.A. 184 and we wish to draw attention to this case. There were clearly irregularities in the conduct of the view of inspection of the Iocus in this case. As the inspection was irregularly conducted the Judge's notes of it should not, in our view, have been regarded as admissible evidence much less as a reason for basing decision.

Olasupo Aremu v. Attorney- General Western Nigeria [1967] N.M.L.R. 62

The appellant was accused of murder and was convicted by the trial judge. The judge visited the place where the identification parade had been conducted by the police because the defence in his address threw doubts on the conduct of the identification parade. At the visit the trial judge made notes of what witness and the appellant said, as witness gave evidence.

HELD

The proper procedure to adopt in such a case is as stated in R. v.. Dogbe.

The Exclusion of Oral by Documentary Evidence Lagos Timber Co. Ltd v. C.A.A. Titcombe (1943) 17 N.L.R. 14

The Plaintiffs sought to give evidence of an oral agreement which had been embodied in a written document which was itself inadmissible in evidence for non-registration under the Lands Registration Ordinance.

HELD:

Such evidence could not be given.

Butter Lloyd, J said at page 14:

The question for decision at this present stage in this case is where an agreement has been put into writing and that document has been rejected as inadmissible in evidence for non- registration under section 23 of cap. 87, can the plaintiffs give evidence of the oral agreement embodied in that document? The principle laid down in Taylor M Evidence, 12 Edition, at page 277 et seq. See seems decisive on this question whether the case be regarded as coming under section 399 or 401, and I must hold that such evidence cannot be given.

S.O Nwabuoku v. P.N. Ottih
[1961] 1 All N.L.R. 487

The plaintiff claimed for an account of rents collected by the defendant as the mortgagee of property and payment of the amount due on the taking of the account. He also claimed in default certain amount and injunction. Neither party pleaded the relevant document. In his evidence, the plaintiff claimed on an oral transaction between the parties in 1955. He gave evidence of this transaction and nothing more. The evidence was not rebutted by the defendant

HELD:

Where a plaintiff adduces oral evidence which establishes his claim against the defendant in the terms of the writ, and that evidence is not rebutted by the defence, the plaintiff is entitled to judgment.

Ademola, C.J.F. (as the then was) said at page 490:

It is to be noted that this document is dated 15th February, 1957. In his particulars of claim the appellant claimed on an oral transaction between the parties in 1955 and gave evidence of this; he gave evidence of the transaction in 1955 and nothing more. It is clear from his judgment that the learned trial Judge gave no consideration whatever to the appellant evidence before him; his evidence was not at any time rebutted by the defendant who did not go in the witness box to give evidence. The evidence of the appellant therefore stands uncontradicted. His evidence giving the terms of the transaction between him and the respondent was in terms of his write. In the absence of any evidence of rebuttal the appellant was entitled to judgment, and I am of the view that the learned Judge's duty was to have entered judgment in his favour at the close of the respondent's case.

Colony Development Board v. Joseph F. Kamson
(1955) 21 N.L.R. 75

In an action by a mortgagee to recover sums due under the mortgage, the defendants desired to adduce evidence to show (a) that they never received the mortgage moneys of which they had acknowledged receipt in the mortgage deed; (b) that repayment was contingent only on the borrowers making adequate profits, there being no term to this effect in the mortgage deed.

HELD:

That such evidence was inadmissible.

Abbott, J. said at page 76:

As to the proposed evidence that the defendants never received the money acknowledged by them in the deed, I feel that such extrinsic evidence was wholly inadmissible. If such evidence were admissible be no mortgage deed would be worth the paper on which it is written.

See further *Kojo v. Solaz* (1938) 4 W.A.C.A. 191*; Mohamman v. Local Government Police* [1970] 2 All N.L.R. 202*; Chief Ibuluya and Others v. Dikibo and Others* (1976) 6 S.C. 97*; Imana v. Robinson* (1979) 3 and 4 S.C. 1.

Lasisi Lasupo Alli v. Chief J O. Ikusebiala [1985] 1 N.W.L.R. (Pt. 4) 630

The land in dispute belonged to the Abogunloko family. Sunmonu Adeleke was at all material times the head of the family. The appellant called evidence to show that at the relevant time, Sunmonu Adeleke was the head of the family and that the principal members of the family knew of and consented to the sale. There was also evidence by Sunmonu Adeleke that at the time of sale he knew the land was family land and that he was introduced to the appellant as the family head. The learned trial Judge refused to act on the oral evidence on the ground that since Sunmonu Adeleke conveyed the land in dispute as "beneficial owner", section 131 f the Evidence Act disallows oral evidence from being given to contradict conveyance in such capacity.

HELD:

(1) Section 131 of the Evidence Act can be used to admit oral evidence in cases where such evidence will not be inconsistent with the terms of the contract in question.

(2) Section 131 can also be used to admit oral evidence in cases where

(i) the capacity in which a person contracted if the written contract or conveyance does not disclose that capacity;

(ii) The person who contracted as 'owner' is not the true owner but has represented himself as such.

Chief Awara Osu v. Ibor Igiri and Others [1988] 1 N.W.L.R. (Pt. 69) 221

The appellants had previously instituted against the respondents Suit No. 14/76 in respect of the same piece of land, which was the subject of the appeal to the Supreme Court.

However, based on the amicable agreement reached between the parties (*Exhibit C*) the appellants withdrew the said suit. When the respondents failed to honour their own part of the agreement, the appellants instituted a fresh action against the respondents. Judgment was given to the appellants by the District Court. The appeal by the respondents was allowed by the learned Chief Magistrate. On further appeal, the High Court allowed the appeal. On further appeal, the Court of Appeal relying on section 131 (1) of the Evidence Act held that extrinsic evidence could not be admitted to prove what was contained in the agreement (*Exhibit C*). The court set aside the judgment of the High Court. Allowing the appeal, the Supreme Court held that section 131 of the Evidence Act did not apply to the case, and even if it did, the Court of Appeal clearly lost sight of subsection (c). This was because there was to be fulfillment of condition precedent before *Exhibit C* could take effect. In the instant case, while appellants granted their own land for the purposes of peace, the respondents granted none. Therefore evidence to alter or explain *Exhibit C* was admissible.

In *Ebueku v. Amola* [1988] 2 N.W.L.R. (Pt 175) 129, the Supreme Court held that by virtue of section 131 (1) of the Evidence Act, oral evidence is inadmissible to prove the terms of settlement in a previous suit where, as in this case, the terms of settlement already form part of the judgment of the court.

Exceptions to the Rule of the Exclusion of Oral Evidence by Documentary Evidence.

Taylor Mbi v. Numan Native Authority 1959 N.R.N.L.R. 11

The appellant was convicted with some other accused persons in the Numan Federal Court of conspiring to defraud the Numan Native Authority. The appellant alleged that he was not in court during the whole course of the trial and that one of the judges was also a witness in the case, and that in fact the judge had also been an accused person in the case. None of these allegations appeared on the record. The court allowed the appeal. Hurley, S.P.J. said:

> *This court is unwilling, in an appeal, to look outside the record for proceedings in the trial court, but we have power to do so under section 131 (1) (a) of the Evidence Act.*

Aguda rightly commented as follows:

With the greatest respect this pronouncement would appear to overlook the provisions of section 133 (1)... makes 131 and 132 applicable only to cases in which some civil right or civil liability is dependent upon the terms of a document in question.

Certainly, the case in hand did not give rise to such a situation.

In *Oluwo v. Church Missionary Trust Association Limited* [1961] 1 All N.L.R. 409, it was held that a collateral oral agreement would be admissible in evidence as to any matter on which a deed is silent, which is separate from it and not inconsistent with it, and might naturally be omitted therefrom. But in this case, there was no sufficient proof of such a collateral oral agreement to the effect that two members of the plaintiff's family would be admitted into the proposed school.

Evidence in Aid of the Interpretation of Documents

G. Gottschalck and Co . v. Elder Dempster and Co. Ltd. (1917) 3 N.L.R. 16

A certain package was short landed from one of the defendant company's ships. The terms of the contract for the carriage of goods were contained in the bill of lading upon which the plaintiffs sued. The package was put over the side of the ship and placed in the custom House shed. Plaintiffs sought to bring evidence of the Custom of port which, according to their contention, extended the defendant company's liability beyond the terms of the bill of lading.

HELD:

No evidence of custom can override the terms of a written contract.

Speed, C.J. said at page 17:

In my opinion the action of the learned Judge was perfectly correct, because it is a well established rule of law that no evidence of custom can override the terms of a written contract.

Chapter 10

FACTS WHICH NEED NOT BE PROVED

Sections 73 to 75 of the Evidence Act.

No fact of which the court must take judicial notice need be proved (S. 73). The court must take judicial notice of the following facts:

(a) all laws, enactments and any subsidiary legislation which are in force in any part of Nigeria;

(b) all public Acts passed by Parliament, including all subsidiary legislation and all local and personal Acts directed by Parliament to be judicially noticed;

(c) the course of proceedings of Parliament and of the Federal and State Legislative Houses of Nigeria;

(d) the assumption of office of the President and of any seal used by him;

(e) all seals of which English Courts take judicial notice; the seals of all the courts of Nigeria; the seals of notaries public; and all seals which any person is authorised to use by any Act of Parliament or other enactment having the force of law in Nigeria;

(f) the existence, title and national flag of every State or Sovereign recognised by Nigeria;

(g) the divisions of time, the geographical divisions of the world, and public festivals, fasts and holidays notified in the Gazette or fixed by Act;

(h) the territories within the commonwealth; the commencement, continuance and termination of hostilities between the Federal Republic and any other State or body of persons;

(I) the commencement, continuance and termination of hostilities between the Federal Repukblic and any other State or body of persons;

(j) the names of the members and officers of the court and of their deputies and subordinate officers and assistants, and also of all officers acting in execution of its process, and of all legal practitioners and other persons authorised by law to appear or act before it;

(k) the rule of the road on land or at sea;

(l) all general customs, rules and principles which have been held to have the force of law in any of the superior courts of law or equity in England and in Nigeria; and

(m) the course of proceeding and all rules of practice in force in the High Court of Justice in England and in the High Court of the States (S. 74(1)).

In all the above cases and also in all matters of public history, literature, science or art, the court may resort for its aid to appropriate books or documents of reference (S. 74(2)). If the court is called upon by any person to take judicial notice of any Act, it may refuse to do so unless and until such person produces any such book or document as it may consider as necessary to enable it to do so (S. 74(3)).

No fact need be proved in any civil proceedings which the parties or their agents agree to admit at the hearing, or which before the hearing, they agree to admit by any writing under their hands, or which by any rule or pleading in force at the time they are deemed to have admitted by their pleadings. However, the court may, in its discretion, require the facts admitted to be proved otherwise than by such admissions (S. 75).

Judicial Notice refers to facts which a Judge can be called upon to receive and act upon either from his general knowledge of them or from inquiries to be made by himself for his own information from sources to which it is proper for him to refer. See *Mrs. Oyelowo v. Dr. Oyelowo* [198] 2 N.W.L.R. (Pt. 56) 239.

Judicial Notice: Facts of which the Court must take Notice

James Adetipe v. Jimoh Omisakin Amodu and Another [1969] N.M.L.R. 62

In Suit HOS/99/64 the respondents as plaintiffs claimed in their writ, declaration of title to a particular farmland and injunction to restrain the defendant/appellant. When the matter came for trial both parties asked leave of court to argue a preliminary issue as to whether the defendant/appellant could succeed on the plea of res judicata raised in his pleadings in respect of Suit No. 40/50. The issue which arose was whether the court which heard the suit described as "Land Court of Ife" was properly constituted under the Native Courts Ordinance. Counsel for the respondents referred the court to the list of established courts set out in the schedule to the notice listing Native Courts in the Western

Provinces at page 48 Volume 9 of the Laws of Nigeria (1948 edition). This list did not show any such court as the Land Court of Ife. Counsel therefore submitted that the onus which lay on him to show prima facie that the "Land Court of Ife" did not have any jurisdiction in 1950 was discharged and that the onus shifted to the defendant to establish if he could, that he was living.

Lewis, J.S.C. said at 67:

> *It is certainly correct that neither Fakayode, J. nor this Court was shown that alterations had been made to the Schedule to the Notice between 1948 and 1950 but Section 73(1) (a) of the Evidence Act, to which we drew Chief Williams' attention' reads... and by virtue of Section 72 of the Evidence Act such facts need not be proved.*
>
> *The courts are therefore deemed to have judicial notice of subsidiary legislation and we are accordingly entitled ourselves to look and see whether the Schedule to the Notice was in fact amended between 1948 and 1950, notwithstanding the submissions of Chief Williams that to do this would be doing the work of the objector for him. The objective would have been more helpful to the court to have himself shown to the court the appropriate legislature but having regard to the provisions of sections 72 and 73(1) (a) of the Evidence Act we cannot say that he must do so when this court must take judicial notice of legislation and subsidiary legislation.*

Olayiwola and Another v. Joseph Oladipopu Ashiru [1967] 1 All N.L.R. 185

The plaintiff sued in Lagos under the Fatal Accidents Act, 1846, applicable in Lagos. The trial Judge erroneously held that the Act also applied in Western Nigeria concurrently with the Torts Law. The defendants submitted that the Supreme Court should follow its decision in *Ananmbu v. Okafor* [1966] 1 All N.L.R. 205 and dismiss the action, whilst the plaintiff, who conceded his mistake, asked for leave to delete as mere surplusage the reference to that Act in the Statement of Claim; but the defendants objected that the amendment would later the whole basis of the action and would deprive them of the benefit of the period of limitation, contrary to the court's accepted practice.

HELD:

The plaintiff would not have been debarred from relying on the law of Western Nigeria by the fact that he had not pleaded it, since under Section 73(1) (a) of the Evidence Act, the High Court must take judicial notice of the laws in force in any part of Nigeria and it is unnecessary to plead matters of which the High Court takes judicial notice.

By section 73(1) (a) of the Evidence Act, the court must take judicial notice of all laws and enactments, including subsidiary legislation in force in any part of the Federation: *Mayaki v. L.C.C.C.* (1977) SC. 81. See also *Peenok v. Hotel Presidential* (1982) 12 S.C. 1; *Dr. Ekperi v. Okonu* [1986] 5 N.W.L.R. (pt. 41) 370; *Adenuso v. Kano Native Authority* (1956-84) 10 S.C.N.D 109; *Tifi v. Uba* [1987] 3 N.W.L.R. (pt. 62) 707; *Abcos (Nig.) Ltd. v. Kango Wolf Power Tools Ltd.* [1987] 4 N.W.L.R. (Pt. 67) 894.

The court must take judicial notice of a policy of the Government. All that is required by the court is evidence, if any, of what the policy was at the material time: *Ike and Others v. Nzekwe and others* (1975) 2 S.C. 1. See also *Oguebe v. Odunwoke* (1979) 3-4 S.C. 58. The court must take judicial notice of activities and pronouncements of Government: *Uwaifo v. Attorney-General of Bendel State* (1982) 7 S.C. 124. The court must take judicial notice of civil service rules, which provide for the procedure which must be adopted in the removal or retirement from service as well as the general discipline of public servants in the established pensionable cadre: *Shitta-Bey v. Federal Public Service Commission* (1981) 1 S.C. 40. The minutes of the Supreme Military Council would be taken judicial notice of by a court under section 73(1) (c) of the Evidence Act as that Council had taken over the duties of Parliament: *Akinbilgi and Others v. Oba Ademola II and Another* (1979) 4 C.A. 65. A trial Judge has a duty to take judicial notice of legislation, including a Decree, under Section 73 of the Evidence Act and the fact that he did not invite counsel to address him on such legislation will not affect his decision: *Mohammed and Others v. Commissioner of Police* (1987) 4 N.W.L.R. (Pt. 65) 420. See also *Alhaji Kanana v. The Governor of Kaduna State and Another* [1986] 4 N.W.L.R. (Pt. 35) 361. Under section 73(1) (j) of the Evidence Act, a court can take judicial notice of officers of court and legal practitioners authorised to practise in the courts and by virtue of section 73(2), can refer to any appropriate book or document of reference to satisfy itself on the point: *Reuben Umenwa v. Gabriel Umenwa and Another* [1987] 4 N.W.L.R. (Pt. 65) 407.

In default of evidence, judicial notice will be taken of any custom which has been held in the Supreme Court to have the force of law, provided that certain conditions are fulfilled: *Taiwo v. Taiwo* (1958) 3 F.S.C. 80. The courts must take judicial notice of a customary law which has been established by decisions of superior courts: *Ojomu v. Ajao* [1983] S.C.N.L.R. 156. See also *Toriola v. Williams* (1982) 7 S.C. 27; *Shaibu v. Bakare* (1956-84) 10 S.C.N.D. 108; *Orobator v. Mrs Amata* (1980) 7 C.A. (Part 1) 84; *Tofi v. Uba* [1987] 3 N.W.L.R. (Pt. 62) 707; *Awoyegbe and Another v. Chief Ogbeide* [1988] 1 N.W.L.R. (Pt. 73) 695; *Famubo and another v. Adekunle and others* [1988] 2 N.W.L.R. (Pt. 79) 729; *Garba v. Inspector-General of Police*, 1956 N.N.L.R. 32.

Judicial Notice: Facts of which the Court may take Notice

Yinusa Bakare v. Rasaki Ishola [1956] W.R.N.L.R. 106

In an appeal from the decision of a Magistrate's Court awarding the plaintiff/respondent damages against the defendant/ appellant for slander it was shown that there had been a fight preceded by an altercation between the parties and that in the heat of anger the defendant/appellant had in the presence of others spoken of the plaintiff in Yoruba the words which were alleged to be *"Ole ni o Elewon, iwo ti o sese ti ewon de yi"* which in English meant: "You are a thief. Ex-convict you who have just come out of prison".

HELD:

The words complained of were mere vulgar abuse as they had been spoken while the parties were exchanging words which led to blows, that is, as usual in this country, while they were abusing each other, and that it was a matter of common knowledge of which the court took judicial notice that people commonly abuse each other as a prelude to a fight and call each other in Yoruba "Ole; Elewon" meaning in English "Thief; Ex-convict", which abuses no one took seriously as they were mere words of anger.

Francis Izedomwen v. Inspector-General of Police [1957] W.R.N.L.R. 57

The appellant, a police constable of the Nigeria Police Force, was convicted of accepting a reward beyond his proper pay and emoluments for having released on bail a person who was in his custody. He appealed on the ground that there was no proof of what was his "proper pay and emoluments" and that the case for the prosecution being that he had demanded a reward he was wrongly charged under Section 99 of the Criminal Code. He also appealed against sentence.

HELD:

The Magistrate was right in taking judicial notice of the fact that the appellant would receive proper pay and emoluments under sections 3 ad 57 of the Police Ordinance and that the quantum thereof is immaterial.

Yesufu Garba v. Inspector-General of Police [1956] N.R.N.L.R. 32

The appellant who was a police officer, employed in the investigation branch of the Nigeria Police at Kano was charged with an offence under section 116(1) of the Criminal Code. He was convicted and sentenced to six months imprisonment. On appeal, it was contended that the Magistrate failed to consider the duties of the appellant at the time of the alleged offence.

HELD:

The duties of a police officer are set out in section 4 of the Police Ordinance and the Court will take judicial notice of them.

In *Chief the Hon. Rotimi Williams and others v. The West African Pilot* [1961] All N.L.R. 866, it was held that the court may take judicial notice of the fact that a particular newspaper is a national daily in Nigeria and has readers outside Nigeria. In *The Queen: Ex Parte Adebo* [1962] 2 All N.L.R. 195, it was held that it is a matter of judicial knowledge that the office of Chief, often, if not invariably, has appurtenant to it a right to salary and other rights. In *Mrs. Oyelowo and Dr. Oyelowo, supra*, it was held that the fact that most societies in Nigeria are patrilineal is that which courts in Nigeria can judicially notice. Thus the onus is on a person claiming that his own society is matrilineal to prove it. In *Kwawam v. Chellaram* (1960) 5 F.S.C 29, it was held that the court may take judicial cognisance of the fact that fashions change in textile designs as in most other things. In *Anokwu v. Commissioner of police* [1975] N.M.L.R. 402, it was held that the terms and abbreviations of which a court can take judicial notice are limited. The prosecution should ensure that esoteric terms and abbreviations are explained to the court in evidence, for example N.C.E.

In *Jamaledine v. Federal Board of Inland Revenue* (1956-84) 10 S.C.N.D. 106, it was held that apart from the facts enumerated in section 73 of the Evidence Act, other facts which the court may take judicial notice of are such facts which are so notorious or of regular occurrence, in the ordinary course of nature or business, that they have become familiar to the Judges. For facts not judicially noticed, see *Mekete v. N.B.C.* [1961] 1 All N.L.R. 482; *Locknan v. The State* (1972) 5 S.C. 22; *Onibudo v. Akibu* (1982) 7 S.C. 60; *Mgberekpe v. Commissioner of Police* (1966-67) 10 E.N.L.R. 135.

Formal Admissions

Ndiakaeme and others v. Obidike Egbonu and Others (1941) 7 W.A.C.A. 53

The matter involved the ownership of a piece of land in Okigwe District. The appellants raised *res judicata* by virtue of two judgments of the Native Court of Uruala given separately.

The Court said at page 55:

> *But before leaving the matter we think it desirable to point out that in our view the learned trial Judge was wrong to go into the question of whether the land now in dispute is the same as that in dispute in the Uruala Native Court in 1933, and to find that identity was not proved. The identity was one of the agreed facts in the case, it was relied upon by both parties in their pleadings, and since one of the objects of pleadings is to shorten proceedings by ascertaining what facts are agreed so that evidence need not be led to prove them, the court should have accepted this agreed fact as established without proof.*

See also *Okai v. Ayikai* (1946) 12 W.A.C.A. 31; *S.S.N.L. v. Ayuafe* (1976) 9-10 S.C. 135; *Iga v. Amakiri* (1976) 11 S.C. 1; *Nwankwere v. Ugorji* (1956-84) 10 S.C.N.D. 38; *Oilfield Supply Centre v. Johnson* [1987] 2 N.W.L.R. (Pt. 58) 625. On judicial notice, see further; *Saraki v. Kotoye* [1990] 4 N.W.L.R. (Pt. 143) 144; *Folami v. Cole* [1990] 2 N.W.L.R. (Pt. 133) 445; *I.A.I.L. v. Chika Bros Ltd* [1990] 1 N.W.L.R. (Pt. 124) 70; *Osafile v. Odi* (No. 1) [1990] 3 N.W.L.R. (Pt. 137) 130; *Oyewunmi v. Oguneran* [1990] 3 N.W.L.R. (Pt. 137) 182; *Agbani v. Okogbue* [1991] 7 N.W.L.R. (pt. 204) 391; *Katto v. C.B.N.* [1991] 9 N.W.L.R. (Pt. 214) 126; *Sadig v. Bundi* [1991]8 N.W.L.R. (Pt. 210) 443; *Romaire v. Romaine* [1992] 4 N.W.L.R. (Pt. 238) 650; *Agidigbi v. Agidigbi* [1992] 2 N.W.L.R. (Pt. 218) 473; *Olabanji v. Omokewu* [1992] 6 N.W.L.R. (Pt. 250) 671; *NEPA v. Alli* [1992] N.W.L.R. (Pt. 295) 279; *Finnih v. Imade* [1992] 1 N.W.L.R. (Pt. 219) 511; *Usman v. Umaru* [1992] 7 N.W.L.R. (Pt. 254) 377; *Ayoke v. Bello* [1992] 1 N.W.L.R. Pt. (218) 380; *Jatau v. Dung* [1993] 3 N.W.L.R. (Pt. 283) 558; *Mumu v. Agor* [1993] 8 N.W.L.R. (Pt. 313); *Awaye Motors Co. Ltd. v. Adewunmi* [1993] 5 N.W.L.R. (Pt. 292) 236; *Oko v. Ntukidem* (1993) 2 N.W.L.R. (Pt. 274) 124. *Bendel Newspapers Corp. v. Okafor* [1993] 4 N.W.L.R. (Pt. 289) 617; *Sambo v. State* [1993] 6 N.W.L.R. (Pt. 300) 399.

Chapter 11

PROOF OF PREVIOUS CONVICTION

Sections 225 and 226 of the Evidence Act.

Proof of previous conviction becomes necessary when evidence of character is necessary. For instance, if an accused person leads evidence as to his good character, then the prosecution can lead evidence as to previous conviction of the accused to drown his evidence of good character. Although this is not the only use of previous conviction, it is the most regular and constant one.

Sections 225 and 226 of the Evidence Act make provisions on the mode of proof of previous conviction. When it is necessary to prove a conviction of a criminal offence, the same may be proved

(a) by the production of a certificate of conviction containing the substance and effect of the conviction only, purporting to be signed by the registrar or other officer of the court in whose custody is the record of the conviction;

(b) if the conviction was before a Native Court by a similar certificate signed by the clerk of court or scribe of the court in whose custody is the record of the conviction; or

(c) by a certificate purporting to be signed by the Director of Prisons or officer in charge of the records of a prison in which the prisoner was confined (S. 225(1)).

If the person alleged to be the person referred to in the certificate denies that he is such person the certificate shall not be put in evidence unless the court is satisfied by the evidence that the individual in question and the person named in the certificate are the same (S. 225(2)). Section 225 (3) provides for the proof of previous conviction outside Nigeria. By the subsection, a previous conviction in a place outside Nigeria may be proved by the production of a certificate purporting to be given under the hand of a police officer in the country where the conviction was had, containing a copy of the sentence or order and the finger prints of the person or photographs of the finger prints of the person so convicted, together with evidence that the finger prints of the person so convicted are those of the accused person. A certificate so given will be prima facie evidence of all facts set therein without proof that the officer purporting to sign the same did in fact sign it and was empowered so to do.

Section 226 provides for additional mode of proof. A previous conviction may be proved against any person in any criminal proceedings by the production of such evidence of the conviction and by showing that his finger prints and those of the person convicted are the finger prints of the same person. By the section, a certificate on the finger prints could be signed by or on behalf of the central registrar, the superintendent of a prison in which any person has been detained in connection with any criminal proceedings or by a police officer who has had custody of any person charged with an offence in connection with any proceedings. Such certificate will be evidence of its content. The central registrar means the person in charge of the principal registry of criminal records established under the provisions of the Prevention of Crimes Act.

What constitutes previous conviction

R.v. Osita Chukwu Agwuna and Others (1949) 12 W.A.C.A. 456

A copy of a previous seditious utterance by the first appellant (in respect whereof he had been convicted) was admitted as evidence upon the trial of the four appellants. The admissibility of the document was raised as a ground of appeal.

HELD:

The only kind of previous conviction which a court is entitled to take into account when assessing sentence is one in which the conviction took place before the commission of the offence for which the accused is instantly charged and convicted.

Black, P. said at page 461:

With regard to the first appellant, the question arises as to the reason which caused the trial Judge to impose on him a more severe sentence (two and half years' imprisonment with hard labour) than that imposed on the second appellant whose language at the Glover Hall was much more violent than the first appellant's. No reason was given by the learned Judge for this distinction, but it would seem from the record that the sentence on the first appellant was imposed after he had admitted what was described as a previous conviction. Assuming that was the reason, we are of opinion that the learned Judge proceeded on a wrong principle in giving the first appellant a more severe sentence, for this appellant was not convicted on account of his speech at the Tom Jones Hall until 25th January, 1949, i.e after the making of the speech in respect of which he was convicted by Gregg, J. The conviction in question was therefore not a previous conviction in the proper sense of the word.

Mode of proving previous conviction

Sunny Blues v. Commissioner of Police (1959) W.R.N.L.R. 234

The appellant had been convicted and sentenced by the Magistrate at Sapele on two counts. The first count was one of being a reputed thief with no visible means of subsistence and unable to give a good account of himself contrary to section 250(4) of the Criminal Code, Cap. 42. The second count was one of being found wandering in a public place under such circumstances as to lead to the conclusion that he was there for an illegal purpose contrary to section 250(6) of Cap. 42.

He appealed on a number of grounds of which was an evidence of previous conviction.

HELD:

(1) That whilst section 224(1) of the Evidence Ordinance provided for the modes of proving previous convictions by certificates signed by certain authorised persons, section 224 (A) (a) of the same Ordinance, inserted by the amending Ordinance, No. 69 1955, provided for additional modes of proof by the certificate of a police officer as had been done in the present case.

(2) That the proper method of proving previous convictions as evidence of antecedent conduct was not merely by the production of a certificate of such convictions but by going further to put the same to the accused in open court for him to admit or deny and that in the present case there was nothing on the record to show that this latter procedure was ever carried out at the trial, no attempt having been made also to identify the appellant as the person with aliases mentioned in the certificate of conviction which had merely been produced and placed before the trial Magistrate who misdirected himself on the evidence by stating that the appellant had not denied the contents of the certificate.

NOTE:

It would appear that the amendment introduced by Ordinance No. 6 of 1955 is part of the present section 226 of the Act.

Maye Rukuba v. Commissioner of Police

[1967] N.M.L.R. 415

The appellant was convicted of the offence of house trespass contrary to section 352 of the Penal Code by the Magisrate's Court Jos. Before the learned trial Magistrate passed sentence on the appellant, the record of previous convictions was produced. It was then recorded that appellant admitted nine previous convictions.

HELD:

That was not enough.

Reed, S.P.J. said at page 418:

Before the Chief Magistrate passed sentence the record of previous convictions was produced. It is (sic) then recorded that the appellant admitted nine previous convictions. That is all we know and it is not enough. Either the record of previous convictions should have been exhibited to form part of the record of the trial or the Chief Magistrate should have recorded details of each conviction which the appellant admitted - date, court, offence and sentence. Some of the convictions may be for offences not involving dishonesty which would have no relevance to the sentence passed on the appellant by the chief Magistrate. We shall therefore treat the appellant as a first offender but the offence was a very serious one and we pass the maximum sentence of imprisonment permitted by section 348 of the Penal Code, namely imprisonment for one year.

Bako Bahar v. Yauri Native Authority Police
[1970] 2 All N.L.R. 256

Bako Bahar and others were tried and convicted in an Area Court on the charge of using criminal force, punishable under section 265 of the Penal Code. The trial court accepted the word of the prosecutor that Bako Bahar had previous convictions.

HELD:

That was not evidence and it was wrong to act on it. The Court further held that previous convictions are not relevant unless for a similar offence.

Jones, S.P.J. said at page 260:

In considering sentence the trial court accepted the word of the prosecutor that appellant had two previous convictions. This was not evidence, because the prosecutor was not a witness. Even if it had been evidence, the prosecutor did not say what those two previous convictions were for. They would be relevant only if they had been for the same type of offence as that for which the appellant was not convicted.

In *Amadu Gwaquarawa v. Kano N.A. Police* (1969) S.C. O.P.E. 108, the Chief Justice of the Northern States said with regard to the acceptance by a court of the prosecutor's statement that the accused was an habitual criminal:

> *We cannot too strongly condemn this practice... This court has repeatedly pointed out that previous convictions alleged against an accused person must either be admitted by him or proved against him before sentence and he must have an opportunity of denying them and putting the prosecution on proof of them.*

See also *Din v. African Newspapers (Nig) Ltd* [1990] 3 N.W.L.R. (Pt. 139) 302.

Chapter 12

TYPES AND PROOF OF DOCUMENTS

Sections 2, 78 to 90 and 100 to 113 of the Evidence Act and the Illiterates Protection Act.

The production of documents forms an essential part in the proceedings of the court. A party who relies on a document to prove his case must either produce the document itself or a copy thereof. In either case, it is known as documentary evidence, as opposed and distinct from oral evidence given by the witness in court. Section 2(1) of the Act defines a document as follows:

> *'Document' includes books, maps, plans, drawings, photographs and also includes any matter expressed or described upon any substance by means of letters, figures or marks or by more than one of these means, intended to be used or which may be used for the purpose of recording that matter.*

The definition is wide, generic and omnibus. It covers virtually all written substances.

Documents are of two types: Public and Private. Public documents are documents forming the acts or records of the acts of the sovereign authority, official bodies and tribunals and public officers, legislative, judicial and executive whether of Nigeria or elsewhere. They also include public records kept in Nigeria of private documents (S. 109). The Act does not define private documents beyond saying that "all documents other than public documents are private documents" (S. 110).

While sections 111 and 112 provide for the proof of public documents within the meaning of section 109; section 113 provides for the proof of other official documents within the meaning of the same section. Sections 103 to 107 deal with proof of attested documents, and section 108 provides for the comparison of signature, writing, seal or finger impressions with others admitted or proved. Affidavit evidence, which is a most regular documentary evidence in judicial proceedings, is provided for in sections 78 to 90.

A court may in any civil proceeding make an order at any stage of such proceeding directing that specified facts may be proved at the trial by affidavit with or without the attendance of the deponent for cross-examination, notwithstanding that a party desires his attendance for cross-examination and that he can be produced for that purpose (S. 78). Before an affidavit is used in the court for any purpose, the original must be filed in the court (S. 79). Any affidavit sworn before any Judge, officer or other person in the Commonwealth to take affidavits, may be used in the court in all cases where affidavits are admissible (S. 80). (See also S. 81). The court may permit an affidavit to be used, notwithstanding that it is defective in form according to the Act if the court is satisfied that it has been sworn before a person duly authorised (S. 84). A defective or erroneous affidavit may be amended and re-sworn by leave of the court, on such terms as to time, costs or otherwise as seem reasonable (S. 85).

Every affidavit used in the court must contain only a statement of facts and circumstances to which the witness deposes either of his own personal knowledge or from information which he believes to be true (S. 86). An affidavit must not contain extraneous matter, by way of objection, prayer, legal argument or conclusion (S. 87). When a person deposes to his belief in any matter of fact, and his belief is derived from any source other than his own personal knowledge, he must set forth explicitly the facts and circumstances forming the ground of his belief (S. 88). When such belief is derived from information received from another person, the name of his informant must be stated, and reasonable particulars shall be given respecting the informant, and the time, place and circumstances of the information (S. 89). Finally, section 90 makes provisions to be observed by persons before whom affidavits are taken.

There is one aspect we should also take here and it is documents which do not comply with the Illiterates Protection Act. By section 3 of the Act, any person who writes any letter or document at the request, on behalf, or in the name of any illiterate person must also write on such letter or other document his own name as the writer and that he was so instructed to write the letter or document and that it was read over to the illiterate person who signed it or made his mark. While section 4 of the Act provides penalty for a writer for non-compliance with section 3, section 7 defines a writer as "any person who shall write any letter or document at the request, on behalf, or in the name of any illiterate person". The definition does not include a legal practitioner. The Act does not define an illiterate. Similarly, the Act does not provide for the effect of non-compliance with the provisions on the subsequent admissibility of the document in court.

Types of Documents

R.v. Taoridi Lawani
1959 L.L.R. 97

At the trial of the accused for manslaughter, the prosecution sought to tender in evidence a police 'Accident Report' book in which entries were made by a police constable who had since died both from and outside his personal knowledge.

HELD:

A Police 'Accident Report' book is not a public or other official book within the meaning of section 38 of the Evidence Ordinance.

Ballemy, J. said at page 98:

As to the first condition, the question arises, is Police Book A/67 a 'public or other official book, register or record' within the section? It cannot possibly be said to be a 'register' or 'record'. Is it a 'public or other official book?' I have no hesitation in answering that question in the negative. Public documents are defined in section 108 of the Evidence Ordinance. The relevant words are 'documents forming the acts or records of the acts of public officers'. In my view, the kind of 'acts' which section 108 has in view is indicated in section 112 of the Evidence Ordinance. In my opinion, it does not cover the inquiries which a police officer may make, whether under the Criminal Procedure Ordinance or otherwise, which may or may not result in action. Therefore I rule that the entries are not admissible on this ground.

In *Nwosu v. Okonkwo* (1956-84) 10 S.C.N.D. 79, it was held that a survey plan is a document within the definition contained in the Evidence Act. In *Wachukwu v. Elewa and Others* [1985] H.C.N.L.R. 1393, it was held that both Particulars of Claim and the Survey Plan are public documents within the meaning of section 108 of the Evidence Act and are admissible. In this respect it is necessary to note that the two documents bear the official stamp of the High Court Registry. This shows that they are in the custody of the High Court. The two documents are signed at the back by the Commissioner for Oaths, a public officer. See further *The State v. Mgbagwu and Others* [1972] 2 E.C.S.L.R. 462; *Okeke Obidite and Others* [1965] 1 All N.L.R. 50; *Isibor v. The State* [1970] 1 All N.L.R. 248; *Esonwune Nwadike and Another v. Martin Nwa]dike and Others* [1987] 4 N.W.L.R. (Pt. 65) 394.

Proof of Public Documents.

The Queen v. The Governor of the Western Region of Nigeria Ex parte Alasan Babatunde Ajagunna II (1957) W.R.N.L.R. 104

On an application for a writ of certiorari for the removal into the High Court for the purpose of being quashed an order made by the Governor of approval and recognition of the appointment of a chief, the court directed the Governor to file an affidavit in reply to the point in issue as to whether the applicant who previously held the office of chief had been deposed or not. An affidavit was sworn to on behalf of the Governor affirming that the applicant had been deposed in exercise of the powers conferred by section 22(1) of the Western Region Appointment and Recognition of Chiefs Law, 1954. It was contended on behalf of the applicant that the affidavit was not satisfactory proof of the order.

HELD:

The affidavit was sufficient proof of the making of the order.

Taylor, J. said at page 106:

I do however accept the affidavit sworn to by Mr. Holden and the facts therein contained as I do the copy of the order of deposition signed by His Excellency and attached to the affidavit. I continually asked Mr. Ayoola to show me good cause why I should not accept the affidavit and its contents as representing the true state of things and though counsel challenged the contents of the affidavit he was unable to advance any sound reason why I should not do so other than a statement that if I made the order nisi then from his cross-examination of the deponent he would be able to show that in fact no such order of deposition could have been made on the way in question... I do not find enough substance in these contentions to make me hold that affidavit is untrue with the serious repercussions it would have on the deponent.

Bubble Up International Limited v. Seven-Up Company Limited [1971] U.I.L.R. 154

Both the applicants and the objectors were companies incorporated in the United States of America. The applicants claimed that they were proprietors of the trade mark "Bubble Up" and device in class 44 in respect of all goods included in the class and had long been using this trade mark which had been registered as a distinctive trade mark in the United States since 1921 in connection with their products. They also claimed to have built up considerable goodwill for the trade mark in many countries. Consequent upon their application for the registration of the trade mark and the subsequent advertisement in the Nigerian gazette, the defendants lodged an objection claiming that the acceptance of the trade mark for registration was an error in view of the trade marks 7 Up, Seven Up and Up in Class 42 and 44 in respect of the same good or description of goods of which the defendants were registered as proprietors.

HELD:

> Where the public document of a foreign country is tendered in evidence in a court in Nigeria, the document, to be admissible, must be in accordance with the provisions of section 112 of the Evidence Act, and that in the instant case, the public document of the Republic of Chile which the applicant company sought to tender was inadmissible as it did not comply with the provisions of the Act.

Kassim J. said at pages 156 and 157:

> *When during his address A.O. Abudu for the plaintiff/applicant company referred to Exhibit XX5 attached to the affidavit in support of the applicant's application, which is a copy of a decision rendered by the Ministry of Economics in the Republic of Chile dated the 21st June, 1961, Mr. Garrick for the objector/defendant company raised an objection and said that the document was hearsay, that it was not a certified true copy, that the law of Chile was a foreign law, which ought to be proved as a fact, and it was not known whether the plaintiffs in the Chile case were the applicants. Mr. Abudu replied and referred to paragraphs 12, 13, 14 and 18 of the affidavit of Mr. Ryan and said that the judgment was admissible though not certified, and that it was not open to the objectors to challenge the evidence without a counter-affidavit.... It is apparent that Exhibit XX5 does not comply with this section (referring to section 112(1) of the Evidence Act), and is therefore, inadmissible, and so are all judgments, orders or other judicial proceedings exhibited or tendered in this proceedings which do not conform with the provision of this subsection 112 of Cap. 62.*

Yeriba Mika v. The Queen
[1963] 1 All N.L.R. 220

The conviction rested mainly on a statement said to be a confession made by the accused to a constable through an interpreter and reduced to writing. It was not produced at the trial. It had been tendered before the Magistrate. It was said that it was lost and that all possible search had been made for it. Oral evidence was of what the appellant had stated; but the testimonies of those who spoke to it varied substantially.

HELD:

> (1) The exhibits clerk of the Magistrate's Court ought to have been called to testify that the writing had got lost and could not be found after all possible search had been made for it. Oral evidence of the confession was admitted. Made before oral evidence of the confession was admitted.

(2) In any event the oral evidence of what the appellant had stated was unreliable.

Taylor, F.J. said at page 224:

In our view it would be most unsafe in the circumstances of this case on appeal to convict on the oral evidence such as it is and in the light it has been shown above. As we have said before, without the confession, the evidence falls far short of that required to sustain a conviction... The appellant is therefore acquitted and discharged.

Bisichi Tin Company Limited v. Commissioner of Police [1963] 2 All N.L.R. 11

The case for the prosecution was that the company's employees had mined in the area comprised in a mining lease which had expired. The lease was not produced and no certified copy was tendered. The prosecution witnesses said that it had expired on the relevant date. Neither, said he had seen it; but one said that he had 'seen the records'. A third witness said the area was Crown land. No objection was taken of any of this evidence.

HELD:

(1) To prove that the lease had expired, it was necessary to prove its terms and the date of its commencement. It was necessary to prove the contents of the lease.

(2) The mining lease being a public document, its contents might be proved by secondary evidence but the secondary evidence must be certified copy, and not oral evidence.

(3) This being a criminal case, the fact that the oral evidence was not objected to did not make it admissible.

Hurley, C.J. said at page 13:

But by subsection 2 (c) of section 96 of the Evidence Ordinance the secondary evidence admissible in respect of the original document mentioned in subsection (1) (e), that is, public documents, is a certified copy of the document but no other kind of secondary evidence. Therefore oral evidence under section 94 (e) was inadmissible to prove the mining lease in question...

R. v. Kwaku Amoyaw (1943) 9 W.A.C.A. 152

The trial court admitted oral evidence of a confession made by the appellant, recorded in writing and marked by the thumb impression, without the production of the written confession or evidence that its production was impossible. The appellant was represented by counsel at the trial, but no objection was taken to the admission of the oral evidence, and the appellant in his evidence did not dispute its accuracy.

HELD:

The written confession was the best evidence and the oral evidence of the confession was inadmissible; but no injustice having been done to the appellant by its wrongful admission, the appeal was dismissed..

See further *Cardoso v. St. Mathew Daniel and Others* [1966] 1 All N.L.R. 25; *Minister of Lands Western Nigeria v. Dr. N. Azikiwe* [1969] 1 All N.L.R. 11; *Ogbuinyiya and Others v. Okudo and Others* [1979] 6-9 S.C. 32; *Ajeja v. Ajayi and Another* [1969] 1 All N.L.R. 72; *Uwawah and Others v. Boyo and others* [1971] 1 N.M.L.R. 233; *Boyo v. The State* [1970] 1 All N.L.R. 318; *National Electric Power Authority v. Alhaji El-fandi* [1986] 3 N.W.L.R. (Pt. 32) 884; *Oboidina Family and Others v. Ambrose Family and Others* [1969] N.M.L.R. 24.

Proof of Execution of Private Documents

Odulaja v. Inspector-General of Police (1955-56) W.R.N.L.R. 3.

The appellant was charged with forgery and uttering. In finding the appellant guilty of forgery, the learned Magistrate relied on the evidence of the Registrar of the Court, who was acquainted with the handwriting of the appellant, that the receipt was in the appellant's handwriting. Furthermore, he rejected the evidence of a handwriting expert and gave satisfactory reasons for doing so.

HELD:

The learned trial Magistrate did not misdirect himself in law in accepting and applying the evidence of handwriting given by the Court Registrar while rejecting that of the handwriting experts. See also *R.v. Onitiri* (1946) 12 W.A.C.A. 58.

Cases in which Proof of Execution of Handwriting is Unnecessary

Nathaniel Okeke v. Akunkwe Obidife and Others [1965] 1 All N.L.R. 50

The widow and children of a person who was killed in a lorry accident sued for damages, alleging in the particulars of negligence some specific acts of negligence. The plaintiffs called a passenger, who testified that it was raining, and a police officer, who without objection from the defence put in the file on the accident with the driver's statement, in which he said that he was driving at 30 to 35 miles an hour, that the road was slippery, that the front tyres bent to the right and the lorry overturned before he could control it. The defence called no evidence. The trial Judge held that on the evidence, the accident could not have occurred without negligence of some sort on the driver's part; and he awarded damages. On appeal, it was argued *inter alia* that the Judge ought not to have relied on the driver's statement as the policeman to whom it was made was not called as a witness.

HELD:

In a civil case, formal proof of a document can always be waived, and the defendant must be treated as having waived any objection to the statement.

Affidavits

The Queen v. The Governor of the Western Region of Nigeria (1957) W.R.N.L.R. 104

On an application for a writ of certiorari for the removal unto the High Court for the purpose of being quashed an order made by the Governor of approval and recognition of the appointment of a chief, the court directed the Governor to file an affidavit in reply to the point in issue as to whether the applicant who previously held the office of chief had been deposed or not. An affidavit was sworn to on behalf of the Governor affirming that the applicant had been deposed in exercise of powers conferred by section 22(1) of the Western Region Appointment and Recognition of Chiefs Law, 1954. It was contended on behalf of the applicant that the affidavit was not satisfactory proof of the order.

HELD:

The affidavit was sufficient proof of the making of the Order.

Taylor, J. said at pages 105 and 106:

Mr Ayoola contends that the affidavit filed is not satisfactory proof of the order which has to be proved by one of the methods set out in section 112 of the Evidence Ordinance... I do however accept the affidavit sworn to by Mr. Holden and the facts therein contained as I do the copy of the order of deposition signed by His Excellency and attached to the affidavit. I continually asked Mr. Ayoola to show me good cause why I should not accept the affidavit and its contents as representing the true state of things and though counsel challenged the contents of the affidavit he was unable to advance any sound reason why I should not do so other than a statement that if I made the Order nisi then from his cross-examination of the deponent he would be able to show that in fact no such order of deposition could have been made on the day in question... I do not find enough substance in these contentions to make me hold that the affidavit is untrue with the serious repercussions it would have on the deponent.

See also *Onitiri v. Onitiri* (1956-84) 10 S.C.N.D. 85.

NOTE:

Affidavit evidence is documentary evidence. It is an important feature of the trial process. As a matter of practice, a trial in the High Court in civil matters can hardly be concluded without parties making use of affidavit evidence one way or the other, particularly in interlocutory matters. Apart from interlocutory matters parties make use of affidavit evidence in originating summons where

(a) the sole or principal question at issue is or is likely to be, one of the construction of a written law or of any instrument made under any written law, or of any deed, will, contract or other document or some other question of law or

(b) there is unlikely to be any substantial dispute of fact. See Order 1 rule 2 of the High Court (Civil Procedure) Rules, 1987. See also *Darman v. Minister of Internal Affairs and Others* [1981] 2 N.C.L.R. 431; *National Bank of Nigeria and Another v. Alakija and Another* (1978) 2 L.R.N. 78; *Doherty v. Doherty* [1968] N.M.L.R. (Pt. 2) 241; *Attorney-General Bendel State v. Attorney-General of the Federation* [1986] 1 N.W.L.R. (Pt. 17) 471; *Fayinmi v. The Speaker of Western House of Assembly* [1962] 1 All N.L.R. 205.

Contents of an Affidavit

Banque De Il, Afrique Occidentale v. Alhaji Baba Haba Sharfodi 1963 N.N.L.R. 21

The plaintiffs' Suit was entered on the undefended list. They claimed under a written agreement between themselves and the first defendant as principal and the second and third defendants as guarantors. Notice of intention to defend signed by the defendants' solicitor was delivered on behalf of all the defendants. It was supported by two affidavits, one sworn by the first defendant. The solicitor's affidavit stated in paragraph 2 that the deponent was informed and he verily believed that the sum claimed in the suit was not yet due; in paragraph 3 that the deponent had studied the written agreement and was of the opinion that it was not binding on the defendants; and in paragraph 4 that all the defendants had a good defence to the suit. The plaintiffs objected to paragraphs 3 and 4 as contravening the provisions of sections 85 and 86 of the Evidence Act.

HELD:

Paragraph 3 was for the most part an expression of opinion and not a statement of facts or circumstances, and the only part which was not an expression of opinion could not stand alone, and paragraph 4 contained only an opinion and a legal conclusion; and these paragraphs must be struck out.

Chief R.I. Osian v. Flour Mills of Nigeria Ltd. [1968] 2 All N.L.R. 13

This was an application for a stay of execution of judgment pending the determination of an appeal to the Supreme Court. The main ground for the application was contained in paragraph 5 of an affidavit which read thus:

> *I verily believe that if the judgment debt and costs awarded against the Defendants/Applicants were paid to the Plaintiff/Respondent there would be no reasonable probability of getting back the said judgment debts and costs in the event of the appeal succeeding wholly or in part.*

HELD:

(1) Where the information contained in an affidavit is derived from sources other than the personal knowledge of the deponent, he must state the source of his information and belief in compliance with sections 87 and 88 of the Evidence Act. In this application the failure of the deponent to state the source of his information and belief rendered his affidavit worthless; consequently the application must be refused.

NOTE

It is difficult to support this decision on any rational basis. It does not appear from the averment that the belief was from a source other than that of the deponent. It was a belief of the deponent and so the issue of disclosure of an informant is, with respect, neither here nor there. But the learned trial Judge was perfectly entitled to hold as he did that the affidavit did not show sufficient evidence to justify the deponent's assertion.

J.O. Wachukwu v. Emmanuel Elewa and Others [1985] H.C.N.L.R. 1393

The plaintiff/respondent filed two actions at two different High Courts in the Rivers State - PHC/49/84 and PHC/118/83. The defendants applied to the High Court that Action PHC/49/84 be either struck out as they alleged, because it constituted an abuse of the judicial process of the court or be transferred to the court where PHC/118/83 was being heard and consolidated with it. In their affidavits, the defendants/applicants *inter alia* averred that the plaintiff's relationship with other members of the family was not cordial (paragraph 9); that the family is already being strained to its limits in the two suits (paragraph 10); and that the plaintiff should not be allowed to use his status as a legal practitioner to file multiplicity of suits against the defendants. An objection was raised to the effect that the paragraphs offended against section 86 of the Evidence Act.

HELD:

(1) A legally acceptable language of an affidavit is that of averment of fact. Once it speaks the language of fact within the meaning of section 86 of the Evidence Act, the affidavit is said to have complied with the requirements of the law.

(2) The paragraphs are not objections, prayers, legal arguments or conclusions within the meaning of section 86 of the Evidence Act. See also *Nneji and Others v. Chief Chukwe and Others* [1988]3 N.W.L.R. (Pt. 81) 184; *Federal Board of Inland Revenue v. Babooye* (1974) 1 F.R.C.R. 124; *Ali Eli-Khadra v. International Metal Industries Ltd.* (1976) 2 F.R.C.R. 84; *In the Matter of West African Metal and Chemical Ltd.,* FRC/L/M20/73 delivered on 9/8/76 (Unreported). *Momodu and Others v. Momoh and Another* [1986] 5 N.W.L.R. (Pt. 43) 649; *Governor of Lagos State v. Chief Ojukwu* [1986] 1 N.W.L.R. (Pt. 8) 621.

Swearing to Affidavit

Iris Winifred Horn v. Robert Rickard 1963 N.N.L.R. 67; [1963] 2 All N.L.R. 41

This was a motion by the defendant/applicant asking for an order to give security for costs. The motion was supported by an affidavit sworn by counsel for the defendant/applicant. On a preliminary objection, it was held that an affidavit sworn to by counsel representing a party to the proceedings is unobjectionable in principle provided it does not by reason of its subject matter offend against the rule that a client's communications to his counsel are privileged, or the requirement that counsel should not put himself in a position where he may be subject to cross-examination or in any way enter personally into the dispute. Applying these principles to this particular case, the affidavit filed by the counsel for the defendant/applicant could not be said to be objectionable. The court held *per in curiam* that the swearing of affidavits by members of the bar is in the main an undesirable practice. If counsel alone has the knowledge necessary to swear to the affidavit and the facts to which he is to swear are likely to be in dispute, he should for the purposes of the application withdraw from the case and brief other counsel. See also *Obadara and Others v. The President of Ibadan West District Council Grade A Customary Court* [1965] N.M.L.R. 39; *Administrator-General and Public Trustees v. Ikemefuna and Another* (1974) 4 E.C.S.L.R. 78; *Aladeusi v. Alhaji Dangana* 1975 N.N.L.R. 190; *Akinola v. Solanke* [1985] H.C.N.L.R. 876; *Cerakie and Another v. Okoye and Another* [1973] 3 E.C.S.L.R. 155.

M.H. Ambakederemo v. Rivers State Utilities Board
Suit No. PHC/370/84 delivered on 16/9/86 (Unreported)

This was an application for an order (a) granting the defendant/applicant leave to amend their statement of defence and (b) to deem the proposed amended statement of defence attached to the affidavit in support of the application as duly ordered, filed and served. Learned State Counsel, Mrs. Sylverline O. Iragunima swore to an affidavit in which she averred to reasons why the amendment was necessary. The issues learned State Counsel swore to were not controversial.

HELD:

Since there is no controversy in the affidavit, counsel was free to swear to it.

The learned trial Judge said:

The rationale behind the basic principle and practice is so clear. Counsel by nature of his professional function of counsel qua advocate is only expected to perform his duties of advocacy in the court. He is not expected to mix up his professional functions with any other function. Concisely put, he cannot give evidence in the case in which he is appearing as counsel. The law and practice do not allow him to perform both functions in any given case. he must only perform one of the functions. If he is appearing as counsel in court, his only function is that of advocacy and related matters and no more. But if he decides to be a witness, he cannot then be an advocate at the same time. So far so good. However in cases where there is no controversy or there is likely to be no controversy or dispute or contest on the issues involved, counsel can swear to an affidavit in a case

> *in which he is representing a party. For instance, he can swear to formal facts not touching on any controversial or disputable substance of the case. In other words, counsel is free and should feel free to swear to affidavit in which his functions as counsel will not clash with any other proprietory interest in the case, to the extent that he will not be exposed to cross-examination on the fact he has deposed to. The dividing line appears thin. The dichotomy is not easy to draw. But counsel who intends to swear to an affidavit should always remind himself that he can only do so when the issues giving rise to the affidavit are formal, not controversial and never in dispute or will never be in dispute. The golden rule, if I may say so, is that the moment counsel is in doubt as to where the pendulum is likely to tilt, he must resolve the doubt in favour of not swearing to the affidavit. By that cautious decision, he must have saved himself from all the embarrassment in the court.*

In *Usman v. Minister of Federal Capital Territory and Another* [1985] H.C.N.L.R.X, it was held that a purported affidavit and sworn to before a person not duly authorised is not in law an affidavit.

On defective affidavits generally, see *Ikwukolam v. Ogbonnaya* (1980) 1 R.S.L.R. 43; *Usman v. Minister of Federal Capital Territory and Another, supra; Otu v. Fadison (Nig.) Ltd. and another*, Suit No. PHC/370/86 delivered on 24/2/86 (Unreported). On unchallenged facts in an affidavit, see generally *Azeeze v. The State* [1986] 2 N.W.L.R. (Pt. 23) 541; *Agbaje v. Ibru S.F.Ltd.* (1972) 5 S.C. 50; *National Bank v. Are Brothers* (1977) 6 S.C. 97; *Sotuminu v. Ocean Steamship (Nig) Ltd.* [1987] 4 N.W.L.R. (Pt. 66) 691.

Documents Not Complying With Illiterates Protection Act: Who is an Illiterate

Malam Kantoma v. Paterson Zochonis and Company Ltd. 1964 N.N.L.R. 54

The appellant signed a guarantee indemnifying the respondent company in respect of a third person's indebtedness to the company. The guarantee was in English. The appellant was not literate in English but was able to read and write in Arabic.

HELD:

> The appellant was not illiterate in the sense in which that word is to be construed in the Illiterates Protection Act, and he did not come within the provisions of the Act.

Taylor F.J. stated as follows:-

> *I have always understood the word 'illiterate' to refer to a person totally illiterate in the case that he is unable to read or write in any language. To hold that a person is literate or not literate because he is unable to read or write in a particular language, even if the document concerned was written in that language, is in my view to stretch the meaning of the word to an absurdity.*

NOTE

The Illiterates Protection Act does not define an illiterate. This is rather unfortunate. The lack of statutory definition has given rise to various interpretations, some of which are quite contradictory. With respect, the interpretation of Taylor, F.J. is absurd. For the purposes of the Act, a person may be literate in one language and not be literate in the other. The interpretation of the learned Judge will only mean that literacy will be imputed on a party to an agreement written in a language he does not write or speak merely because he has entered into the agreement in that language. This does not make any sense. The learned Judge was however right when he held that an illiterate under the Act includes "a person who, though not totally illiterate, is not sufficiently literate to read and understand the contents of the document. In *S.C.O.A. Zaria v. Okon* (1959) 4 F.S.C. 220, the Federal Supreme Court arrived at a different decision. The court held that the person who could only write his name qualified as an illiterate within the meaning of the Act. This is correct. In *Ntiashagwo v. Amodu and Another* (1959) W.R.N.L.R. (Pt. 4) 273, Charles, J. rightly defined an illiterate person as "a person who is unable to read with understanding, and to express his thoughts by writing in the language used in the document made or prepared on his behalf. See generally *Lawal v. G.B. Ollivant (Nig.) Ltd.* [1972] 1 All N.L.R. (Pt. 1) 207; *Jiboso v. Obadina* (1962) W.R.N .L.R. 303.

Effect of Non-Compliance with Act.

The Act does not provide for the effect of non-compliance with its provisions on the subsequent admissibility of the document in court. The courts have however pronounced on the effect. In *United Africa Company of Nigeria Limited v. Edems and Ajayi*, 1958 N.R.N.L.R. 33, Smith, J. held that the object of the Illiterates Protection Act is to protect an illiterate person from possible fraud. Strict compliance with it is obligatory as regards the writer of a document. In *Akokwere of Okan v. Emayabor* (1959-60) W.R.N.L.R. 83, Dufus, J. held that the Illiterates Protection Law, 1956 was, as the title itself stated, a law to protect and not to penalise illiterates and the fact that the writer did not carry out the provisions of that law could not mean that the document was for that reason alone void and of no effect.

In *S.C.O.A. Zaria v. Okon*, supra, an illiterate defendant denied signing a financial document as a surety. He also contended that the document he signed was not explained or interpreted to him before he signed it. It was held that on the evidence before the court, the defendant did not understand the nature of the document he signed. In *Eke v. Odolofun* [1961] 1 All N.L.R. 404 Madarikan J. (as he then was) examined some of the above authorities and held that the failure to comply with the Act rendered the document inadmissible and that the decision in *Akohwere of Okan v. Emayabor, supra.* that such non-compliance alone did not render a writ void and of no effect, appeared to be inconsistent with the general stream of authorities.

In *Djukpan v. Orovuyovbe* [1967] N.M.L.R. 287, the Supreme Court held that so far as non-compliance with section 6 of the Illiterates Protection Act is concerned, the court does not consider the section, unlike section 3, in so much for the protection of the illiterate as a penal provision in respect of the writer and non-compliance would not as much affect admissibility. In *Barclays Bank D.C.O. v. Hassan* [1961] All N.L.R. 836, Charles J. abandoned the position he took in *Ntiashaswo v. Amadu, supra* that a document which did not comply with the provisions of the Act was inadmissible. He said:

> *I am satisfied from further consideration of my remarks in* Ntiashashwo's *case that non-compliance with the requirements of the Illiterates Protection Act by the preparer of a document renders the document void, were too widely stated and inaccurate on that account. What is the exact general effect of such non-compliance on the enforceability of a document and its admissibility as evidence need not be considered here. It is sufficient to say that the document is not rendered void in the strict sense, as obviously the illiterate can rely on it. (*Akokwere of Akan v. Emayabor and Another*). But it is unenforceable by the preparer against the illiterate in respect of legal rights created by it in favour of the former (*S.C.O.A. Zaria v. Okon*).*

From the above line of cases, the general consensus can be summarised thus. A document which does not comply with the Act is not void ab initio as it could be enforced in favour of the illiterate who seeks remedy under it. This is so because the Act is designed to protect an illiterate against fraud emanating from his more privileged literate counterpart in a transaction. Accordingly, such a document is admissible in evidence in favour of the illiterate.

On the chapter, see further: *Nsirim v. Nsirim* [1990] N.W.L.R. (Pt. 138) 285

Chapter 13

STATEMENTS ADMISSIBLE UNDER SECTION 91

Section 91 of the Evidence Act.

Section 91 of the Evidence Act provides for admissibility of documentary evidence as to facts in issue. By the section, in any civil proceedings where direct oral evidence of a fact would be admissible, any statement made by a person in a document and tending to establish that fact shall, on production of the original document, be admissible as evidence of that fact if the following conditions are satisfied:

(a) f the maker of the statement either had personal knowledge of the matters dealt with by the statement; or where the document in question is or forms part of a record purporting to be a continuous record, made the statement (in so far as the matters dealt with thereby are not within his personal knowledge) in the performance of a duty to record information supplied to have, personal knowledge of those matter; and

(b) if the maker of the statement is called as a witness in the proceedings subject however to the exceptions in the proviso therein stated (S. 91(1)).

In any civil proceedings, the court may at any stage of the proceedings, if having regard to all the circumstances of the case it is satisfied that undue delay or expense would otherwise be caused, order that such a statement as is mentioned in subsection (1) shall be admissible as evidence or may without any such order having been made, admit such a statement in evidence:

(a) notwithstanding that the maker of the statement is available but is not called as a witness;

(b) notwithstanding that the original document is not produced, if in lieu thereof there is produced a copy of the original document or of the material part thereof certified to be a true copy in such manner as may be specified in the order or as the court may approve, as the case may be (S. 91(2)).

Nothing in the section will render admissible as evidence any statement made by a person interested at a time when proceedings were pending or anticipated involving a dispute as to any fact which the statement might tend to establish (S.9(3)).

For the purposes of the section, a statement in a document will not be deemed to have been made by a person unless the document or the material part thereof was written, made or produced by him with his own hand, or signed or initialed by him or otherwise recognised by him in writing as one for the accuracy of which he is responsible (S. 9(4)).

For the purposes of deciding whether or not a statement is admissible as evidence, the court may draw any reasonable inference from the form or contents of the document in which the statement is contained, or from any other circumstances. The court may, in deciding whether or not a person is fit to attend as a witness act on a certificate purporting to be the certificate of a registered medical practitioner, and where the proceedings are with a jury, the court may in its discretion reject the statement notwithstanding that the requirements of the section are satisfied with respect thereto, if for any reason it appears to it to be inexpedient in the interest of justice that the statement should be admitted (S. 91(5)).

Section 91 has two main restrictions which must be mentioned. First, the section applies only to statements in documents, and section 2 of the Act defines a 'statement' within the meaning of the Act as including "any representation of fact, whether made in words or otherwise". Second, the section applies only to civil proceedings. This is so clear in subsections (1) and (2) thereof.

Diab Nasr v. Berini Beirut-Riyad (Nig.) Bank Limited [1968] 1 All N.L.R. 274

The plaintiff claimed against the defendant the delivery of the original deed of lease dated 16th May, 1962 and registered as No. 2778 for Plots Nos. XRL 3042 and 3043 situate at Apapa, Lagos. The issue was on the admissibility of the contents of Exhibit 23, the solicitor's letter to the defendant containing what the plaintiff claimed as the main proposals of the tacit arrangement.

HELD:

In the circumstances in which Exhibit 23 was put in evidence, the maker of it, i.e. the plaintiff, even though he acted through his agent, his solicitor, gave oral evidence indicating that he was the author of the contents of Exhibit 23. Therefore on that basis the Judge was right to deal with the contents of Exhibit 23 as if the document was evidence of its contents.

Coker, J.S.C said at page 293:

At this juncture we comment briefly on a point of law which arose whilst this aspect of the case was being argued. Chief Williams for the defendant submitted that the letter, Exhibit 23, should not be regarded as evidence of its contents in view of the provisions of section 90 of the Evidence Act. That section precludes the admission as evidence of written statements when the maker of such statements is not called as a witness and the other conditions of admissibility under that section are not shown to exist. We think the argument overlooked some of the peculiar features of this case. The letter, Exhibit 23, was put in evidence by Diab Nasr himself. He had given evidence that he instructed his solicitors to write the letter and he thereafter testified as follows: 'Exhibit 23 speaks of a tacit arrangement between us and the bank.... the main terms of the tacit arrangement are contained in Exhibit 23'... We think therefore that on that basis the Judge was right to deal with the contents of Exhibit 23 as if the document was evidence of its contents.

Alhaji Etiko v. M. Aroyewun [1959] 4 F.S.C. 129

This is an appeal by the defendant from the judgment of the Lagos High Court, awarding to the plaintiff a declaration of title to certain land at Odunfa Street, Ebute Metta and damages for trespass and an injunction. The second ground of appeal alleged that the "learned trial Judge was wrong in law in comparing the plan on Exhibit 'E' (the conveyance to the plaintiff) with the plan attached to the statement of claim when the plan was not in evidence".

HELD:

Where there is no difficulty in identifying the land, a declaration of title may be made without it being based on a plan. The court relevantly discussed sections 90(1) and 129 of the Evidence Act.

Abott, Ag. C.J.F. (as he then was) said at pages 130 and 131:

Mrs. Kotun dealt with the first and fourth grounds together. So far as the first is concerned, the error alleged in the first ground is that the Judge wrongly applied section 90(1) of the Evidence Ordinance to the recital 'E'. I am of opinion that the trial Judge correctly applied section 90(1) of the Evidence Ordinance in this case...In my opinion, the provisions of subsection (1) of section 90 of the Evidence Ordinance have been satisfied, and the recitals in Exhibit 'E' are admissible in evidence as proof that the land in dispute formed part of the land edged red on the plan attached to Exhibit 'F'... I entirely agree with the learned trial Judge as to the admissibility of the recitals in

Exhibit 'E' for the purpose for which he admitted them and with the conclusion at which he arrived as a result. To my mind, this was exactly the type of difficulty which section 90(1).. was designed to meet.

Adekunle Coker v. Albert Farhat (1952) 14 W.A.C.A. 216

The plaintiff's case was that he bought the premises in dispute in 1950 with a conveyance from the vendor containing recitals proving the vendor's title and right to convey, *viz*: that A had conveyed in fee simple to B; who made a deed of settlement in 1895 settling property including the premises in dispute upon the trusts mentioned in that deed that B's widow made a will containing a proviso, which was recited, and finally this, that the vendor became the beneficiary of the property comprised in the settlement. The deed of settlement was tendered in evidence, but not the will, nor was any foundation laid for leading secondary evidence on its contents. The trial Judge gave judgment to the plaintiff of the basis of the conveyance and its recitals as being proof of the vendor's title to convey and right to possession. The defendant appealed. The argument turned mainly on evidence. For the plaintiff it was that his vendor had personal knowledge of the matters recited in the conveyance but as he was dead, it was not necessary to call him as a witness. He relied on section 90(1). For the defendant the argument was that before a statement in a document can become evidence of a fact under section 90(1), the requirement that direct oral evidence of the fact would be admissible had to be satisfied (which related to the will mentioned above, as it had not been tendered in evidence, and to section 96(1) of the Evidence Ordinance).

HELD:

No foundation was laid of the facts to be proved as required by section 96(1) of the Evidence Ordinance so as to make secondary evidence of the will admissible. Without proof of the facts required the vendor could not have given direct oral evidence of the contents of the will, therefore his recital in the conveyance ought to have been accepted as establishing any facts alleged by it.

Foster-Sutton, P. said at page 218:

He also argued that before a statement contained in a document can become evidence of a fact under section 90(1) of the Evidence Ordinance, the requirement that direct oral evidence of the fact would be admissible has to be satisfied, and, he submitted, that could not be said to be the case here. Apart from the fact that a recital that, by virtue of diverse meagre assurances and acts and operations of law of and concerning the relevant construction to the said recited proviso contained in the said will and ultimately the said hereditaments became the property of and vested in the said vendor' can hardly be said to be satisfactory evidence of the fact that the property in question had become vested in the vendor, the argument put forward on behalf of the respondent seems to me to prove the provision of section 96(1) of the Evidence Ordinance which sets out the facts to be proved before secondary evidence of the contents of a document becomes admissible.

Mrs. C.A. Ogunsanya v. Madam A. Taiwo [1971] 1 All N.L.R. 147

The plaintiff claimed title through one Adebiyi to whom she alleged that one Raji Akintola as the Mogaji or head of the Ajengbe family and two other members of that family had sold two plots of land in the layout one of which is the subject-matter of the present proceedings. At the trial she produced the conveyance executed in favour of her vendor, Adebiyi by Raji Akintola and the two members of the family. The conveyance, dated 8th October, 1981, was admitted in evidence as Exhibit A1.

HELD:

(1) Section 90(1) of the Evidence Act provides that oral evidence is required, plus other conditions, to make admissible as evidence a statement made by a person in a document and tending to establish a fact whereof direct oral evidence would be admissible.

(2) In this case, the document, Exhibit A1 was executed by Raji Akintola himself and so the provisions of subsection (4) of section 90 of the Evidence Act were satisfied.

Armels Transport Ltd. v. Madam Atinuke Martins [1971] 1 All N.L.R. 27

The plaintiff claimed damages from the defendant for the negligent driving by the defendants' driver of an omnibus which collided with the plaintiff's tipper on the Lagos/Ikorodu Road. The trial Judge judgement to the plaintiff. reliance was placed by the trial Judge on Exibit J, The sketch of the accident, who in his judgement said "I would prefer to accept the evidence of the police officer as shown in the sketch of the accident (Exhibit J). This proves that the omnibus had left its side of the road and had careered to the wrong side of the road before the collusion.

HELD:

The point shown on the plan as the point of impact not being within the personal knowledge of the policeman and not being admissible by virtue of section 90 of the Evidene Act was unadmissible, being hearsay evidence.

Chief Igunbor Igbodin and Others v. Chief Ugbende Obianke [1976] 1 N.M.L.R. 212

The plaintiffs claimed in the lower court against the defendants declaration of title to land, trespass and injunction. The plaintiffs called witnesses in support of their claim. Several witnesses gave evidence at the instance of the defendants and put in several documents in evidence. The learned trial Judge expunged 24 exhibits and entered judgement for the plaintiffs. the defendants in the appeal, complained of the expunction of the documentary evidence, Exhibits D -C8, G, H, J - R and S which they argued were admissible and properly admitting at the hearing.

HELD:

It is settled law that documentary evidene can be admitted in court proceedings through any witness by consent or without objection and section 90(2) of the Evidence Act which governed proceedings in Bendel State High Court gave the learned trial Judge power to admit such doucuments, notwithstanding that their makers were available and not called as witnesses.

(2) The court was satisfied that the learned trial Judge had not acted on all the admissible evidence before him. A trial *de novo* was ordered.

Marian Olutunde Agbeja and Another v. Olusola Idowu Agbeja and Another [1985] 3 N.W.L.R. (Pt. 11) 11

The plaintiffs brought a suit praying the court to order letters of administration in respect of the Estate of one D.O. Agbeja who died intestate. The 1st plaintiff claimed that she was married to the deceased at the Marriage Registry in Lagos on 14th January, 1954. She obtained forms necessary to obtain letters of administration filled them and sent same to the 1st defendant to sign. She refused on the ground that her mother was married to the deceased on 25th December, 1947 under native laws and custom, and that the purported marriage having taken place during the continuance of the earlier marriage in 1947. At the trial, the defendants proved the 1947 marriage under native law and custom.

The learned trial Judge held that the 1st plaintiff could not succed in her claim because the earlier marriage in 1947 between the deceased and the mother of the 1st defendant made her marriage to the deceased in 1954 a nullity. He had earlier admitted the marriage certificate as Exhibit A.

HELD:

(1) Section 90(1) of the Evidence Act only provides for the admissibility of a statement in evidence on certain conditions and there is no presumption of the correctness of such statement.

(2) In this case, Exhibit A, the Marriage Certificate of the marriage between the deceased and the 1st plaintiff was admitted in evidence in conformity with section 90(1) of the Evidence Act.

In *Are and Another v. Ipaye and Others* [1986] 3 N.W.L.R. (Pt. 29) 416, the Court of Appeal held that section 90(3) refers to statements made or particularly the person who seeks to tender them and not documents *per se* and since the defendants neither adduced evidence nor tendered a document in proof of the case referred to (Exhibit G being a document relating to another piece of land and the parties being different from those in their action) comments made thereto would not form part of the reasons for the judgment and if they do they would be expunged as irrelevant.

In *Chief Apena and Others v. Chief Aiyetobi* [1989] 1 N.W.L.R. (Pt. 95) 85, it was held that a Surveyor who prepares a survey plan in respect of a parcel of land in dispute in a pending case and tenders it in evidence is not a 'person interested' within the context of section 90(3) of the Evidence Act.

Chapter 14

DOCUMENTARY EVIDENCE

Sections 93 to 99 of the Evidence Act.

The contents of documents may be proved either by primary or by secondary evidence (S. 93). Primary evidence means the document itself produced for the inspection of the court. Where a document has been executed in several parts, each part shall be primary evidence of the document. Where a document has been executed in counterpart, each counterpart being executed by one or some of the parties only, each counterpart shall be primary evidence as against the parties executing it. Where a number of documents have all been made by one uniform process, as in the case of printing, lithography or photography, each shall be primary evidence of the contents of the rest; but where they are all copies of a common original, they shall not be primary evidence of the contents of the original (S. 94).

Secondary evidence includes

(a) certified copies given under the provisions hereinafter contained;

(b) copies made from the original by mechanical processes which in themselves ensure the accuracy of the copy and copies compared with such copies;

(c) copies made from or compared with the original;

(d) counterparts of documents as against the parties who did not execute them;

(e) oral accounts of the contents of a document must be proved by primary evidence except in the case mentioned in section 97 (S. 96).

By section 97, secondary evidence may be given of the existence, condition or contents of a document in the following cases:

(a) When the original is shown or appears to be in the possession or power of the person against whom the document is sought to be proved, or by any person legally bound to produce it, and when, after the notice mentioned in section 98, such person does not produce it;

(b) when the existence, condition or contents of the original have been proved to be admitted in writing by the person against whom it is proved or by his representative in interest;
(c) when the original has been destroyed or lost and in the latter case all possible search has been made for it;
(d) when the original is of such a nature as not to be easily movable;
(e) when the original is a public document within the meaning of section 109
(f) when the original is a document of which a certified copy is permitted by the Act, or by any other law in force in Nigeria to be given in evidence;
(g) when the originals consist of numerous accounts or other documents which cannot conveniently be examined in court, and the fact to be proved is the general result of the whole collection;
(h) when the document is an entry in a banker's book (S. 97(1)).

The secondary evidence admissible in respect of the original documents referred to in the several paragraphs of subsection (1) above is as follows:

(a) in paragraphs (a), (c) and (d) any secondary evidence of the contents of the document is admissible;
(b) in paragraph (b) the written admission is admissible ;
(c) in paragraph (e) or (f) a certified copy of the document, but no other kind of secondary evidence is admissible;
(d) in paragraph (g) evidence may be given as to the general result of the documents by any person who has examined them, and who is skilled in the examination of such documents;
(e) in paragraph (h) the copies cannot be received as evidence unless it be first proved that the bank in which the entries copied were made was at the time of making, one of the ordinary books of the bank, and that the entry was made in the usual or ordinary course of business, and that the book is in the custody and control of the bank, which proof may be given orally or by affidavit by a partner or officer of the bank, and that the copy has been examined with the original entry and is correct, which proof must be given by some person who has examined the copy with the original entry and may be given orally or by affidavit (S. 97(2)). When a seaman sues for his wages he may give secondary evidence of the ship's articles and of any agreement supporting his case, without notice to produce the originals (S. 97(3)).

Secondary evidence of the contents of the documents referred to in paragraph (a) of subsection (1) of section 97 shall not be given unless the party proposing to give such secondary evidence has previously given to the party in whose possession or power the document is, or to a legal practitioner employed by such party, such notice to produce it as is prescribed by law; and if no notice is prescribed by law, then such notice as the court considers reasonable in the circumstances of the case. However, such notice will not be required in order to render secondary evidence admissible in any of the following cases, or in any other case in which the court thinks fit to dispense with it:

(a) when the document to be proved is itself a notice;
(b) when, from the nature of the case, the adverse party must know that he will be required to produce it;
(c) when it appears or is proved that the adverse party has obtained possession of the original by fraud or force;
(d) when the adverse party or his agent has the original in court;
(e) when the adverse party or his agent has admitted the loss of the document (S. 98).

Section 99 provides inter alia for proof of incorporation of bank. First, the fact of any bank having duly made a return to the Commissioner of Inland Revenue in Great Britain may be proved in any legal proceedings by production of a copy of its return by the affidavit of a partner or officer of the bank, or by the production of a copy of a newspaper purporting to contain a copy of such return published by the said Commissioners of Inland Revenue. Second, the fact that any savings bank is established under the Savings Bank Act, may be proved by a certificate purporting to be under the hand of the Director of Posts and Telegraphs or officers of the postal department in charge of such savings bank. Third, the fact of any banking company having been incorporated under any charter before or after passing of the Evidence Act may be proved by the production of a certificate of a partner or officer of the bank that it has been duly incorporated under such charter.

Primary Documentary Evidence

Esso West Africa Inc. v. L. Oladiti [1968] N.M.L.R. 453

During the hearing of an action for a sum of money said to be the balance of the price of goods sold and delivered to the defendant by the plaintiff, counsel for the defendant sought to tender a document which was one of the copies of a document signed in quadruplicate by one of the plaintiff's agents acknowledging that the defendant was entitled to a credit of a sum of money in his account with the plaintiff. The Document, a carbon copy was however signed through one single process with the original.

HELD:

(1) If many copies of an agreement are made by the process of typing with carbon papers, each copy, including the carbon copies is primary evidence of the provisions of the agreement provided, they are all signed or executed by the parties to the agreement. Such copies do not come within section 94 of the Evidence Act, but are akin to counterparts each of which has been executed by the parties which are declared to be primary evidence under subsections (2) and (3) of section 93(2). (2) The process of "printing, lithography and photography" mentioned in section 93(4) of the Evidence Act is not meant to be exhaustive of such processes but are mentioned only as examples of the type of uniform processes intended. (3) Under section 93(4) of the Evidence Act, each copy of a printed matter is primary evidence of the other but only secondary evidence of the material which forms the basis of the print.

Aguda, J. (as he then was) said at page 456:

In my view, the processes of 'printing', 'lithography' and 'photography' mentioned in this subsection is not meant to be exhaustive of such process but are mentioned only as examples of the type of uniform process intended. Under this section, each copy of a printed matter is primary evidence of the other, but only secondary evidence of the material which forms the basis of the print. Similarly, I hold the view that where a number of documents have all been made by one single act by the use of carbon papers each of such documents is primary evidence of the other but secondary evidence of the material which forms the basis of the documents. Therefore in this case the document now being sought to be tendered is primary evidence of the contents of the top copy which is usually referred to as the original since the process of signing all the copies consists of one single act. In this regard there is support for the view expressed above in the case of A.O. Coker v. S.A. Ayode and Others, Unreported, but see Ibadan Suit No. 1/286/57 (decided, December 4, 1963) noted in (1964) Nigerian Law Journal p. 132 in which it was held that "where a letter is typed from a draft, each copy of the letter is primary evidence of the contents of the other copies, including the top, but not of the draft from which the copy was made". Cf. Abed Brothers Limited v. Niger Insurance Company Limited and Another [1974] 4 E.C.S.L.R. 525 at 539.

Michael Oguntonade v. Commissioner of Police [1959] W.N.L.R. 289

The appellant was charged with conspiracy, attempt to obtain money by false pretences and also with stealing. During the trial, officials of the National Bank, Ibadan and the Bank of West Africa, Ibadan, were called to tender the Bank's statements of accounts of the Production Board with the Banks. There was no compliance with section 96(2) (e) of the Evidence Ordinance.

HELD:

> The Bank statements tendered were primary evidence. They are a part and parcel of what constitutes "Bankers Book" which are used in the ordinary business of the bank. They are therefore admissible.

Taylor, J. said at pages 291 and 292:

> *The first question that arises is whether these exhibits are pimary or secondary evidence within the meaning of the Ordinance. To do this I think it necessary to digress a little and enquire into the object of the Ordinance which is obviously taken from the Bankers Books Evidence Act of 1879 of England. This object is stated in Halsbury's Laws of England, Volume 1, the 1st Edition at page 645, section 1301 as follows: 'The main object of these provisions is to enable evidence to be procured and given; to relieve bankers from the necessity for atending and producing their books. They enable a party who formerly had the right to issue a subpoena duces tecuum to compel bankers to produce their books and to attend and be examined on them, to obtain an order for leave to inspect and take copies of the books'.... The object of the provision is therefore to allow third parties to make copies of entries in banker's books and when such copies have been made to allow them to be tendered in evidence but subject to the very strict provisions in section 96(2) (e) of the Evidence Ordinance... There is no room for doubt that on these authorities these exhibits are not copies of secondary evidence within the meaning of the Ordinance. They are in fact primary evidence.*

Secondary Documentary Evidence

In *Esso West Africa Inc. v. Y. Alli* [1968] N.M.L.R. 414 Aguda, J. (as he then was) held that by virtue of section 94 of the Evidence Act, photostat copies of documents are not primary but secondary evidence of the original and as such inadmissible, and if the party to be affected fails to raise objection to such admission, the court may, and indeed in criminal cases must reject such evidence on its own motion, and where the court admits such inadmissible evidence, it is the duty of the court not to act on it, but to decide the case on legal evidence.

In *Abed Brothers Limited v. Niger Insurance Company Limited and Another, supra,* Wheeler, J. held that invoice booklets which contained carbon copies of the invoices are mere copies of an original document not made by same uniform process within the meaning of section 93(4) of the Evidence Law, 1963 of Eastern Nigeria.

> *"The words printing, lithography or photography each govern the expression 'are uniform process', and each of those words connotes mechanical process of some kind (to use the words which, significantly enough, appear in section 94 (b) of the Evidence Law). Whereas documents made with the use of carbon paper substantially involve not a mechanical process but a manual process, and it involves no great manupilation in the use of carbon paper to end up with a series of documents which do not conform with each other, although I do not for a moment suggest that, occurred in this case, my opinion, therefore, is that Exhibits 43 and 44 were not admissible in evidence, and I have not taken any of their contents in my consideration of the issue of damages" Per Wheeler, J. See also Ojo v. Adejobi and Others (1978) 3 S.C. 65 at 73.*

Cases in which Secondary Evidence may be Given

Among other things, before secondary evidence of the contents of a document could be properly given, the person who gives the evidence must have seen it himself prior to the testimony. *(The Nigeria Safety Insurance Co. Ltd. v. Zaria Co-operative Credit Marketing Union Ltd.* (1978) 1 N.C.A.R. 1). There is no absolute legal bar to the admissibility of secondary evidence of documents such as there is to proving alteration of deeds by extrinsic evidence *(Okpanku v. Amachi* (1956-84) 10 S.C.N.D. 76). Before secondary evidence of a document can be given, a case must be made out under section 96 of the Evidence Ordinance; but in the present suit the plaintiff did not give any evidence to show that his letter of acceptance and receipts reached the hands of the defendant. *(Iphie v. Plateau Auditing Company* 1957 N.R.N.L.R. 212). No foundation was laid of the facts to be proved as required by section 96(1) of the Evidence Ordinance so as to make secondary evidence of the will admissible *(Coker v. Farhat* (1952) 14 W.A.C.A 216). The mining lease being a public document, its contents ought be proved by secondary evidence but the secondary evidence must be a certified copy and not oral evidence *(Bisichi Tin Company Limited v. Commissioner of Police*, 1962 N.N.L.R. 71). The combined effect of section 96(2) (c) (e) and (f) of the Evidence Act is that in the case of public documents, the only type of secondary evidence permissible is a certified true copy of the document and none other *(Dobadina Family and Another v. Ambrose Family and Others* [1969] N.M.L.R. 24). See also *Isibor v. The State* [1970] 1 All N.L.R. 248. In the case of public documents the only type of secondary evidence permissible is a certifed true copy of the document and none other. The document now marked Exhibit '2' was not a certified true copy but a photostat copy and it was therefore inadmissible as secondary evidence of a public document which it purported to be. There was no objection to its admissibility when it was produced but it was not within the competence of parties to a case to admit by consent or otherwise a document which, by law, was inadmissible *(Minister of Lands, Western Nigeria v. Dr. N. Azikiwe and Others* [1969] 1 All N.L.R. 49).

By virtue of section 96(1) (c) of the Evidence Ordinance, secondary evidence may be given of the existence, condition or contents of a document when the original has been destroyed or lost and in the latter case all possible search has been made for it, and that by virtue of section 94(e) of the Ordinance the nature of the secondary evidence that may be given includes oral accounts of the contents of the document by some person who has himself seen *it (The Minister of Lagos Affairs v* The Federal Administrator-General and Others (1961) W.N.L.R. 159). Although section 95 of the Evidence Act requires primary evidence in proof of documents, yet secondary evidence of a document can be given if, *inter alia*, section 96(1) (c) of the Act is complied with. Where there is evidence of the loss and search for the original document, the trial Judge should admit secondary evidence of the document if he believes the evidence *(Okpanku v. Amachi, supra)*. The Exhibits Clerk of the Magistrate's Court ought to have been called to testify that the writing had got lost and could not be found after all possible search has been made, before oral evidence of the confession was admitted under section 96(1) (c) of the Evidence Act (*Mika v. The Queen* [1963] 1 All N.L.R. 220). See also *Giovanni v. Luigh* (1956-84) 10 S.C. N.D. 73.

The phrase "in the usual and ordinary course of business" relating to the Books of the Bank in section 96(2) (e) of the Evidence Act did not imply that the Books had to be in daily use. It was sufficient if the Bank kept the Books so as to be able to refer to them when necessary (*Yassin v. Barclays Bank D.C.O.* [1968] N.M.L.R. 380. The Bank statements tendered were primary evidence. They are part and parcel of what constitutes "Bankers Books" which are used in the ordinary business of the bank. They are therefore admissible. The prosecution by calling the bank officials to produce the bank statements did not avail itself of the provisions of section 96(2) (e) by inspecting such Books and having extracts made *(Oguntonade v. Commissioner of Police* (1959) W.R.N.L.R. 289). And *in Nwadike and Another v. Nwadike and Others* [1987] 4 N.W.L.R. (Pt.

65) 394, the Court of Appeal held that in the case what has been used are photocopies of documents which are recognised to be secondary evidence within the meaning of section 94 (a) of the Evidence Act. The point should be made that section 94 (a) anticipates certified copies of secondary evidence.

Notice to Produce

J.O. Iphie v. Plateau Auditing Company 1957 N.R.N.L.R. 212

The plaintiff sued for a balance of salary as an accountant engaged by the defendant. At the hearing, counsel for the defendant merely said 'claim disputed'. The plaintiff gave evidence that the defendant engaged him orally to check the monthly accounts of his tavern and that he sent to the defendant a letter of acceptance, a copy of which he tendered. Objection was made that no notice to produce the original had been given, but the magistrate received the document, apparently under proviso (b) to section 97 of the Evidence Ordinance.

HELD:

> Proviso (b) to section 97 of the Evidence Ordinance relates to a case where the document forms the basis of the action so that the action itself acts as a notice - which was not the case either in regard to the letter of acceptance or to the receipts.

In *Odionye v. Anyansi and Brunton Ltd. and Others* [1963] 2 All N.L.R. 44, it was held that a notice to produce a document when served on a party does not by itself entitle the opposite party to lead secondary evidence of the document unless possession of the original was admitted by the party served with the notice or the opposite party established at the trial that the document was at the time of service of such notice, in the possession of the person whom the notice was served or of his privy or some other agent or other person over whom the party served had some control and from whom he could have obtained the document. In *Adekunle v. African Continental Bank Ltd.* [1971] N.M.L.R. 324, it was held that a party making allegations in proof of which he is in possession of document is not entitled to say that he received no notice to produce, especially when the allegations have not been admitted by the other side. See further *Uwawah and Others v. Boyo and others* [1971] N.M.L.R. 233; *Olowu v. Desalu* (1955) 14 W.A.C.A. 662. *Din v. African Newspapers* (Nig) Ltd. [1990] 3 N.W.L.R. (Pt. 139) 392.

Chapter 15

BURDEN OF PROOF

Sections 135 to 143, 145 to 147 of the Evidence Act.

Both the Constitution and the Evidence Act make provisions on burden of proof. While the constitutional provision relates only to burden of proof in criminal matters, the Evidence Act provides for burden of proof in respect of both criminal and civil matters. By the Constitution of the Federal Republic of Nigeria 1999, "every person who is charged with a criminal offence shall be presumed to be innocent until he is proved guilty: provided that nothing in this section shall invalidate any law by reason only that the law imposes upon any such person the burden of proving particular facts" (S. 36(5)).

The Evidence Act, in its section 135 provides that whoever desires any court to give judgment as to any legal right or liability dependent on the existence of facts which he asserts must prove that those facts exist. When a person is bound to prove the existence of any fact, it is said that the burden of proof lies on that person. The burden of proof in a suit or proceeding lies on that person who would fail if no evidence at all were given on either side (S. 136).

In civil cases the burden of first providing the existence or non-existence of a fact lies on the party against whom the judgment of the court would be given if no evidence were produced on either side, regard being had to any presumption that may arise on the pleadings (S. 137(1)). If such party adduces evidence which ought reasonably to satisfy a jury that the fact sought to be proved is established, the burden lies on the party against whom judgment would be given if no more evidence were adduced; and so on successively, until all the issues in the pleadings have been dealt with (S. 137(2)). Where there are conflicting presumptions, the case is the same as if there were conflicting evidence (S. 137(3)).

If the commission of a crime by a party to any proceeding is directly in issue in any civil or criminal proceeding, it must be proved beyond reasonable doubt (S. 138(1)). The burden of proving that any person has been guilty of a crime or wrongful act is, subject to the provisions of section 141, on the person who asserts it, whether the commission of such act is or is not directly in issue in the action (S. 138(2)). If the prosecution prove the commission of a crime beyond reasonable doubt, the burden of proving reasonable doubt is shifted on to the accused (S. 138(3)).

The burden of proof as to any particular fact lies on that person who wishes the court to believe in its existence unless it is provided by any law that the proof of that fact shall lie on any particular person. But the burden may in course of a case be shifted from one side to the other (S. 139). The burden of proving any fact necessary to be proved in order to enable a person to adduce evidence of some other fact; or to prevent the opposite party from adducing evidence of some other fact lies on the party concerned. It is the duty of the court to determine admissibility of evidene under the section (S 140).

Where a person is accused of any offence, the burden of proving the existence of circumstances bringing the case within any exception or exemption from, or qualification to the operation of the law creating the office with which he is charged is upon such person. The above provision and the provisions of sections 138 and 142 will not diminish in any respect the obligation of the prosecution to establish guilt of the accused person (S. 141). When any fact is especially within the knowledge of any person, the burden of proving that fact is upon him (S. 142). See also S. 143.

When the question is whether persons are partners, landlord and tenant or principal and agent, and it has been shown that they have been acting as such, the burden of proving that they do not stand, or have ceased to stand, to each other in those relationships is on the person who affirms it (S. 145). When the question is whether any person is the owner of anything of which he is shown to be in possession, the burden of proving that he is not the owner is on the person who affirms that he is not the owner (S. 146). Where there is a question as to the good faith of a transaction between parties, one of whom stands to the other in a position of active confidence, the burden of proving the good faith of the transaction is on the party who is in a position of active confidence (S 147).

Nature of Burden of Proof

Murana B.O. Elemo and others v. Fasasi A.S. Omalade and Others [1968] N.M.L.R. 359

Beckley, J. said at page 361:

> *Burden of proof has two distinct and frequently confusing meanings. (1) It means the burden of proof as a matter of law and pleadings - the burden as it has been called of establishing a case whether by preponderance of evidence or beyond reasonable doubt and (2) the burden of proof in the sense of introducing evidence. As regards the first meaning attached to the term 'burden of proof' this rests upon the party whether plaintiff or defendant who substantially asserts the affirmative of the issue. It is fixed at the beginning of the trial by the state of the pleadings and it is settled as a question of law, remaining unchanged throughout the trial exactly where the pleadings place it and never shifting in any circumstances whatever. In deciding which party asserts the affirmative, regard must of course be had to the substance of the issue and not merely to its grammatical form which latter the pleader can frequently vary at will. Moreoever, a negative allegation must not be confounded with the mere traverse of an affirmative one. The true meaning of the rule is that where a given allegation whether affirmative or negative forms an essential part of a party's case, the proof of such allegation rests on him .(2) Burden of adducing evidence. It is this second sense that the term is ore generally sued. While the burden of proof in the first sense is always stable, the burden of proof in the second sense may shift constantly more as one scale of evidence or the other preponderates. In this sense the onus probandi rests upon the parties who would fail if no evidence at all, or no more evidence as the case may be were given on either side. That is it rests before evidence is gone into upon the party asserting the affirmative of the issue and it rests after evidence is gone into upon the party against whom the tribunal at the time the question arises would give judgment if no further evidence were adduced.*

See also *Bello v. Inspector-General of Police* (1956) 1 F.S.C. 48; *Alonge v. Inspector-General of Police* (1959) 4 F.S.C. 203; *Kate Enterprises Limited v. Daewoo Nigeria Limited* [1985] 2 N.W.L.R. (Pt. 5) 116; *Custom v. Barau* (1982) 10 S.C. 48; *Odulaja v. Haddad* (1973) 11 S.C. 357; *Imana v. Robinson* (1979) 3-4 S.C. 1; *Lewis and Peat v. Akhimien* (1976) 7 S.C. 157; *George v. U.B.A.* (1972) 8-9 S.C. 264; *Akinfosile v. Ijose* (1960) 5 F.S.C. 192.

General Burden of Proof

In *Omorhirhi and others v. Ematerwere* [1988] 1 N.W.L.R. (Pt. 73) 746, the Supreme Court held that the elementary principle regarding the burden of proof is that generally, criminal cases are proved beyond reasonable doubt for in criminal cases there is a compelling presumption of innocence which must prevail unless the evidence proves beyond doubt that the accused was guilty of the offence charged. In civil cases on the other hand, the standard required is proof by preponderance of evidence; proof by putting the totality of the testimony adduced by both parties on an imaginary scale, the evidence of the plaintiff and his witnesses on one side of the scale and that of the defendants and his witnesses on the other side, then weighing them together to find out which side preponderates. When the act which constitutes the tort in civil proceedings is also a crime, then that act, which is a crime, and which is directly in issue must be proved beyond reasonable doubt whether the proceedings be civil or criminal. Otherwise a person who alleges that he was assaulted might fail to prove the assault in a criminal prosecution and yet obtain judgment in civil proceedings. See also *Okuarume v. Obabokor* [1966] N.M.L.R. 48; *Achonu v. Commissioner of Police* [1967] N.M.L.R. 387; *R. v. Nwokarofor and Others* (1944) 10 W.A.C.A. 221; *Adetola v. R.* (1960) W.N.L.R.5; *Archibong v. Ita* (1954) 14 W.A.C.A. 520.

In *Okechukwu and Sons v. Ndah* [1967] N.M.L.R. 368, it was held that the burden of proof of any issue rests before evidence is gone into, upon the party asserting the affirmative of the issue; but after all the evidence has been completed the burden rests on the party against whom the tribunal at the time in question would give judgment if no further evidence were adduced. See also *Bala and Others v. Mrs. Bankole* [1986] 3 N.W.L.R. (Pt. 27) 141. *In Noibi v. Fikolati* [1987] 1 N.W.L.R. (Pt.52) 619 it was held that he who asserts must prove. Once a plaintiff has proved his case and the defendant raises an issue in his defence within his exclusive knowledge, the burden is on him to prove that issue. In *Chukwukole and Another v. Unachukwu* (1979) 3 C.A. 141, it was held that it is elementary principle of law that the burden of proof on the pleadings rests upon the party, whether plaintiff or defendant, who substantially asserts the affirmative of the issue. It is settled at the beginning of the trial by the state of the pleadings. Whether in a particular case the burden of proof has been discharged to the satisfaction of the court depends on the evidence adduced. See also *Are v. Adisa and Others* [1967] N.M.L.R. 304.

Burden of Introducing Evidence: Civil Cases.

In *The Nigerian Safety Insurance Co. Ltd. v. Zaria Co-operative Credit Marketing Union Ltd.* (1978) 1 N.C.A.R. 1, the Court of Appeal held that the burden is on the plaintiff in a civil action to show that he is entitled to the claim sought. See also *Echeazu and Others v. Awka Community Council and Others* (1980) 7 C.A. (Pt.1) 103. *In Fashanu v. Adekoya* (1974) 6 S.C. 83 it was held that the plaintiff has the onus of proving his case and that where he fails to get the appropriate findings relevant to the reliefs he had sought he must fail. *In Elias v. Disu* [1962] 1 All N.L.R. 214, it was also held that the onus is on the plaintiff to prove that he is entitled to the relief sought. The onus does not shift to the defendant. In *Juli Pharmacy v. Ethoven Ltd.* [1985] H.C.N.L.R. 700, it was held that the plaintiff must rely on the strength of his own case to establish his claim and not on the weakness of the defence. In *Olowu and Others v. Olowu and Others* [1985] 3 N.W.L.R. (Pt. 13) 372, it was held that a plaintiff can succeed only on the strength of his case. Therefore, the onus is upon him to prove to the satisfaction of the court the assertions made in his pleadings of the contention upon which he rests his case. Where a plaintiff has failed to discharge the onus of proof upon him at the close of the pleadings, a defendant is not obliged to adduce any evidence in rebuttal. Where a plaintiff has not sufficiently proved his case, he cannot rely on the weakness of the defendant's case and the proper judgment is for the defendant. Where however, a plaintiff alleging a fact, pleads that fact and produces evidence in proof of it, the onus will shift to the defendant to adduce evidence in rebuttal.

In *Attorney-General Anambra State v. Onuselogu* [1987] 4 N.W.L.R. (Pt. 66) 547 it was held that it is the duty of the plaintiff to prove his case and not rely on the weakness and shortcomings of the defence. But in *Niger Construction Ltd v. Okugbeni* [1987] 4 N.W.L.R. (Pt. 67) 787, it was held that although a plaintiff should rely on the strength of his own case, it is also true that he is entitled to rely on any evidence from the defence which goes to prove or support his case. Similarly, in *Akinola and Another v. Oluwo and Others* [1962] 1 All N.L.R. 224, it was held that the rule that in establishing his claim a plaintiff must succeed on the strength of his own case and not on the weakness of the defendant's case does not apply where the defendant's case itself supports that of the plaintiff and contains evidence on which the plaintiff is entitled to rely. See also *Woluchem v. Gudi* (1981) 5 S.C. 291.

In *Nasr v. Benni* [1968] 1 All N.L.R. 274, it was held that section 136(1) of the Evidence Act sufficiently describes the position about burden of proof in civil cases and it is clear that a defendant who is satisfied that the plaintiff has failed to comply with the subsection is entitled to rely on the evidence of the plaintiff without calling any evidence.

In *Osawam v. Ezeimka* (1978) 6-7 S.C. 135, it was held that in civil cases while the burden of proof in the sense of establishing the case initially lies on the plaintiff, the proof or rebuttal of issues which arise in the course of procedings may shift from the plaintiff to the defendant and vice versa as the case progresses. In *Uzuegbu v. Progress Bank of Nigeria Limited* [1988] 4 N.W.L.R. (Pt. 87) 236 it was held that it is an established principle of law that, for the plaintiff to succeed, the burden of proof expected of him, generally is to establish his case on balance of probabilities, i.e on preponderance of evidence. See also *Elias v. Omo-Bare* (1982) 5 S.C. 25; *Elebute v. Odekilekun* [1969] 1 all N.L.R. 449.

See further *Olujinle v. Adeagbo* [1988] 2 N.W.L.R. (Pt. 75) 238; *Owoade and Another v. Omibola and Others* [1988] 2 N.W.L.R. (Pt.77) 413; *Balogun v. Labiran* [1988] 3 NWLR (Pt.80) 66 *Johnson and Another v. Maja and Others* (1951) 13 W.A.C.A. 290; *Akinfosle v. Ijose* (1960 5 F.S.C. 192; *Oloto v. Administrator-General and Others* (1946) 12 W.A.C.A. 76: *Diken v. Odeniyi* (1960) W.N.L.R. 102; *Igbokwe and Others v. University College Hospital Board of Management* (1961) W.N.L.R. 173; *Udee v.Bonjust* (1954) 14 W.A.C.A. 533; *Lagos Municipal Transport Service v. Ibechim* 1961 L.L.R. 146; *Dahiru Cheranci v. Alkali Cheranci* 1960 N.R.N.L.R. 24

Burden of Introducing Evidence: Criminal Cases

In *Alonge v. Inspector-General of Police* (1959) 4 F.S.C. 203, it was held that the commission of a crime by a party must be proved beyond reasonable doubt. The burden of proving that any person is gulity of a crime rests on the person who asserts it, and this is the law laid down in section 137 of the Evidence Act. The burden of proof lies on the prosecution and it never shifts. In *Nwankere v. Adewunmi* [1967] N.M.L.R. 45, it was held that section 137 (1) of the Evidence Act applies where "the commission of a crime by a party to any proceedings is directly in issue" in any proceedings, civil or criminal. In *Ikoku v. Oli* [1963] 1 All N.L.R 194, it was held that section 137(1) only applies where there is a specific allegation of crime in the pleadings, so that the commission of a crime can properly be said to be a basis or foundation of the claim or defence, as the case may be. Facts directly in issue are to be distinguished from facts which come collaterally into question. See also *Jules v. Ajani* (1980) S.C. 965; *Torti v. Ukpabi* (1984) 1 S.C.N.R. 24; *Okuamme v. Obabokor*

[1965] All N.L.R. 360 In *Adesanya v. Ewedemi* [1962] 1 All N.L.R., it was held that section 137 (1) which requires that the commission of crime, if it is directly in issue in any proceedings, civil or criminal, must be proved beyond reasonable doubt, applies only where there is a specific allegation of crime in the pleadings so that its commission can properly be said to be a basis or foundation of the claim or defence. See also *R.v. Bada and Another* (1944) 10 W.A.C.A. 249.

The Shifting of Burden of Proof

In *Aouad v. Nzirimo and Another* (1944) 10 W.A.C.A. 73, the plaintiff sued the defendants claiming a certain sum of money being balance of cost of goods supplied for sale on basis of profit-sharing. The plaintiff gave evidence on shortage of stock, pleading the items of the shortage. It was held that once plaintiff established a shortage, the onus was on the defendants to account for the shortage. In *Akosa v. The Commissioner of Police* (1950) 13 W.A.C.A 43, the West African Court of Appeal held that the burden was on the Crown to prove the identity of property in respect of which a restitution order is made, but although the burden of introducing evidence rests on the Crown in the first instance, it may shift to the defence. In the circumstances of this case the onus has shifted to the appellant and he had not discharged it. In *Ohuka and Others v. The State* (No.2) [1988] 4 N.W.L.R. (Pt. 86) 36, the Supreme Court held that by virtue of section 137(3) of the Evidence Act, once the prosecution proves its case beyond reasonable doubt, the burden of proving reasonable doubt is shifted on to the accused. In the instant case involving murder, since the prosecution has proved its case beyond reasonable doubt, the 4th and 5th appellants cannot be said to have discharged the onus imposed on them by section 137(3) of the Act.

In *The Queen v. Ohaka* [1962] 1 All N.L.R. 545, it was held that where any fact is peculiarly within the knowledge of an accused, the burden of proving that fact is upon him. Where a charge relates to a presumption of guilty intent, the burden is on the accused to show circumstances which on the balance of probablities will rebut that presumption or which brings him with any express exemption from that presumption. In *Abdul-Raham v. Commissioner of Police* [197] N.M.L.R.87, it was held that by virtue of section 141 of the Evidence Law, the fact that the appellant was a pilot of the Pan African Airlines was peculiarly within his knowledge and the burden of proving it lies on him. See also *Koladele v. Commissioner of Police*

[1971] N.M.L.R. 109. In *Attoney General, Eastern Nigeria v. Osiala* [1964]... [1964] N.M.L.R. 104, it was held that the question of having a licence or permit are facts peculiarly within the knowledge of the person charged, therefore the prosecution is not bound to aver it on the charge; not required to give even prima facie evidence of it, notwithstanding that generally speaking the onus lies upon the prosecution to prove their case. See also *Bakare v. The State* [1987] 1 N.W.L.R (Pt. 52) 579; *N.M.S.I. v. Afolabi* (1978) 2 S.C. 79.

Criminal Cases: Discharge of the Burden: The Prosecution

In *Ogunwole v. The State* (1979) 2 C. A. 191, it was held that the onus is on the prosecution to prove its case beyond all reasonable doubt, and call witnesses material to its case. The onus never shifts. In *Echemanzu v. The State* (1956-84) 10 S.C.N.D. 123, it was held that in a criminal case, the onus is on the prosecution to prove its case. Where the prosecution has failed to prove the charge against the accused, it is not the duty of the accused to establish his innocence. See also *Yusufu v. The State* (1956-84) 10 S.C.N.D. 124, where it was held that in a criminal charge, the fact that the accused is more likely to have been guilty than anyone else is not enough to sustain the charge, in the absence of proof beyond reasonable doubt that it was the accused who committed the offence. See also *Eke v. The Queen* (1956-84) 10 S.C.N.D. 137; *Dogo v. The State* (1956-84) 10. S.C.N.D. 126; *Dauda v. The State* (1956-84) 10 S.C.N.D. 127; *Dedewo v. The State* (1956-84) 10 S.C.N.D. 125.

In *Inspector-General of Police v. Oguntade* [1971] 2 All N.L.R. 11, it was held that it is not correct to say that it is a cardinal principle of law that if there is any doubt at all however slight the benefit should go to the accused person. The correct statement of the law on this point superimposes the word "reasonable" between "any" and "doubt". In *Adio v. The State* [1986] 2 N.W.L.R. (Pt. 24) 581 it was held that a case is said to be proved beyond reasonable doubt either by direct oral evidence or by circumstantial evidence . In *Lori v. The State* (1980) 8-11 S.C. 81, it was held that the basic necessity before a verdict of guilty in a criminal charge can be pronounced is that the jury or the Judge as the case may be must be satisfied of the guilt of the accused beyond reasonable doubt. See also *Uguni v. The State* (1956-84) 10 S.C.N.D. 127; *Abdul and Others v. The State* (1979) 2 C.A 198, *Jaja v. The State* (1981) 3 C.A. 230; *Ikebudu v. Borno Native*

Authority 1966 N.N.L.R. 44; *Attorney-General v. Palm line Ltd* (1958) 3 F.S.C. 64; R *v. Motor* (1944) 10 W.A.C.A 251; *Inspector-General of Police v. Ewekay* (1957) L.L.R. 11; *Gachi v. The State* [1965] N.M.L.R. 333; *Nwagu v. The State* [1966] 1 All N.L.R. 213.

Criminal Cases: Discharge of the Burden: The Defence

1. Proof of Insanity and Intoxication.

In *The Queen v. Adeyefa* (1962) W.N.L.R. 235, the accused was charged with murder. Learned counsel for the accused did not call any medical evidence as to the state of mind of the accused but submitted that the prosecution ought to have subjected the accused to medical examination at the time he committed the offence. It was held that the onus of proving the defence of insanity rests upon the defence and not upon the prosecution. See also *Idowu v. The State* [1972] 5 S.C. 10; *The Queen v. Bui* [1964] N.N.L.R 45; *The State v. Moradehun* [1971] N.M.L.R. 15; *The State v. Uwa* (1965) 9 E.N.L.R. 95; *Chukwu v. The State* (1972) 1 N.M.L.R. 328; *Walai v. The State* (1956-84) 10 S.C.N.D. 132; *Ikebuaku v. The Queen* (1956-84) (10 S.C.N.D. 132; *Sanusi v. The State* (1956-84) 10 S.C.N.D. 135; *Attorney-General v. Oninkoyi* (1956-84) 10 S.C.N.D. 133; *Ayinla v. The Queen* (1958-84) 10 S.C.N.D. 133; *Makosa v. The Queen* (1956-84) 10 S.C.N.D 134;.*Dania v. The State (1978) 1 N.C.A.R. 31;* Onaholo v. The State*(1980)* 7 C.A. (Pt. 1) 190; *Akhimien v.The State* [1987] 1 N.W.I.R. (pt. 52) 598; *Onakpoya v. The Queen* (1959) 4 F.S.C 150.

2. **On proof of facts especially within the knowledge of the accused,** see *Otti v. Inspector-General of Police* 1956 N.R.N.L.R. 1; *Joseph v. Inspector-General of Police* 1957 N.R.N.L.R. 120; *Arase v. Arase* (1981) 5 S.C. 33.
3. **On proof of customs offenes**, see *Chairman of the Board of Customs and Excise v. Baye* (1960) W.N.L.R. 178; *Ebiri and Another v. Board of Customs and Excise* [1967] N.M.L.R. 35; *Board of Customs and Excise v. Ntukidem* (1970-72) 1 R.S.L.R. 68; *Board of Customs and Excise v. Garba and Another* (1978) 2 L.R.N. 184; R. *v. Akinsanya* (1961) W.N.L.R. 222; *Board of Customs and Excise v. Bayo* (1960) W.N.L.R. 18; *Edet v. Board of Customs and Excise* (1965) N.M.L.R 188; *Board of Customs and Excise v. Abubakar* [1978] 1 L.R.N. 380; Nadar v. Board of Customs and Excise [1965] 1 All N.L.R. 33*; Board of Customs and Excise v. Aligor* (1974) 1 F.R.C.R. 243; *Ayeni v. Board of Customs and*

Excise [1965] 2 All N.L.R. 97; *Board of Customs and Excise v. Ewusie* 1 F.R.C.R. (1976) 119.

Proof of Alibi

The word alibi means elsewhere and since it is a matter peculiarly within the knowledge of an accused person. If he was at some particular place other than where the prosecution says he was at any material time what has been called the evidential burden, that is, the burden of adducing or eliciting some evidence tending to show this, rests on him. But apart from this evidential burden, there is no burden of proof on an accused person who puts forward an alibi as his defence. See generally *Yanor and Another v. The State* [1965] N.M.L.R. 337; *Gachi and Others v. The State* [1965] N.M.L.R. 333; Adeyeye and Others v. The State [1986] N.M.L.R. 48; *Adamu v. The State* 1971 N.N.L.R 89; *Okolo v. Commissioner of Police* 1977 N.N.L.R. 1; *Njovens and Others v. The State* 1973 N.N.L.R. 76; *The State v. George* (1970 -72) 1 R.S.L.R. 25; *Ugboaja and Others v. Commissioner of Police* (1963) 7 E.N.L.R. 153; *The State v. Dikeocha and Others* (1966-67) 10 E.N.L.R. 155; *Obiaje and Others v. Commissioner of Police* 1976 N.N.L.R. 21; *Abudu v. The State* [1985] 1 N.W.L.R. (pt. 1) 55.

Civil Cases: Discharge of Burden

In *Okuaniwe v. Obabokor* [1965] 1 All N.L.R. 361, it was held that in civil cases the preponderance of probability may constitute sufficient ground for a verdict, but this general rule is subject to section 137(1) of the Evidence Act, which requires proof beyond reasonable doubt if the commission of crime by a party to a proceeding, whether civil or criminal, is directly in issue. Dealing with section 137(1), Unsworth, F.J. said in *Ikoku v. Oli* [1962] All N.L.R. 194 at pages 199 to 200:

> *"the subsection only applies where there is a specific allegation of a crime in the pleading so that the commission of a crime can properly be said to be the basis or fore-data of the claim or defence as the case may be. For example, the subsection will apply where a defendant in an action for which is pleaded jusification of an allegation that the plaintiff had committed a criminal offence or where a petitioner sought divorce under the matrimonial Causes Act, on the grounds of rape, sodomy or bestiality".*

See also *Atedoghu v, Alade* (1957) W.R.N.L.R.184; *Nwankwere v..Adewumi* (1963) W.N.L.R. 278; *Bello v. Inspector-General of Police* (1956) I F.S. C. 48.

Matrimonial Causes: Discharge of the burden

It has frequently been held that, as with all other matrimonial offences, the standard of proof required in respect of adultery is proof beyond reasonable doubt. But it has been held that it is rare to obtain direct evidence, there would be no protection for the wronged spouse if the rule were otherwise. See *Akinyemi v. Akinyemi* [1963] 1 All N.L.R. 340. See also *Sowande v. Sowande* (1960) L.L.R. 58; *Lewis v. Lewis* (1960) L.L.R. 215; *Oloko v. Oloko and Another* (1961) W.N.L.R. 101; *Ikpi v. Ikpi* (1957) W.R.N.L.R. 59.

On the chapter generally, see further: *Ude v, Osuji* [1990] 5 N.W.L.R. (Pt.151) 488; *Gwani v. Ebule* [1990] 5 N.W.L.R. (Pt.149) 201; *Uzoka v. State* [1990] 6 N.W.L.R. (Pt. 159) 680; *Igwe v. Alozieuwa* [1990] 3 N.W.L.R. (Pt.141) 735; *Okpular v. State* [1990] 7 N.W.L.R. (Pt.164) 581; *Highgrade Maritime Service Ltd v. F.B.N.Ltd* [1991] 1 N.W.L.R. (Pt.167) 290; *Osho v. Foreign Finance Corporation* [1991] 4 N.W.L.R. (Pt.184) 157; *Mohammed v. State* [1991] 5 N.W.L.R. (Pt.192) 438; *Ogoala v. State* [1991] 2 N.W.L.R. (Pt.175) 509; *Oje v. Babalola* [1991] 4 N.W.L.R. (Pt.185) 267; *Ibe v. State* [1992] 5 N.W.L.R. (Pt 244) 642; *Balogun v. U.B.A. Ltd* [1992] 6 N.W.L.R. (Pt.247) 336; *Amaeze v. Anyaso* [1993] 5 N.W.L.R. s(Pt. 291) 1; *Eseigbe v. Agholor* [1993] 9 N.W.L.R. (Pt. 316) 128; *Ojomo v. Incar* (Nig) Ltd [1993] 7 N.W.L.R. (Pt. 307) 534; *Egboghonome v. State* [1993] 7 N.W.L.R. (Pt.306) 383; *Onyegbu v. State* [1994] 1 N.W.L.R.(Pt. 320) 328; *Kasa v. State* [1994] 2 N.W.L.R. (Pt. 325) 143; *Edokpolo v. Asemota* [1994] 7 N.W.L.R. (Pt. 356) 314.

Chapter 16

PRESUMPTIONS

Sections 4, 54, 114, 144 and 149 of the Evidence Act.

Whenever it is provided by the Evidence Act that the Court may presume a fact, it may either regard such fact as proved unless and until it is disproved, or may call for proof of it. Whenever it is directed by the Act that the court shall presume a fact, it must regard such fact as proved unless and until it is disproved (s. 4) (a) and (b).

Every judgment is conclusive proof as against parties and privies, of facts directly in issue in the case, actually decided by the court, and appearing from the judgment itself to be the ground on which it was based, unless evidence was admitted in the action in which the judgment was delivered which excluded in the action in which that judgment is intended to be proved (s. 54).

The court shall presume every document purporting to be a certificate, certified copy or other document, which is by law declared to be admissible as evidence of any particular fact and which purports to be duly certified by any officer in Nigeria who is duly authorised thereto to be genuine, provided that such document is substantially in the form and purports to be executed in the manner directed by law in that behalf. The court shall also presume that any officer by whom any such document purports to be signed or certified, held, when he signed it, the official character which he claims is such paper. (S. 114).

Other sections of the Act deal with presumptions as to different types of documents. They include presumption as to documents produced as record of evidence in court (S. 115); presumption as to gazettes, newpapers and other documents (S. 116); presumption as to documents admissible in the Commonwealth without proof of seal or signature (S. 117); presumption as to powers of attorney (S. 118); presumption as to public maps and charts (S. 119); presumption as to books (S. 120); presumption as to telegraphic messages (S. 121) and presumption as to due execution of documents not produced (S. 122). Others include presumption as to documents twenty years old (S. 123);

presumption as to date of document (S. 124); presumption as to stamp of a document (S. 125); presumption as to sealing and delivering (S. 126); presumption as to alterations (S. 127); presumption as to age of parties to a document (S. 128); presumption as to statements in documents twenty years old (S. 129); presumtption as to deeds of corportations (S. 130); and presumption of death from seven years absence and other related facts (S. 144).

The court may presume the existence of any fact which it thinks likely to have happened, regard being had to the common course of material events, human conduct and public and private business, in their relation to the facts of the particular case, and in particular the court may presume:

(a) that a man who is in possession of stolen goods seen after the theft is either the thief or has received the goods knowing them to be stolen, unless he can account for his possession;
(b) that a thing or state of things which has been shown to be in existence within a period shorter than that within which such thing or state of things usually cease to exist, is still in existence;
(c) that the common course of business has been followed in a particular case;
(d) that evidence which could be and is not produced would, if produced, be unfavourable to the person who withholds it;
(e) that when a document creating an obligation is in the hands of the obligor, the obligation has been discharged (S. 149).

Presumption of Intention

Phillip Dim v. The Queen
(1952) 14 W.A.C.A. 154

The appellant was convicted of murder. The facts were that he left his room in the small hours of the morning and went to his wife's room and injured her badly with a pickaxe-head. She died of the injuries. The defence was that the appellant suffered from a "black out" at the time of the offence.

HELD:

A person is taken to intend the natural and probable consequences of his acts; intent to murder was a necessary inference to be drawn from the acts of the appellant in this case.

R.v. Arubi
(1933) 11 N.L.R. 27

It was proved against the accused that he wrote the document containing the defamatory matter the subject of the prosecution. It was also proved that the document was received in the ordinary course through the post. The accused was convicted in the Divisional Court of publishing the defamatory matter and he appealed by way of case stated to the Full Court.

HELD:

The receipt of the document in the ordinary course through the post raised a presumption that the accused who wrote it posted it and that by posting it he delivered it with intent that it should be read by the addressee, and that this amounted to publication under section 374 of the Criminal Code. See also *Peneva v. Motor and General Insurance Co. Ltd.* [1975] 2 All N.L.R. 261.

Maye Nungu v. R..
(1953) 14 W.A.C.A. 379

The appellant and his younger brother had had a dispute about the burning of some trees in the appellant's farm; and later further words were exchanged in the course of which the younger brother said he had supplied money for the appellant to marry. The appellant was highly annoyed at this and taking up an axe struck his brother on the head with the wooden elbow of the half. The blow caused a wound. The brother died almost immediately. The appellant was convicted of murder. On appeal, it was argued that there was no intent to kill or do grevious harm.

HELD:

Although the appellant turned away the cutting edge, he must have intended to cause grevious harm, which was the natural and probable consequence of striking on the head with the half of the axe weighted with an iron head with such force as to inflict the wound described.

Verity C.J. said at page 380:

It may be arguable from the turning away of the cutting edge of the axe that the appellant had no intention of killing the deceased and did not believe that to strike him with the wooden half would cause his death... He must in our view have intended the natural and probable consequence of that act and by reason of subsection (2) of section 316 of the Criminal Code, a person is guilty of murder if he intends to do the person killed some grevious harm.

Presumption of Guilty Knowledge

R. v. Isa Braimoh and Another
(1943) 9 W.A.C.A. 197

On 3rd May, first accused was released from Kaduna prison where he spent seven months, and went to second accused's house to stay. Second accused was a warder in the prison, but first accused was not in his gang. On 5th and 7th May, thefts occurred in the neighbourhood, and on 9th May second accused sent some of the stolen property to his brother at Enugu with instructions to sell them at any price he thought good. The first accused was convicted of shopbreaking and stealing the goods, and the second accused was convicted of receiving them. The second accused appealled on the ground that there was no evidence that he knew or ought to have known the property had been stolen.

HELD:

The circumstances fully justified a finding of guilty knowledge. The appeal was dismissed.

The court said at page 199:

In the present case we are of opinion that the circumstances in which the appellant lodged the first accused, so recently a convict in a prison in which the second accused was a warder, sent the stolen goods to Enugu so shortly after the date at which they were stolen and advised his brother to sell the cloth 'at any prices that you think good' fully justified the Judge in holding that there was guilty knowledge and in convicting the appellant of the offence with which he was charged.

R. v. Palmer Iyakwe
(1944) 10 W.A.C.A. 180.

The only evidence to connect the accused with the burglary and stealing was the fact that five months after it, he was in possession of stolen shoes and passed them to another defendant to sell for him.

HELD:

The accused ought not to have been found guilty of burglary and stealing but of receiving the shoes knowing them to have been stolen.

In R. *v. Jumbo* 1960 L.L.R. 192, it was held that the accused who was found to be in possession of stolen goods as a result of a burglary committed a few hours earlier could be presumed to be the burglar. See also *R. v. Opara* (1961) W.N.L.R. 127. Cf. *Lawani v. Police* (1952) 20 N.L.R. 87.

In *Eze v. The State* [1985] 3 N.W.L.R. (Pt. 13) 429, it was held that the presumption of "recent possession" as contained in section 148(1) of the Evidence Act is not a presumption of law but a presumption of fact. Section 148(a) is the Nigerian equivalent of the English doctrine of recent possession. For section 148(a) to apply to a set of facts, there should be evidence that

(i) the accused was found in possession of some goods;
(ii) those goods were recently stolen;
(iii) the accused failed to account for his possession of those goods.

The presumption that a person in recent possession 65of stolen property is either the thief or the receiver with guilty knowledge is merely an inference which the court of trial is at liberty to draw (not must draw) from the facts and surrounding circumstances of each particular case. An accused found in possession of a recently stolen property must state how he came about the property to the satisfaction of the court in order to rebut the presumption of fact in section 148(a).

In *Nwachukwu v. The State*[1985] 3 N.W.L.R. (Pt. 11) 218, it was held that the doctrine of recent possession under section 148(a) applies in this case because the appellant was found lying on the bag containing the money, the subject matter of the robbery, or soon after the fact of robbery and in the circumstances revealed in the evidence the court could draw the inference that the appellant was in possession of the bag and was one of the robbers. In *Bozin v. The State* [1985] 2 N.W.L.R. (Pt. 8) 467, it was held that the five matters enumerated in section 148 of the Evidence Act, which the court may, in particular presume are neither exhaustive nor conclusive and do not derogate from the general statement of the section that the court may presume the existence of a fact which it thinks likely to have happened, having regard to the common course of material events or having regard to the common course of human conduct. See also *The State v. Aiyeola* [1969] 1 All N.L.R. 303; *Omogodo v. The State* (1981) 4 S.C. 5; *Koladele v. Commissioner of Police* 1971 N.N.L.R. 33.

Presumption of Continuance

Alhaji Rotimi v. Adegunle and Another
(1959) 4 F.S.C. 19.

The appellant hired a lorry with driver from the first respondent. While the lorry was driven during the period of hire by the driver, with the appellant on board, an accident occurred, as a result of which the appellant suffered injury and damage for which he claimed against the two respondents. The main bulwark of the defence was (a) that the lorry and driver were, at the time of the accident, under the control and direction of the appellant, and (b) that at the material time the driver was the agent of the appellant.

HELD:

> *The onus of proving that the driver was, at the material time, under the control of the appellant lay upon the respondent who had failed to discharge that onus. The court was of opinion that the presumption was in favour of the fact that the driver continued to be under the control of the first respondent. See also* Shamanda v. James *1960 L.L.R. 192;* Oghogho v. Karunwi "Busy Bee" *1957 L.L.R. 22*

Course of Business

In *R. v. Ugwuoso and others* (1943) 9 W.A.C.A. 73, it was held that an accused charged with an offence and to whom a caution has been administered is presumed to understand it. "There is nothing to disturb the presumption in this case and the accused to do not aver that they did not understand the caution". (At p. 74). *In Ashard v. Commissioner of Police* 1963 N.N.L.R. 80, the court presumed that the statement made by the appellant not under caution but as a witness was duly set forth in the case diary as required by section 121(g) of the Criminal Procedure Code. The statement being an item in the case diary was therefore admissible in the trial as evidence against the appellant.

Withholding of Evidence

See also Mukete and others v. Nigerian Broadcasting Corporation and Another [1961] All N.L.R. 482.

In *Adeyemi v. Commissioner of Police* [1961] All N.L.R 387, the appellant was convicted by a Senior Magistrate of a charge containing counts of stealing money and other property from two different persons, and of obtaining money and other property from a third person with intent to defraud by falsely pretending that he was in a position to hire Customary Court members. In the course of the trial it was alleged that the complainants had made a report to a paramount chief, who was not called as a witness, to the effect that the appellant had obtained monies from them and that the chief had advised him to return the same. The appellant denied that the chief had spoken to him or advised him as alleged or that he had received the monies or the other properties from the complainants or made representations to them as alleged.

It was held that as the appellant had denied that the chief had spoken to him or advised him as alleged, if the chief's evidence were necessary at all it was necessary for the prosecution's case and it was a misdirection for the learned Senior Magistrate to have held that the failure of the appellant to call the chief as a witness was fatal to the case for the defence. The provisions of section 148 of the Evidence Ordinance as to the presumption that evidence that could be and is not produced would, if produced, be unfavourable to the person who withholds it, cannot be applied in a criminal case so as to shift the onus of proof from the prosecution. See also *Mandillas and Karaberis Limited* and *Another v. Inspector-General of Police* (1958) 3 F.S.C. 20; *Tewogbade v. Akande* [1968] N.M.L.R. 404. In *Enahoro v. The Queen* [1965] N.M.L.R. 267, it was held that section 148(d) of the Evidence Act does not lay upon an accused person any burden of disproving the case for the prosecution or any part of it. It does not also mean that where an accused person fails to call a witness in circumstances where he is expected to call him, that the accused is withholding the witness.

In *Bello v. Kassim* [1969] N.M.L.R. 148, it was held that section 148(d) deals with the failure to call evidence, and not the failure to call a particular witness. A party is not bound to call a particular witness if he thinks he can prove his case otherwise. In *Ogbodu v. The State* [1987] 2 N.W.L.R. (Pt. 54) 20, it was held that the presumption in section 148 (d) applies in a criminal case, to the prosecution only when it withholds evidence, that is, fails to call evidence, not when it fails to call a particular witness. In *Asariyu v. The State* [1987] 4 N.W.L.R. (Pt. 67) 709, where the prosecution failed to call an inmate of the appellant's house to testify in the case, the court held that the provision of section 148(d) is concerned with the withholding of evidence and not with the failure of a party to call a particular witness. In *Olunlade v. Awijo* (1956-84) 10 S.C.N.D. 117, it was held that non-production of a witness by a party to a civil action does not necessarily raise the presumption under section 148(d).

In *Shittu and Another v. Mrs. Osibanjo and Another* [1988] 3 N.W.L.R. (Pt. 83) 483, it was held that if there was any family meeting of the Adewunmi family at which the defendants/respondents were appointed administrators or the family sanctioned the counter-claim for letters of administration filed at the trial court, they would have produced it. Their failure to produce it raises a presumption that if produced, it would be unfavourable to them within the meaning of section 148(d) of the Evidence Act. In *Akunfe v. The State* [1988] 3 N.W.L.R. (Pt. 85) 729, where the prosecution failed to tender a medical certificate in a murder trial, the Supreme Court held that the trial court was entitled to draw the presumption under section 148(d). See also *Uzuegbu v. Progress Bank of Nigeria Limited* [1988] 4 N.W.L.R. (Pt. 87) 236.

In *Trustees Reformed Ogboni v. Shiriki* [1985] H.C.N.L R. 1357, it was held that section 148(d) of the Evidence Act applies to the non-production of documents and not to the non-production of witnesses. Similarly, in *Olayide v. B.A.I.C. Ltd.* (1985) H.C.N.L.R. 569, it was held that the subsection operates against the defendants who failed to tender voucher as they know it will be against them. See also *Sendan and Another v. The State* [1968] N.M.L.R. 208.

NOTE.

The two decisions of *Shirika* and *Olayide* should be taken in relation to the facts of the case and not as a general principle of law. This is because section 148(d) talks about evidence and not only documents. But since documents are also evidence, the courts in the two cases rightly related the *ratio* to the facts of the cases. Apart from this, the general principles cannot pass the test of the subsection. See further *Onah v. The*

State [1985] 3 N.W.L.R. (Pt. 12) 236; *Opolo v. The State* (1977) 11-12 S.C. 1; *Adisa v. Adili* [1985] H.C.N.L.R.447.

In *Awosile v. Sotunbo* [1986] 3 N.W.L.R. (pt.29) 471, it was held that before a court can get along with the presumption in section 148 (d) of the Evidence Act, there must be proof that (a) the evidence exists; (b) that it could be produced; (c) that it has not been produced; and (d) that it has been withheld by the person who could produce it. See also *Tawogbade v. Akande* [1968] N.M.L.R. 404.

Documents Creating Obligation in the Hands of Obligor

In *Macauley v. Seriki and Another* (1925) 6 N.L.R. 92, the plaintiff sought to recover the sum of two hundred pounds which he stated he had lent to the defendants in February, 1920 and for which they had given him a written receipt, which was produced in evidence. The defendants admitted giving the receipt, but stated that at the time it was given, the money had not actually passed between the parties and that they had not received it at any subsequent date. It was admitted that the receipt had been in the possession of the plaintiff since it was given to him in February 1920 and no satisfactory evidence was given on behalf of the defendants proving that they had earlier made any demand on the plaintiff either to return the receipt to them or to give them the money which they denied having received.

HELD:

> The giving of the receipt by the defendants was presumptive, although not conclusive, evidence of their having received the money, that the evidence to rebut that presumption must be of a very conclusive nature, that the evidence given by the defendants fell short of that standard, and that the fact that they had allowed the receipt to remain in the hands of the plaintiff for nearly five years was inconsistent with their contention that they had not received the money. Judgment was therefore entered for the plaintiff for the amount claimed.

In *R. v. Iregbu* (1938) 4 W.A.C.A. 32, the appellant was convicted of slave dealing contrary to section 369 of the Criminal Code. The appellant having arranged with the parents of a girl to marry her and having paid part of the bride price, he was allowed to take her to Ikot-Ekpene. He returned without her and gave at least two untrue explanations of her non-return and she has never been found since. After recording his disbelief of the appellant's stories, the learned trial Judge finished his judgment with these words: "I must presume also that this girl was taken or transferred by the accused to be held or treated as a slave".

HELD:

A court can make a presumption of this nature when it is a presumption which must irresistibly be made from the evidence, i.e. when there is no other reasonable presumption which fits all the facts. The court held that such was not the case here.

Kingdom, C.J. said at page 32:

There are other possibilities which there is nothing to rebut. The facts, for instance, are equally consistent with the appellant having murdered the girl or again with the girl having been accidentally drowned, and the appellant being afraid to say so in case he should be charged with murder. The assumption that she has been sold as a slave is, in fact, only one of many which might be made to account for her disappearance. For these reasons we think the conviction cannot be upheld.

Presumptions as to Judgment

In *Ojiako and Others v. Ogueze and Others* [962]1 All N.L.R. 58, the plaintiffs/respondents obtained in the High Court a declaration of title to certain lands against the defendants/appellants. They also obtained judgment for damages for trespass and injunction. Title to the lands in dispute was the subject matter of an earlier action brought in a Native Court by one Osakwe against three of the defendants/appellants. The Native Court gave judgment in the matter. But after some time, the Native Court without setting that judgment aside, re-opened the case but never brought the re-opened proceedings to a conclusion. The plainitiffs respondents then commenced these proceedings in the High Court, relying on the judgment of the Native Court. The High Court held that the Native Court had improperly re-opened the earlier case and that the original judgment, not having been set aside, remained in force. It gave judgment to the plaintiffs/respondents.

HELD:

(1) The Native Court, having delivered judgment in the proceedings before it, had no power effectively to re-open those proceedings; and the original judgment, not having been set aside by competent authority, must be regarded as a subsisting one (2) Where no question of nullity arises, once the judgment of a competent court is perfected it is valid until set aside by competent authority.(3) There can be no presumption against the validity of such a judgment.

Rebuttable presumption of Law: presumption of Innocence

In *Kinnami v. Bornu N.A.* 1957 N.R.N.L.R. 40, the court held *per incuriam* that there is a presumption that an accused person who denies an accusation is innocent, which makes it the duty of the accuser to prove his guilt. Therefore, until the accuser has made out his case, there is no reason for hearing witnesses brought by the accused person, and when the accuser has not produced evidence to make out his case, the accused person must be discharged. Bairamian S.J.P. (as he then was) said at page 42: "We wish to remind courts of trial that when a person is accused of an offence, he is presumed to be innocent. That was so in Roman law, it is so in English law, and it is so, we are advised, in Moslem law too. This presumption of innocence lays the duty on the accuser to produce witnesses to prove his accusation, and this presumption and the accuser's duty must always be borne in mind. See also *R. v. Eka* (1945) 11 WACA 39; *Obiode and Others v. The State* [1970] 1 All N.L.R. 35; *Okoko v. The State* [1964] 1 All N.L.R. 423.

But in *Ibeziako v. Commissioner of Police* [1963] 1 All N.L.R. 61, the Supreme Court held that the procedure laid down in the Criminal Procedure Code where the Magistrate is empowered to draft a charge if he is of the opinion that the accused has committed an offence, is not contrary to the constitutional presumption of innocence under section 21(4) of the 1960 Constitution. With respect, the decision can hardly be support on any rational basis. Once the trial Magistrate drafts the charge against the accused when he is of the opinion that the accused has committed an offence, it is difficult to contend that he is still the independent umpire. He has, by his findings, and subsequent drafting of the charge, removed himself from being an independent umpire and assumes the role of a quasi-prosecutor. Viewing from this angle, it is submitted that violence is done to the constitutional presumption of innocence. *Ibeziako* is therefore bad law. See further *Mohammed v. Commissioner of Police* [1967] N.M.L.R. 83; *Lafia v. Commissioner of Police* [1971] 2 All N.L.R. 231; *Wambai and Another v. Kano N.A.* [1965] N.M.L.R. 15.

Presumption of Marriage

In *Adegbola v. Folaranmi and Others* (1921) N.L.R. 89, Harry Johnson married according to native law and custom, Oniketan by whom he had one daughter, Adegbola, the plaintiff. He was subsequently seized as a slave and shipped to the West Indies where he lived for about forty years, his wife and child remaining at home. In the West Indies, Harry Johnson was converted to the christian faith and became a member of the Roman Catholic Church. Prior to 1876 Harry Johnson married a woman, afterwards known as Mary Johnson, in a Catholic Church and after living in the West Indies for some three years they came to Lagos and were received in the Roman Catholic Church there. In 1876, Harry Johnson bought the land which is the subject matter of this action, and built a house thereon. Harry Johnson's wife, Oniketan, was alive on his return to Lagos and was still living with the plaintiff, who used to visit the father in Lagos. The father died intestate in 1900. Affirming the decision of the Divisional Court, it was held that notwithstanding that no certificate of the marriage was produced, the court presume on the facts that Harry Johnson and Mary Johnson had contracted a valid christian marriage and the courts of the Colony of Lagos must recognise such marriage.

It is submitted that the decision is wrong in law. Harry Johnson had no capacity to contract a christian marriage while his marriage under native law and custom with Oniketan was subsisting. It is sad that the court did not consider this very vital aspect. The point should be made however, that the position could have been different by now because the court is entitled to presume that Oniketan died if Harry Johnson did not hear from her after a period of seven years; if that was the factual position. Otherwise, no.

In *Smith v. Smith* (1924) 5 N.L.R. 105, it was held that although the fact that natives married according to the rites of the Church of England, raise a presumption that they intend that their lives, their actions and their property should be regulated by English laws and standards, this is not conclusive evidence of such an intention, and that in deciding the question the court should be guided by consideration of the position of life occupied by the parties and their conduct with reference to the property in dispute. *Cf. Cole v. Cole* (1898) 1 N.L.R. 15. In R. *v. Ajiyola and others* (1943) 9 W.A.C.A. 22, where both the co-accused of the appellant and a witness who described herself as his wife, gave evidence after swearing on the bible, the court held that there was a presumption that they were both husband and wife of a christian marriage. Accordingly, the court held that the wife was not competent as a witness other than upon the application of her husband. Similar decision was given in *The Queen v. Adesina* (1958) 3 F.S.C. 25.

The presumption is rather sophisticated. It is a matter of experience that time without number persons married under customary law give evidence on oath by swearing on the bible. It is therefore not safe to come to the conclusion that any person who swears on the bible and who is married has conducted a christian marriage. See also *R. v. Udom and Others* (1947) 12 W.A.C.A. 227; *R. v. Laoye and Another* (1940) 6 W.A.C.A. 6; *Inspector-General of Police v. Ango and Others* (1955-56) W.R.N.L.R. 168; *Akpolokpolo v. Commissioner of Police* (1960) W.N.L.R. 89.

In *Omoge v. Badejo* [1985] H.C.N.L.R. 1075, it was held that the law will presume strongly in favour of the validity of a marriage where a great length of time has elapsed since its celebration and such a presumption can only be rebutted by strong satisfactory and conclusive evidence. Similarly, in *Joledo v. Joledo* [1985] H.C N.L.R. 1267, it was held that where there is evidence of marriage having been performed in this country in accordance with the rules of the church and parties to it have lived as husband and wife and cohabited together, everything necessary to ensure the validity of the marriage should be presumed in the absence of decisive evidence to the contrary. See generally *Lawal and Others v. Younan and Sons and Others* (1959) W.R.N.L.R. 155; *Adepeju v. Aderet.* W.N.L.R. 154.

Presumption of Legitimacy

In *Elumeze v. Elumeze* [1969]1 All N.L.R. 311, it was held that section 147 of the Evidence Act, provides for the presumption of legitimacy. Section 147 of the Evidence Act has been substituted by section 115(3) of the Matrimonial Causes Act, No. 18 of 1970. It provides inter alia:

> *Where a person was born during the continuance of a valid marriage between his mother and any man, or within 280 days after the dissolution, the mother remaining unmarried, the court shall presume that the person in question is the legitimate son of that man.*

In *Cole and Another v. Akinyele* (1960) 5 F.S.C. 84, Brett, F.J. said at page 88:

> *In Re Adadevoh (1951) 13 W.A.C.A. 304, Sir John verity, C.J. pointed out that the encouragement of promiscuous intercourse must always be contrary to public policy, but the law both of England and Nigeria, including the prsumptions as to the legitimacy of any child born by*

a married, woman clearly leans against holding anyone to be a bastard filius nullius, and I know of no principle of public policy to exclude the rule under which the second appellant, as the acknowledged son of his father, born at a time when his father was free to marry who he chose, is to be regarded as legitimate.

Presumption of Sanity

In *The Queen v. Ogor* [1961] 1 All N.L.R. 70, it was held that where the question of insanity is raised by the defence, the onus is on the defence to discharge it. It is discharged if the court, considering the wide evidence, is satisfied on the balance of probabilities that the accused's insanity has been proved. That position results from the presumption in section 27 of the Criminal Code, that every person is of sound mind until the contrary is proved and from the degree of proof required where the onus of proof rests on the accused. In *Salawu v. The State* [1971] N.M.L.R. 249, it was held that everybody is presumed to be of sound mind until the contrary is proved and the burden is on the defence to prove insanity. In *Ayinla v. The Queen* (1956-84) 10 S.C.N.D. 133, it was held that the presumption of sanity is rebutted when the accused shows on the balance of probability that he was insane when he committed the offence for which he was charged. Where the accused does not adduce sufficient evidence to discharge the burden of proof, it is proper for a trial Judge to conclude that the accused was sane when he committed the offence.

Presumption of Negligence

In *Asekele and Another v. Boboye* (1962) W.N.L.R. 12, it was held that the maxim of *res ipsa loquitur* applied where a driver by a sudden application of his brakes to a fully loaded vehicle at a corner on a wet day caused an accident. In *Olaiya v. Ososami* (1959) W.R.N.L.R. 264, where the defendant's agent negligently operated a crane in the course of building operations which fell on the plaintiff whilst he was returning from school along a foot path normally used by members of the public and school children, the court held that the maxim applied. See also *Duclaud v. Ginoux and Another* [1969] N.M.L.R. 18; *Lagos Municipal Transport Service v. Ibechim* 1961 L.L.R. 146; *Igbokwe and Others v. Univeristy College Hospital Board of Management* (1961) W.N.L.R. 173; *Anichebe v. Onyekwe* [1965] N.M.L.R. 108; *Thompson v. Adefope* [1969] 1 All N.L.R. 322.

Regularity: Ominia Praesumuntur Rita Esse Acta

In *Re Randle, Nelson and Another v. Akofiranmi* [1962] All N.L.R. 130, it was held that where a testamentary instrument is *ex facie* perfectly regular as regards all of the formalities of signature and attestation and no question of incapacity or fraud exists, a presumption of due execution arises to which great weight must be given.

In *Ayiwoh v. Akerede* (1951) 20 N.L.R. 4, the respondent had sued as attorney of the landlord for arrears of rent and recovery of possession. Objection was raised on his Power of Attorney which was attested to by a solicitor's clerk who was not a notary public. The learned trial Magistrate ruled that it was admissible. The appeal was upheld. Robinson, J. said at page 5: "A solicitor's clerk is certainly not enough. I see therefore, no presumption in favour of this Power of Attorney and as its due execution has not been proved by any of the recognised ways - see Phipson, page 506 - it ought to have been rejected."

In *Aminu v. Goualin Ltd.* (1956-84) 10 S.C.N.D. 113, it was held that by virtue of section 129 of the Evidence Act, recitals in deeds which are at least twenty years old raise the presumption that the statements contained therein are true, in the absence of any evidence to the contrary.

In *John v. Adebanjo* (1956-84) 10 S.C.N.D. 112, it was held that section 129 of the Evidence Act relieves a party of the burden of proving facts in the recitals and gives the recitals their probative value and sufficient evidence, but also casts upon the other party the burden of proving the contrary. Section 129 would not apply where the statements contained in the recitals have proved inaccurate. In *Williams v. Akinwunmi* [1966] 1 All N.L.R. 115, it was held that the presumption in section 129 is obligatory. It saves the party who can invoke it from proving certain facts in the first instance, and puts the onus on the other side. In *Cardoso v. Daniel* [1986] 2 N.W.L.R. (Pt. 20) 1, it was held that in order to secure the benefit of the presumption conferred by section 129, the document must relate to a contract, otherwise the presumption is inapplicable to the document merely because the document is twenty years old. Section 129 clearly implies that for the necessary presumption of evidence to be raised, the Deeds, Instruments, Act of Parliament or statutory declaration must be twenty years old at the date of contract. By the basic rule of construction, namely, that words must in general be given their plain ordinary meaning, there could be no grounds whatsoever for applying the provision of section 129 to cases other than those, in which the purported age of the document was referable to a specific contract. *Odeneye v. Savage* [1964] N.M.L.R. 115, and *Williams v. Akinwumi* [1966] 1 All N.L.R. 115 are cases in which the courts either did not advert to the necessity for determining the age of the document in relation to a contract or else equated "the date of the contract" to the present proceedings. These decisions which purport to equate "the date of the contract" with the "date of the present proceedings" were manifestly unsupportable and were further overruled. For the future, the true implication of section 129 of the Evidence Act is that a deed to be competent for the presumption contemplated must be twenty years old "at the date of the contract" in respect of which the deed is sougt to be relied upon, and not twenty years old at the date of the proceedings at which such a deed is being offered in evidence. See *Johnson and Others v. Lawanson and another* [1971] N.M.L.R. 380.

In *Sanya v. Johnson* [1974] 4 E.C.S.L.R. 691, it was held that under section 129, the recital in a title deed is presumed to be evidence of the truth of the facts recited therein; it is nevertheless not conclusive evidence. By virtue of the section, recitals in a document of the age specified, are presumed in favour of the vendor. But it is not conclusive evidence, as it cannot operate as an estoppel against a stranger to the contract who is able to show that he has a better title than the person named in the recital. In *Omosanya v. Anifowoshe* (1959) 4 F.S.C. 94, it was held that under section 129, although a recital is to be taken as evidence of the truth of the facts recited, it is not conclusive evidence and does not relieve a vendor from the necessity of showing a good root of title. See also *Cheranci v. Cheranci* 1960 N.N.L.R. 24; *Ogiamien and Another v. Ogiamien* [1967] 1 All N.L.R. 191; *Sale and others v. Board of Customs and Excise* [1966] N.M.L.R. *Kenrow Ltd. v. Moss* [1987]; 4 N.W.L.R. (P t.65) 362 *Bukar v. The Queen* (1956-84) 10 S.C. N.D. 111.

Presumption of Undue Influence

In *Aduke v. Onyenubi* [1968] N.M.L.R. 477, it was held that the presumption of undue influence does not arise merely because the relationship betwen the parties can be described as fiduciary, as for instance that of principal and agent. It arises only in the case of relationships of the special and limited class referred to above where the fiduciary relationship naturally raises the presumption.

On presumption generally, see further *Suwa and Another v. The State* - [1965] N.M.L.R. 405; *Waziri v. Ugye and Others* 1977 N.N.L.R. 129; *Board of Customs and Excise v. Udo* (1966-67) 10 E.N.L.R. 52; *Ototo v. Administrator-General and Others* (1946) 12 W.A.C.A. 76; *Arum v. The State* (1974) 4 E.C.S.L.R. 368; *Queen v. The African Press Limited* (1957) W.R.N.L.R. 1; *Aghenghen v. Waghaeghor* (1956-84) 10 S.C. N.D. 114; *Edaun v. Orie* (1956-84) 10 S.C. N.D. 115; Kalio and *Another v. Woluchem and Another* (1985) 1 N.W.L.R.(Pt. 4) 610; *Okeowo v. Sanyaolu* [1986] 2 N.W.L.R. (Pt. 23) 471; *Alibe v. Bornu Native Authority* 1970 N.N.L.R. 79; *Ebueku v. Amola* [1988] 2 N.W.L.R. (Pt. 75) 128; *Owoade and others v. Adeleke and Others* [1988] 2 N.W.L.R. (Pt. 77) 413; *Ogbole v. Onal* [1990] 1 N.W.L.R. (Pt. 126) 357; *Ottih v. Nwanekwe* [1990] 3 N.W.L.R. (Pt. 140) 550; *Ogbuanyiya v. Okudo* (N0. 2) [1990] 4 N.W.L.R. (Pt. 146) 551; *Oyenuga v. I.C.L. Ltd.* [1991] 1 N.W.L.R. (pt. 168) 415; *Imo v. State* [1991] 9 N.W.L.R. (Pt. 213) 1; *Onwujuba v. Obienu* [119] 4 N.W.L.R. (Pt. 213) 16; *Ajomole v. Yaduat* (N0. 2) [1991] 5 N.W.L.R. (Pt. 191) 266; *Akibu v. Oduntan* [1991] 2 N.W.L.R. (Pt. 171) 1; Yongo v. C.O.P. [1992] 8 N.W.L.R. (Pt. 257) 36; *Laguro v. Toku* [1992] 2 N.W.L.R. (Pt. 223) 278; *Anyanwu v. Mbara* [1992] 5 N.W.L.R. (Pt. 242) 386; *Odubeko v. Fowler* [1993] 7 N.W.L.R. (Pt. 308) 637; *Ekpenyong v. State* [1993] 5 N.W.L.R. (Pt. 295) 513; *Dabup v. Kolo* [1993] 9 N.W.L.R. (Pt. 317) 254; *Megwalu v. Megwalu* [1994] 7 N.W.L.R. (Pt. 359) 718; *Opeola v. Opadiran* [1994] 5 N.W.L.R. (Pt. 344) 368.

Chapter 17

ESTOPPEL

Sections 54, 55, 151 to 154 of the Evidence Act.

Estoppel is a rule which bars a party in litigation in Court either from asserting or denying a particular fact, as the case may be. There are many types of estoppel: Estoppel by record, estoppel by deed, estoppel by agreement and estoppel by conduct, to mention the main ones.

Every judgement is conclusive proof, as against parties and privies, of facts directly in issue in the case, actually decided by the court, and appearing from the judgement itself to be the ground on which it was based; unless evidence was admitted in the action in which the judgement was delivered which is excluded in the action in which that judgement is intended to be proved (S. 54). If a judgement is not pleaded by way of estoppel it is as between parties and privies deemed to be relevant fact, whenever any matter, which was, or might have been, decided in the action in which it was given, is in issue, or is deemed to be relevant to the issue, in any subsequent proceeding. Such a judgement is conclusive proof of the facts which it decides, or might have decided, if the party who gives evidence of it had no opportunity of pleading it as an estoppel (S. 55).

Part VIII of the Evidence Act is headed Estoppel, thus giving the impression that it is only the four sections under the part that deal with estoppel. This is wrong. Apart from the four sections that we will deal with here, the two sections examined above also relate to estoppel. Part VIII contains sections 151 to 154.

When one person has, by his declaration, act, or omission intentionally caused or permitted another person to believe a thing to be true and to act upon such belief, neither he nor his representative in interest shall be allowed, in any proceedings between himself and such person or such person's representative in interest, to deny the truth of that thing (S. 151). No tenant of immovable property, or person claiming through such tenant, shall, during the continuance, be permitted to deny that the landlord of such tenant had, at the beginning of the tenancy, a title to such immovable property. Similarly, no person who came upon any immovable property by licence of the person in possession thereof shall be permitted to deny that such person had a title to such possession at the time when such licence was given (S. 152).

No bailee, agent or licensee is permitted to deny that the bailor, principal or licensor by whom any goods were entrusted to any of them respectively, was entitled to those goods at the time when they were so entrusted. However, any such bailee, agent or licensee may show that he was compelled to deliver up any such goods to some person who had a right to them as against his bailor, principal or licensor, or that his bailor, principal or licensor wrongfully and without notice to the bailee, agent or licensee, obtained the goods from a third person who has claimed them from such bailee, agent or licensee (S. 153).

Every bill of lading in the hands of a consignee or endorsee for valuable consideration representing goods to have been shipped on board a vessel, is conclusive proof of that shipment as against the master or other person signing the same, notwithstanding that some goods or some part thereof may not have been so shipped, unless such holder of the bill of lading had actual notice at the time of receiving the same that the goods had not been in fact laden on board. However, the master or other person so signing exonerate himself in respect of such misrepresentation by showing that it was caused without any default on his part, and wholly by the fraud of the shipper or of the holder or some person under whom the holder holds.

Nature of Estoppel

In *Udo and Others v. Obot and Others* [1989] 1 N.W.L.R. (Pt. 95) 59, it was held that when an estoppel as a general rule, binds a party to a litigation, he is prevented from placing reliance on or denying the existence of certain facts. Therefore, from the point of view of the party in whose favour it operates, an estoppel could be regarded as something which renders proof of certain facts unnecessary. The doctrine of estoppel applies to (a) parties in litigation or their privies in respect of matters raised and finally distinctly decided; (b) issues in litigation which merely form part of matters to be decided; and (c) conduct of the parties. Oputa, J.S.C. said at page 68:

> *To use the language of naval warfare, an estoppel must always be either a mine layer or a mine sweeper: it can never be a capital unit. Its function is either to place an obstacle in the way of a case which might otherwise succeed or else to remove an impediment out of the way of a case which might otherwise fail.*

In *Egbe v. The Hon. Justice Adefarasin* [1987] 1 N.W.L.R. (Pt. 471) 1, it was held that estoppel is but a part of the law of evidence. It is no other than a bar to testimony and its sole office is either to place an obstacle in the way of a case which might otherwise succeed or to remove an impediment out of the way of a case which might otherwise fail. An estoppel is thus either a mine layer or mine sweeper. It is never a capital unit. See *also Gbadamosi and Others v. Alhaji Bello* [1985] 1 N.W.L.R. (Pt. 2) 211.

In *Iga and Others v. Amakiri and Others* (1976) 11 S.C. 1, it was held that if a person by his words or conduct wilfully endeavours to cause another to believe in a certain state of things which the first knows to be fake and if the second believes in such state of things and acts upon his belief, he who knowingly made the false statement is estopped from averring afterwards that such a state of things does not exist at the time. Again, if a man either in express terms or by conduct, makes a representation to another of the existence of a state of fact which he intends to be acted upon in a certain way and it be acted upon in the belief of the existence of such a state of facts, to the damage of him who so believes and acts, the first is estopped from denying the existence of such a state of facts. Thirdly, if a man whatever his real meaning may be so conduct himself that reasonable man would take his conduct to mean a certain representation of fact and the latter was intended to act upon it in a particular way, and he with such belief, does act in that way to his damage the first is estopped from denying the facts as represented. See also *United Nigeria Insurance Co. Ltd. v. Oshinuga.* FCA/L/84/82 dated 26/2/83.

In *Odjevwedje v. Echanokpe* [1987] 1 N.W.L.R. (Pt. 52) 633, it was held that the principle of estoppel applies to the case where a point, fundamental to the decision, taken or assumed by the plaintiff and traversable by the defendant has not been traversed. In that case also, a defendant is bound by the judgment, although it may be true enough that subsequent light or ingenuity might suggest some traverse which has not been taken. In *Horicon Ltd. v. Wasurum* [1987] 4 N.W.L.R. (Pt. 66) 646, it was held that if a man either in express terms or by conduct, makes a representation to another of the existence of a state of facts which he intends to be acted upon in the belief of the existence of such state of facts, to the damage of such a person who so believes and acts, such a man is estopped from denying the existence of such a state of facts.

In *Oke v. Atoloye* [1986] 1 N.W.L.R. (Pt. 15) 241, it was held that there are many types of estoppel, namely estoppel per *rem judicatam*, estoppel by conduct - like active participation in the previous suit, estoppel by taking actual benefit from the previous suit, estoppel by inaction - by merely standing-by when one's vital interest should have compelled one to intervene. On issue estoppel see *Duru v. Dim* (1956-84) 10 S.C.N.D. 97; *Ezeanyanwu v. Meze* (1956-84) 10 S.C.N.D. 103. On distinction between issue estoppel and *res judicata*, see *Ladega v. Durosimi* (1978) 3 S.C. 91. On distinction between *res judicata* and estoppel by conduct, see *Synan v. Kale* [1969] 1 All N.L.R. 256.

In *Ijale v. A.G. Leventis* [1965] 1 All N.L.R. 176, it was held that estoppel is sometimes spoken as a rule of evidence only. This is not correct. Lord Wright said "Estoppel is often described as a rule of evidence, as it may be so described. But the whole concept is more correctly viewed as substantive rule of law".

Generally speaking, it is always the defendant that raises the defence of issue estoppel. Although the plea of estoppel is a shield for the protection of a defendant it can also validly be employed as a sword by a plaintiff (*Odjevedje and Another v. Echanokpe* [1987] 1 N.W.L.R. (Pt. 52) 633). See also *Iyowuawi* v. *Iyowuawi* [1987] 4 N.W.L.R. (Pt. 63) 61.

Estoppel as a defence must be specifically raised in the pleadings, otherwise it cannot generally be raised on appeal. See *K. Chellaram and Sons v. G.B. Ollivant Ltd.* (1944) 10 W.A.C.A. 77; *Obanye v. Okwunwa and Another* (1930) 10 N.L.R. 8; Sowa and *Another v. Chief Amachree* (1933) 11 N.L.R. 82; *Dedeke and Others v. Williams and Another* (1944) 10 W.A.C.A. 164; *Agusto v. Joshua* [1962] 1 All N.L.R. 312; *Sosan and others v. Dr. Ademuyiwa* [1986] 3 N.W.L.R. (Pt. 27) 241; *Lion of Africa Insurance Co. Ltd. v. Fisayo* [1986] 4 N.W.L.R. [Pt. 37] 674.

Estoppel by Record

The rule of *res judicata* is derived from the maxim of *nemo debet bis vexari pro eadem causa*. It is the *causa* that matters; and a plaintiff cannot by formulating a fresh claim re-litigate the same *causa: Modukolu v. Nkemdilim* [1962] 1 All N.L.R. 587. The principles underlying estoppel by record are

(a) *Interest reipublicae ut sit finis litium* - It is for the common good that there should be an end to litigation.
(b) *Nemo debet bis vexari pro una et eadem causa* - No one should be sued twice on the same ground. No one shall be twice vexed for one and the same cause.

There are two kinds of estoppel by record viz: Cause of action estoppel and issue estoppel. In either case there must be a distinct holding by a former court which a latter court will not allow the parties to reopen and re-litigate. For the plea of *estoppel per rem judicatam* to apply, there must have been a judicial determination of a cause agitated between the real parties upon which a real interest has been settled. Finality is basic and crucial in pleas of *estoppel per rem judicatam.* It is not the mere raising of an issue that is binding on the parties. Rather it is the fact that such issue has been adjudicated upon and decided one way or another. When that is the case, it is not open to the losing party to re-open or re-litigate the issue which had already been decided and which should therefore be considered closed. The doctrine is the product of our adversary system of litigation. The essence of the system is that unless an issue litigated as between opposed parties is distinctly decided upon by a properly constituted court, it remains open to be litigated in the future if it becomes an issue. But once distinctly and actually raised and decided it should be regarded as forever decided: *Udo and Others v. Obot and Others* [1989] 1 N.W.L.R. (Pt. 95). 59 See also *Ogundiran and Another v. Balogun* (1957) W.R.N.L.R. 51; *Ojo v. Abadie* (1954) 14 W.A.C.A. 628; *Daniel and Another v. Iroeri* [1985] 1 N.W.L.R. (Pt. 3) 541; *Dzengwe v. Gbishe and Another* [1985] 2 N.W.L.R. (Pt. 8) 528; *and Cardoso v. Daniel Others* [1986] 2 N.W.L.R. (Pt. 20) 1; *Coker v. Sanyaolu* (1976) 8-10 S.C. 203; *Mercantile Bank of Nigeria Ltd. v. Abusomiran* [1986] 2 N.W.L.R. (Pt. 22) 270; *Sosan and Others v. Dr. Ademuyiwa* [1986] 3 N.W.L.R. (Pt. 27) 241; *Banire and Others v. Balogun* [1986] 4 N.W L.R. (Pt. 38) 746; *Dilibe and Others v. Nwokozor* [1986] 2 N.W.L.R. (Pt. 41) 315; *Ibodo and Another v. Enarofia and Another* (1979) 2 C.A. 1*;* *Alabi v. Ladeji* [1986] 5 N.W.L.R. (Pt. 42) 429; *Bamishebi v. Faleye* [1987] 2 N.W.L.R. (Pt. 54) 51; *Aladegbemi v. Fasanmade* [1988] 3 N.W.L.R. (Pt. 81) 129.

Conditions of Application of Estoppel by Record

It is well known that before the doctrine of *estoppel per rem judicatam* can operate, it must be shown that the parties, issues and subject matter were the same in the previous case as those in the action in which the plea of *res judicata* is raised: *Nwaneri* and *Others v. Oriuwa* (1959) 4. F.S.C. 132. It is trite law that before a judgment can operate as an estoppel in a subsequent proceeding

(a) the parties to the two proceedings must be the same. The term 'parties' includes privies to the parties name in the writ.
(b) The issues in and the subject-matter of the two proceedings must be the same. Estoppel will not operate even if the parties to both suits are the same once the issues and subject-matter of both suits are different.
(c) There must be a valid subsisting judgement: *Oyeneye and Others v. Rosetti* FCA/ / L 71/82 decided on 21/1/83 (unreported). For the principle to apply in any proceedings, all the preconditions to a valid plea of *estoppel inter parties a per rem judicatam* must apply, that
    (1) The same question must be for decision in both proceedings which means that the question for decision in the current suit must have been decided in the earlier proceedings.
    (2) The decision relied upon to support the plea of issue estoppel must be final.
    (3) The parties must be the same, which means that parties involved in both proceedings must be the same:

Fadiora v. Gbadebo (1978) 3 S.C. 219. See also *Alashe v. Ilu* [1964] 1 All N.L.R. 390; *Nkanu v. Onum* (1977) 5 S.C. 13; *Oliko v. Okonwo* [1970] 1 All N.L.R. 86; Shonekan v. Smith [1964] 1 All N.L.R. 168; *Rahaman v. Ajele* (1956-84) 10 S.C.N.D. 89; *Amida v. Oshoboja* (1956-84) 10 S.C.N.D. 92; *Nwehi v. Nwaka* (1956-84) 10 S.C.N.D. 100; *Board of Customs and Excise v. Kalu* [1966] N.M.L.R. 85; *Adebona v. Amao* [1966] N.M.L.R. 404; *Esi v. Chief Secretary* (1973) 11 S.C. 189; *Unisales Commercial Limited v. Dawodu* [1986] 3 N.W.L.R. (Pt. 31) 706; *Larinde v. Ajiko and Another* (1940) 6 W.A.C.A. 108; *Ekpe v. Chief Antai* (1944) 10 W.A.C.A. 19; *Alao v. Akano* [1988] 1 N.W.L.R. (Pt. 71) 431; Nwawuba and Others v. Enemuo and Others [1988] 2 N.W.L.R. (Pt. 78) 581.

The parties must be the Same

In *Thomas Hoare v. Samuel Hoare* (1936) 13 N.L.R. 28, the plaintiff suing as heir-at-law of his deceased father sought a declaration that the will of his grandfather in so far as it affected the real properties mentioned in the deed of settlement is void *ab initio*. There were two previous litigations in 1926 and 1927. The defendants pleaded *res judicata*. It was held that the plaintiff claiming as heir-at-law of his father was affected by the same estoppel. In *Onisango v. Akinkunmi and Others* (1955-56) W.R.N.L.R. 39, it was held that the term "parties" includes not only those named on the record of proceedings - defendants becoming parties after service of the writ - but also those who had an opportunity to attend the proceedings. All people who are substantially interested in the suit of a proceeding and are cognisant of it are bound by any judgment given thereunder. *c.f. Lateju v. Iyanda and Another* (1958) W.R.N.L.R. 3.

In *Santos v. Okosi Industries Ltd. and Another* (1942) 8 W.A.C.A. the West African Court of Appeal said that

> *for the purpose of estoppel per rem judicatam, 'party' means not only a person named as such, but also one.... who, being cognisant of the proceedings and of the fact that a party thereto is professing to act in his interest, allows his battle to be fought by that party intending to take the benefit of the championship in the success.*

See also *Ajaka v. Chief Eyinmosan and Others* (1961) W.N.L.R. 30; *Uwalaka and Others v. Agba and Others* (1955) 15 W.A.C.A. 63; Esiaka and Others v. Obisogwu and Others (1952) 14 W.A.C.A 178; *Ojiake v. Ogbueze* [1962] 1 All N.L.R. 58; *Adenle v. Oyegbade* [1964] 1 All N.L.R. 26; *Allen v. Salako* (1956-84) 10 S.C.N.D. 89; *Onyenobi v. Dabirinze* (1956-84) 10 S.C.N.D. 95; *Chinweze and Another v. Mrs. Masi and Another* [1989] 1 N.W.L.R. (Pt. 97) 254; *Oshoboja v. Dada* [1987] 4 N.W.L.R. (Pt. 66) 569.

Issues and Subject-Matter must be the Same.

In *Agunwa v. Onukwe* [1962] All N.L.R. 537, it was held that the principle of *res judicatam* will apply if the issues involved in the two cases are substantially the same. See *Fakorede v. Attorney-General (West)* (1972) 3 S.C. 81. In *Ofunne v. Okoye* [1966] 1 All N.L.R. 94, it was held that for the purposes of determining the same subject-matter, the Court will consider whether the controversies in the earlier proceedings are also the controversies in the subsequent action. Where the controversies are the same the plea of *res judicatam* will succeed, otherwise not. In *Alhaji Gafai v. United Africa Company Ltd.* [1961]. All N.L.R. 785 where the same cause of action gave rise to the two different forms of relief, the court held that the plaintiff was estopped. In *Okusanya and Another v. Akanwo and Another* (1939) 7 W.A.C.A. 1, it was held by the Judicial Committee of the Privy Council that a claim included in an action which is not a subject of adjudication by the trial court cannot operate as *res judicata* in a subsequent case with respect to that claim. See also *Dedeke and Others v. Williams and Another* (1944) 10 W.A.C.A. 164. *In Ibiyemi and Others v. Olusoji and Another* (1957) W.R.N.L.R. 25, it was held that although the issue before the court is the same as that adjudicated upon in previous suits and the parties are also the same, the plaintiffs have, in the present suit added a small strip of land to the north of the area declared to be that of the first defendant in previous proceedings. All the land which is the subject-matter of the present action has and therefore been previously adjudicated upon, and the plea of *res judicatam* must, for this reason, fail.

In *Odua and Others v. Nwanze* (1934) 2. W.A.C.A. 98, the court held that the plea of *res judicata* must fail as there was no evidence that the parties in one of the judgments relied upon were privies and in the other judgment there was no evidence that the pieces of land involved in the judgment were the same as in the present case. In *Commissioner of Lands v. Abraham and Others* (1948) 19 N.L.R. 1, it was held that the judgment dismissing the Commissioner's previous suit did not operate as estoppel

(a) because there Aromire was sued personally whilst in the suit in hand, he was defending as representative of the Aromire Chieftaincy family and

(b) because the issue was not as to ownership; whilst the previous suit was dismissed merely on the ground that there was no evidence of trespass.

See also *Jia Enterprises (Electrical) Ltd. v. British Commonwealth Insurance Co. Ltd.* [1962] All N.L.R. 363; *Shitta-Bay v. The Chairman, L.E.D.B. and Another* [1962] All N.L.R. 373.

In *Edem v. Chief Edet* (1940) 6 W.A.C.A. 220, the appellants relied upon judgments delivered in 1921 and 1929 to substantiate their plea of *res judicata*. The previous suit was for a declaration of title to land whilst the present suit was for a declaration that the plaintiff had a right to farm on the land. It was however clear from the state of the pleadings and the evidence before the court that the plaintiff's claim was as to titular ownership of the land. The court held that the plaintiff was estopped from instituting the action. See also *Chukwunta v. Chukwu and Others* (1953) 14 W.A.C.A. 341; *Ijanna v. Aina, the Oba of Ibese* (1942) 16 N.L.R. 67; *Rosaline Parker v. Roland Parker* (1964) N.M.L.R. supplement, p. 28.

There must be a Valid Subsisting Judgment

Before a plea of *res judicata* can succeed the judgment must be a final, valid and subsisting one. See *Eko v. Ugwuoma and Others* (1940) 6 W.A.C.A. 206; Abogunde v. Lanlokun (1958) W.R.N.L.R. 69; *Lateju v. Iyanda and Another* (1959) 4 F.S.C. 257; *Ajogodo and Others v. Adegoriola* (1961) W.N.L.R. 177. In *Odu v. John Holt and Company Limited* (1950) 19 N.L.R. 127, there were cross-actions between the parties and they were consolidated. On the day fixed for hearing the plaintiff in the present suit did not appear, and the court, after hearing evidence of the company, gave judgment in its favour and dismissed his claim. He applied to have his action relisted but was refused. He brought a new action with the same claim, and the company applied to have the claim struck out or the action stayed. It was held that there being a judgment dismissing plaintiff's claim, the court could not entertain the same claim in a second action. In *Chief Ekpe v. Chief Antai* (1944) 10 W.A.C.A. 19, the court held that since the previous case and the present case had to do with trespass, the previous one operated as estoppel, although the trial court had no jurisdiction to entertain the matter involving real property. cf. Inyang and Another v. Essien and Another (1957) 2 F.S.C. 39. The doctrine of estoppel will not avail a party where a decision is not meant to be a bar to further proceedings. See *Olawoyin v. Commissioner of Police* [1961] All N.L.R. 130. In *Makanjuda v. Khalil* (1958) W.R.N.L.R. 82, in 1945, the defendant obtained a judgment in a case of trespass against the plaintiff. In 1949, the plaintiff, this time around, obtained judgment against the defendant for declaration of title to the same land. The court held that it was the 1949 judgment which operated as an estoppel in the present suit

See further *Seriki v. Solaru* [1965] N.M.L.R. 1; *Runka v. Katsina Native Authority* (1950) 13 W.A.C.A. 98; *Chapman v. C.F.A.O. and Another* (1943) 9 W.A.C.A. 181; *Chime and Another v. Elikwu and Another* [1965] N.M.L.R. 71; *Adeigbe and Another v. Adebowale* (1959) 4 F.S.C. 142; *Larinde v. Ajiko* (1940) 6 W.A.C.A. 108; *Ojiako and Others v. Onwumaogueze and Others* [1962] All N.L.R. 58; *Yekrorogha v. Barakpali* (1929) 9 N.L.R. 60.

Estoppel by Deed

In *Agboola v. Abimbola* [1969] 1 All N.L.R. 287; it was held that estoppel by deed is a rule of evidence founded on the principle that a solemn and unambiguous statement or engagement in a deed must be taken as binding between parties and privies and therefore as not admitting any contradictory proof.

Estoppel by Agreement: Landlord and Tenant

In *Augusto v. Joshua (No. 1)* [1962)] against a tenant or licensee is contained in section 151 of the Evidence Act. As against the assignee or lessee of the reversion the tenant cannot impeach the validity of his own lease, not controvert the lessor's title, but the assignment itself may be disputed.

Payment of rent to a claiming assignee of the reversion is prima facie evidence of the claimant's title.

Estoppel by Conduct

In *Njoku v. Ekeocha and Another* [1972] E.C.S.L.R. 199, it was held that estoppel by conduct can arise where one party has led another by his conduct to take a step prejudicial to his interest such as has happened in the instant case where the defendants were put in peril of losing their lives by swearing on oath.

In the unreported case of *Riv Biscuits Co (Nig.) Ltd. v. Okezie and Sons Co.,* Suit No. PHC/112/83, delivered on 6/3/86, a Port Harcourt High Court said:

> *I agree entirely with the submission of learned counsel for the plaintiff that the defendant is estopped from asking the court to strike out the case. The doctrine of estoppel by conduct is founded on equity. It is a very old equitable remedy, well secreted and nurtured in the elbows of substantive jurisprudence and common law. It is available to a victim of an organised or clever device or conduct of a party; a conduct which could lazily be likened to a camouflage or smoke screen or even more appropriately, in day to day life, likened to a reservior with a breakable cover, where the victim is lured into by the opposite party and he falls head long, deep down the reservior to his detriment. The doctrine could be stated thus: If a party, having a legal right allows another party to act contrary to that legal right to the latter's detriment, without the former asserting the legal right at the time of the action, or within a reasonable time thereafter, he will be estopped from arrogating to himself the legal right by way of enforcement. The law will presume that by his previous passive and carefree conduct, he has abandoned his legal right or willing to waive it and that it is too late in the day for him to parade the right (which he was aware, he had) within the corridors of the court, with a view to enforcing it. I see such a situation here.*

See also *Iga v. Amakiri, supra; Tika -Tore Press Ltd. v. Abina* (1973) 12 S.C. 79.

On estoppel generally, see further *Oduka and others v. Kasumu and Another* [1968] N.M.L.R. 29; *Synaux v. Kale and Others* [1969] N.M.L.R. 159; *Udofia and Others v. Agusisua and Others* [1973] N.M.L.R. 286; *Attorney-General of Bendel State v. Attorney-General of the Federation and Others* [1982] 3 N.C.L.R. 1; *Alase and Others v. Ilu and Others* [1965] N.M.L.R. 66; *Adogan v. Oshilaja* (1964) W.N.L.R. 86; *Ababio II v. President-Incharge Catholic Mission and Others* (1935) 2 W.A.C.A. 380; *Dugbo and others v. Kporoaro and Others* (1958) W.R.N.L.R. 73; *Oke v. Atoleye* [1986] 1 N.W.L.R. (Pt. 15) 241; *Rowrafric and Far Eastern Ltd. v. Chief Avbenake and Others* [1958] W.R.N.L.R. 92; *Njionye v. Onuoha* (1974) 6 S.C. 111; *Toriola v. Williams* (1982) 7 S.C. 27; *Ikpang v. Edoho* (1978) 6-7 S.C. 221*;* *Owoniyin v. Omotosho* [1961] 1 All N.L.R. 304; *Nwabia v. Aderi* (1958) 3 F.S.C. 112*;* *Bonny v. Yougha* [1969] 1 All N.L.R. 396; *Fadiora v.*

Gbadebo (1978) 3 S.C. 219; *Jack v. Harry* (1978) 6-7 S.C. 159; *Talabi v. Adeseye* (1972) 8-9 S.C. 20; *Ekpoke v. Usilo* (1978) 6-7 S.C. 187; *Lawal v. Dawodu* (1972) 8-9 S.C. 83; *Ibuluya v. Dikibo* (1976) 6 S.C. 97; *Yoye v. Olubode* (1974) 10 S.C. 209; *Amawo v. Attornery-General, North* (1973) 6 S.C. 47; *Rahaman v. Ajele* (1956-84) 10 S.C. N.D. 90; Onotaire v. Onokpasa (1956-84) 10 S.C. N.D. 93; *Iyakin v. Gbajumo* (1956-84) 10 S.C.N.D. 96; *Dieke v. Manfuo* (1956-84) 10 S.C. N.D. 98; *Solagbade v. Apanpa* (1956-84) 10 S.C. N.D. 99; *Ezewani and Others v. Onwadi and Others* [1986] 4 N.W.L.R. (Pt. 33) 27; *Alabi v. Ladeji* [1986] 5 N.W.L.R. (Pt. 42) 423; *Egbe v. Justice Adefarasin* [1987] 1 N.W.L.R. (Pt. 47) 1; *Temco Engineering v. Savannah Bank* [1985] H.C. N.L.R. 239; *E.S.O. Cherubim and Seraphim v. Otubu* [1985] H.C. N.L.R. 943; *Amena v. Makar* [1985] H.C. N.L.R. 675; *Aro v. Faro* [1959] L.L.R. 116; *Iyowuawi v. Iyowuawi* [1987] 4 N.W.L.R. (Pt. 63) 61; *Chief Okpuruwu and Others v. Chief Okpokam and Another* [1988] 4 N.W.L.R. (Pt. 90) 554. *Ezenwa v. Kareem* [1990] 3 N.W.L.R. (Pt. 138) 258; *Udeze v. Chidebe* [1990] 1 N.W.L.R. (Pt. 125) 141. *Nwosu v. Udeaja* [1990] 1 N.W.L.R. (Pt. 125) 188; *Olawuji v. Adeyemi* [1990] 4 N.W.L.R. (Pt. 147) 746; *Ekpenyong v. Etim* [1990] 3 N.W.L.R. (Pt. 140) 594; *Ikpuku v. Ikpuku* [1991] 5 N.W.L.R. (Pt. 193) 571; *Ukaegbu v. Ugoji* [1991] 6 N.W.L.R. (Pt. 196) 127; *M.I.A. and Sons Ltd. v. F.H.A.* [1991] 8 N.W.L.R. (Pt. 209) 295; *Ogunleye v. Jegede* [1991] 6 N.W.L.R. (Pt. 199) 594; *Ayye v. Yar, Aduwa* [1991] 8 N.W.L.R. (Pt. 210) 464 *Akinseye v. Sofa Splints Ltd* [1992] 7 N.W.L.R. (Pt. 252) 241; *Osunrinde v. Ajamogun* [1992] 6 N.W.L.R. (Pt. 246) 156; *Briggs v. Briggs* [1992] 3 N.W.L.R. (Pt. 228) 128; *Igwego v. Ezeugo* [1992] 6 N.W.L.R. (Pt. 249) 561; *Omokhafe v. Esekhomo* [1993] 8 N.W.L.R. (Pt. 309) 58; *A.I.C. Ltd. v. Mannesmann-Anlegendau* [1994] 3 N.W.L.R. (Pt. 334) 596; *Nwaru v.Commissioner of Police* [1994] 5 N.W.L.R. (Pt. 347) 722.

Chapter 18

EFFECT OF WRONGFUL ADMISSION AND REJECTION OF EVIDENCE

Section 227 of the Evidence Act

The wrongful admission of evidence is not of itself a ground for the reversal of any decision in any case where it appears to a court on appeal that the evidence so admitted cannot reasonably be held to have affected the decision and that such decision would have been the same if such evidence had not been admitted (S. 227(1)). Similarly, the wrongful exclusion of evidence is not itself a ground for the reversal of any decision in any case if it appears to the court of appeal that had the evidence been admitted it may reasonably be held that the decision would have been the same (S. 227(2)). The term "decision" here includes a judgment, order, finding or verdict (S. 227(3)).

The two subsections provide for two opposing situations. While under the first subsection, wrongful *admission* of evidence may not be a ground for the reversal of any decision on appeal, a wrongful *exclusion* of evidence may also not be a ground for the reversal of any decision on appeal. In either case, the appellate court will consider whether the wrongful *admission* or wrongful *exclusion* affected the decision of the trial court. By the section if the answer is in the negative, then the appellate court will not disturb the *status quo.*

In *Olukade v. Alade* (1976) 2 S.C. 183, the Supreme Court warned:

> *A court is expected in all proceedings before it to admit and act only on evidence which is admissible in law (i.e under the Evidence Act or any other law or enactment relevant in any particular case) and so if the court should inadvertently admit inadmissible evidence it has a duty generally not to act upon it. The court has the power even to reject inadmissible evidence at the stage of giving judgment.*

See *Igbodin and Others v. Obianke and Others* [1976] 1 N.M.L.R. 212.

In *Minister of Lands Western Nigeria v. Dr. Nnamdi Azikiwe* [1969] 1 All N.L.R. 490, the trial court wrongly admitted a photocopy of a public document instead of a certified true copy within the requirement of section 96(2) (c) of the Evidence Act. There was no objection at the trial of the admissibility of the document. The appellate court nevertheless held that the photocopy was inadmissible. The court said: "It is not within the competence of parties to a case to admit by consent or otherwise a document which by law is inadmissible". Similarly in *Saidu v. The State* (1982) 4 S.C. 41, it was held that it is not the law that in criminal trials documentary evidence which are inadmissible can be admitted in evidence by consent.

In *Owoniyi v. Omotosho* [1961] All N.L.R. 304, the court said: If such evidence is by error or otherwise admitted in evidence, then it is the duty of the trial court to expunge it in giving a judgment; and if the court of trial fails to do so, then an appeal court will reject such evidence and consider the case in the light only of the legally admitted evidence. In *Alashe v. Ilu and Others* [1964] 1 All N.L.R. 390, at the trial a plan, not countersigned as required by section 23(1)(b) of the Survey Act, was tendered by the defendants and without objection. Their counsel conceded that it was wrongly admitted in evidence, but submitted that the plaintiffs should have objected in the High Court. It was held that it is the duty of a Court of Appeal to reject evidence which has been improperly received and to decide a case on legal evidence. The court accordingly rejected the plan. But in *Akunne v. Ekwuno and Others* (1952) 14 W.A.C.A. 59, Foster-Sutton, P. admitted an alleged inadmissible evidence. He said at page 60:

> *Appellant's counsel argued that the evidence of witnesses 5 and 6 for the defence was inadmissible. We declined to allow him to argue that point: the evidence was not objected to, it was cross-examined and its admissibility was not put in question at any stage of the trial. It was also argued, that exhibits 4, 5, 6, and 8 were inadmissible, not being relevant to any issue in the case. As we pointed out to counsel for the appellants, no exception was taken to exhibits 5, 6 and 8 at the trial, but apart from that consideration, in my view, the evidence was clearly admissible under the provisions of sub-section (b) of section 12 of the Evidence Ordinance.*

In *R.v. Adebanjo and Others* (1935) 2 W.A.C.A. 315, Aitken, J. said at pages 321 and 322:

> *It is true that the record dicloses several irregularities in regard to the admission of documents in evidence before a proper foundation for their reception had been laid, but before the end of the case was reached every single document tendered in evidence by the prosecution appears to have been adequately proved... In such circumstances it is hardly for the defence to complain, and though they were not strictly admissible in evidence they were perfectly innocent letters of no probative value whatever. They can therefore be disregarded, just as the learned trial Judge appears to have disregarded them, and*

we have been unable to find any oral evidence on the record which was inadmissible against one or more of the accused.

See *also Okafor and Another v. Okitiakpe* (1973) 2 S.C. 49; *Aderemi v.* Adedire [1966] N.M.L.R. 398; *Total (Nigeria) Ltd. and Another v. Nwako and Another* (1978) 5 S.C. 1.

In *Yassin v. Barclays Bank D.C.O.* [1968] N.M.L.R. 380, the court said: If inadmissible evidence is not objected to and is admitted, it must still be rejected on appeal, but if the evidence can be interpreted as complying with the appropriate statutory requirement, then it is a matter to be taken into consideration when interpreting the evidence that it went unchallenged. In other words, if the evidence can be treated as admissible it is not to be treated as inadmissible because there is a possible interpretation which would render it inadmissible when that possible other interpretation had not been tested by questions from the party who could have objected to the evidence being admitted. In Nigeria the correct test is not whether or not miscarriage of justice had been occasioned by the wrongful admission of evidence: the effect of the wrongful admission of evidence is governed by section 226(1) of the Evidence Act, namely: whether the evidence so admitted cannot reasonably be held to have affected the decision and that such decision would have been the same if such evidence had not been admitted. See also *Massin v. Barclays Bank* [1968] 1 All N.L.R. 171*; Ajayi v. Fisher* (1956) 1 F.S.C. 90; *Raimu v. Akintoye* [1986] 3 N.W.L.R. (Pt. 26) 97; *James v. Mid-Motors* (1978) 11-12 S.C. 31; *Enegokwule v. Okadigbo* (1973) 4 S.C. 113.

Wrongful Admission and Rejection of Evidence not leading to a Reversal of Decision Appealed

In *Aiyeola v. The State* (1956-84) 10 S.C. N.D. 27, it was held that there is a distinction between wrongful admission of inadmissible evidence and wrongful use of otherwise admissible evidence. The wrongful use of otherwise admissible evidence may not necessarily affect the eventual verdict of the trial. In *Nwanyanwu v. The State* (1956-84) 10 S.C.N.D. 28, it was held that the question whether the wrongful reception of a piece of evidence of a trial Judge will affect the decision depends on the circumstances of the case. Where it is possible to exclude the wrongfully admitted evidence and yet have enough material to sustain the decision, the wrongfully admitted evidence and yet have enough material to sustain the decision, the wrongful reception of such evidence would not affect the decision.

In *Alhadi v. Allie* (1951) 13 W.A.C.A. 323, the plaintiff recovered judgment against the defendant for damages for malicious prosecution. The trial Judge admitted as against the defendant certain inadmissible evidence, and to some extent relied upon it on the issue of malice, but there was other evidence supporting the Judge's conclusion. It was held that the misreception of inadmissible evidence was not fatal to the case, since excluding that evidence, there was ample evidence to support the finding of facts.

By virtue of section 266(1) of the Evidence Act, there is no justification for interfering with the judgment of the lower court on the ground of wrongful admission of evidence since the evidence by the despositions thus wrongly admitted could not reasonably have affected the decision and that the decision would have been the same if the depositions had not been admitted: *Akadile v. The State* [1971] 1 All N.L.R. 18. If a document tendered in evidence in civil case and admitted without objection, is clearly admissible under the provisions of a particular written law, but is admitted by a trial court wrongly under the provisions of another written law, it will be grossly unjust for a court of appeal to hold, that the document has been wrongly admitted and to allow the appeal on that ground. By doing so, the court of appeal will be denying the party which tendered the document in the trial court substantial justice based on a mere technicality: *Ayeni v. Dada* (1978) 3 S.C. 5. Where documentary evidence is admissible in civil cases under certian conditions and it is admitted with procedural defect, but with the consent of the parties or without objection, a trial court can justifiably make use of it in arriving at a decision and the appeal court will not upset the decision on the ground of inadmissibility: *Dina v. New Nigerian Newspapers Ltd* [1986] 2 N.W.L.R. (Pt. 22) 353. See also *Commissioner of Police v. Tsalikis* (1943) 9 W.A.C.A. 211.

In *R. v. Edem and Others* (1943) 9 W.A.C.A. 25 where the evidence of a Chief on customary law was wrongly admitted, the West African Court of Appeal held that the conviction could not be disturbed as no miscarriage of justice occurred as a result of the admission of the evidence. In *Timitimi and Others v. Chief Amabebe and Others* (1953) 14 W.A.C.A. 25, the trial court wrongly admitted a judgment of a Native

Court. Since the court did not rely on the judgment, the appeal based on the wrongful admissibility of the judgment was dismissed. In *R. v. Aderogba* (1960) 5 F.S.C. 212, the learned trial Judge wrongly called a witness to help the Crown and also treated him as a witness for the Crown. It was held on appeal that since there was no substantial miscarriage of justice, as the defending counsel was allowed to cross-examine the witness, the appeal based on it was dismissed. In *R. v. Wilcox* [1961] All N.L.R. 631, the learned trial Judge went outside the evidence before him to make use of other evidence in determining exhibits in court. Although the procedure was held irregular on appeal, the appeal was dismissed as there was no substantial miscarriage of justice. And in *Chief Dugbo and Others v. Chief Kporoaro and Others* (1958) W.R.N.L.R. 73, where the learned trial Judge wrongly admitted in evidence an uncertified judgment, the Federal Supreme Court invoked the provisions of section 226(1) of the Evidence Act since the admissibility of the uncertified judgment did not reasonably affect the decision of the case one way or the other. See also *Idundun v. Okumagba* (1976) 9-10 S.C. 227; *Ugbe v. Edigbe* S.C. 736/66 (unreported); *Ayanwale and Others v. Atanda and Another* [1988] 1 N.W.L.R. (Pt. 68) 22.

Wrongful Admission and Rejection of Evidence Leading to a Reversal of the Decision Appealed

In *The Queen v. Thomas* (1958) 3 F.S.C. 8, it was held that as a general rule, where an accused person's conviction is based on inadmissible evidence, the court of appeal will quash the conviction, particularly when the inadmissible evidence is highly prejudicial. See also *The Queen v. Haske* [1961] 1 All N.L.R. 330; *Nwobiala v.Inspector-General of Police* (1960) 5 F.S.C. 43; *Elias v. Disu* [1962] 1 All N.L.R. 214.

In *Schofoluwe v. The King* (1951) 13 W.A.C.A. 264, where the wrongful admission of a deposition affected the decision of the learned trial Judge, the West African Court of Appeal quashed the conviction. In *R.v. Harry and Others* (1938) 4 W.A.C.A. 37, the learned trial Judge wrongly admitted in evidence the dying declaration of a boy. The appellant was convicted of murder. The West African Court of Appeal quashed the conviction. And the appellate court took this line of action despite the finding of the learned trial Judge that

> *even in the absence of the dying declaration I should come to the same conclusion",*

because the evidence left did not justify that conclusion. *c.f* .*R. v. Ogbuewu* (1949) 12 W.A.C.A. 483 where a contrary decision was reached in respect of a wrongful admission of a dying declaration, on the ground that there was sufficient evidence outside the dying declaration to justify the conviction of the appellant.

Wrongful Admission and Rejection of Evidence Leading to an Order of Re-trial

In *Ajayi v. Fisher* (1956) 1 F.S.C. 90, it was held that if there is evidence in a case and although the appeal court thinks that the inadmissible evidence must have influenced the decision, yet it is unable to say that without the inadmissible evidence the decision would or would not reasonably have been different, its proper course will be to order a re-trial. In *Korgba v. The State* [1968] 1 All N.L.R. 97, it was held that where the court was in doubt whether the wrongfully admitted evidence did not affect the decision of the trial court, the court of appeal ordered a re-trial.

In *Ezeani and Others v. Nzene and Others* (1935) 2 W.A.C.A. 342, in an action for special damages arising from wilful damage and looting of properties, the learned trial Judge refused to admit a certified true copy of the criminal proceedings on the matter. The defendants had earlier been convicted in the criminal trial. The West African Court of Appeal, held that the learned trial Judge was wrong in refusing to admit the certified copy of the criminal proceedings. A re-trial was accordingly ordered. In *R.v. Thomas* (1958) 3 F.S.C. 8, the appellant was tried in the High Court and convicted for forgery. On appeal his conviction was quashed by the Federal Supreme Court and a re-trial ordered. One of the reasons for quashing the conviction was that inadmissible evidence was admitted at the trial. The court took the view that the inadmissible evidence was highly prejudicial to the appellant.

In *Abodunde and Others v. R.* (1959) 4 F.S.C. 70, the Federal Supreme Court set down principles that will guide appllate courts in ordering a re-trial. Abbot, F.J. said at page 73;

> *We are of opinion that, before deciding to order a re-trial, this court must be satisfied (a) that there has been an error in law (including the observance of the law of evidence) or an irregularity in procedure of such a character that on the one hand the trial was not rendered a nullity and on the other hand this court is unable to say that there of the Ordinance;(b) that leaving aside the error or irregularity, the evidence taken as a whole discloses a substantial case against the appellant; (c) that there are no such special circumstances as would render it oppressive to put the appellant on*

> *trial a second time;(d) that the offence or offences of which the appellant was convicted, or the consequences to the appellant or any other person of the conviction or acquttal of the appellant, are not merely trivial; and (e) that to refuse an order for re-trial would occasion a greater miscarriage of justice than to grant it".*

See further *Akinfe v. The State* [1988] 3 N.W.L.R. (Pt. 85) 729; *Eyorokoromo v. The State* (1979) 6-9 S.C. 3; *Onuokafor v. The State* (1976) 5 S.C.13; *Arutu v. R.* (1959) 4 F.S.C. 66; *Umojiako v. Ezenamuo* [1990] 1 N.W.L.R. (Pt. 126) 253; *Inyang v. Eshiet* [1990] 5 N.W.L.R. (Pt. 149) 178; *Iwuno v. Dieli* [1990] 5 N.W.L.R. (Pt. 149) 126; *Okaroh v. State* [1990] 1 N.W.L.R. (Pt. 125) 128; *Yongo v. C.O.P.* [1990] 5 N.W.L.R (Pt. 148) 103; *N.A.B. Ltd v. Shuaibu* [1991] 4 N.W.L.R. (Pt. 186) 450; *Glorylux Ass. Ind. v. N.P.F.M.B.* [1993] 7 N.W.L.R. (Pt. 305) 341; *Igiehon v. Omoregie* [1993] 2 N.W.L.R. (Pt. 276) 398; *Agbaje v. Adigun* [1993] 1 N.W.L.R. (Pt. 269) 261.

Chapter 19

COMPETENCE AND COMPELLABILITY OF WITNESSES

Sections 155 to 164 of the Evidence Act.

All persons are competent to testify, unless the court considers that they are prevented from understanding the questions put to them, or from giving rational answers to those questions, by reason of tender years, extreme old age, disease, whether of body or mind, or any other cause of the same kind. A person of unsound mind is not incompetent to testify unless he is prevented by his mental infirmity from understanding the questions put to him and giving rational answers to them (S. 155). A witness who is unable to speak may give his evidence in any other manner in which he can make it intelligible, as by writing or by signs; but such writing must be written and the signs made in open court (S. 156).

A banker or officer of a bank shall not, in any legal proceeding to which the bank is not a party, be compellable to produce any banker's book the contents of which can be proved in manner provided in section 97 or to appear as a witness to prove the matters, transactions and accounts therein recorded, unless by order of the court made for special cause (S. 157). Subject to the provision to section 148, in all civil proceedings the parties to the suit, and the husband or wife of any party to the suit, shall be competent witnesses (S. 158). Subject to the provisions of Part IX of the Act, in criminal cases the accused person, and his or her spouse, and any person and the spouse of any person jointly charged with him and tried at the same time, is competent to testify (S. 159).

Every person charged with an offence is a competent witness for the defence at every stage of the proceedings, whether the person so charged is charged solely or jointly with any other person (S. 160). See also the proviso. Section 161 provides for instances when evidence by a husband or wife is compellable and when competent. By the provision, a spouse of a monogamous marriage is not compellable to disclose any communication made to the spouse during the marriage. It is rather unfortunate that the provision is restricted to monogamous marriages only as opposed to polygamous marriages which is more rampant in the Nigerian society. It is submitted that the provision should include all types of marriages lawfully contracted between two consenting adults. See also section 162.

The parties to any proceedings instituted in consequence of adultery and the husbands and wives of the parties are competent to give evidence in the proceedings, but no witness in any such proceedings whether a party thereto or not, will be liable to be asked or bound to answer any question tending to show that the spouse has been guilty of adultery, unless the spouse has already given evidence in the same proceedings in disproof of the alleged adultery (S. 163). No spouse shall be compelled to disclose any communication made to him or her during marriage by any person to whom the spouse is or has been married; nor shall the spouse be permitted to disclose any such communication, unless the person who made it or that person's representative in interest, consents. The provision will however not apply to suits between married persons or proceedings in which one married person is prosecuted for an offence specified in section 161(1) of the Evidence Act (S. 164).

Competence and Compellability: General Considerations.

All persons are competent to testify unless the court considers that they are prevented from understanding the questions put to them or from giving rational answers to those question by reason of tender years, extreme old age, disease, whether of body or mind or any other cause of the same kind: *Elebanjo v. Tijani* [1986] 5 N.W.L.R. (Pt. 46) 952). There is a long line of authorities establishing that competence is not a matter of age but of understanding: *Okoye v. The State* (1972) 12 S.C. 115. There is nothing in the Evidence Act to the effect that a party in a civil suit is only competent to give evidence upon his own application. A plaintiff is a competent witness for the defence if the defendant wants to take the risk: *Elias v. Disu* [1962] 1 All N.L.R. 214. See also *Obolo v. Aluko* (1976) 3 S.C. 105. Section 159 of the Evidence Act makes the person charged only competent to give evidence for the defence. It does not prevent a person charged separately from an accused person or a person liable to be charged with a completely separate offence from giving evidence for the prosecution. The competency of such a witness to give evidence is covered by section 154(1) of the Act which says that all persons shall (subject to the exception contained in the subsection) be competent to testify: *Ereku v. The Queen* [1959] N.M.L.R. 77.

In *Obolo v. Aluko* (supra), in the High Court, the plaintiff issued a subpoena on the defendant to give evidence at the plaintiff's instance. The trial judge held that "a party could call his opponent as witness and provided he is willing he is a competent witness". He added however that "there is no law to compel the defendant to give evidence for the plaintiff". The Supreme Court held that the defendant is both competent and compellable to testify on behalf of the plaintiff. In *Ekerete v. Eke* (1926) 7 N.L.R. 73, a witness was present in court throughout the entire proceedings. The court held that he was still a competent witness and that the weight to be attached to his evidence was quite a different matter. See also *Ekong v. Okpala* (1972) 5 S.C. 177; *Falaju v. Amosu* [1983] 2 S.C. N.L.R. 209. In *Felix v. Onyinke* (1941) 7 W.A.C.A. 31, it was held that a person sentenced to death was a competent witness.

In *Inspector-General of Police v. Edosomwan* (1957) W.R.N.L.R. 161, where the accomplice has not been charged with any offence and not being before the court on any charge, was held a competent witness for the prosecution. *In R.v. Omisade and Others* [1964] 1 All N.L.R. 233; [1964] N.M.L.R. 67, the accused persons were charged with treasonable felony and conspiracy. Two of the witnesses in the case were facing separate charges for being in illegal possession of arms. The court was of the opinion that they were accomplice. On the issue of competence, it was held that an accomplice who is charged with a similar offence but who is not on trial in the case before the court is a competent witness for the prosecution. See also *Bandailey v. Commissioner of Police* (1946) 12 W.A.C.A. 64; *Yusuf v. N.T.C. Ltd.* (1977) 6 S.C. 39.

Children

In *Omosivbe v. Commissioner of Police* (1959) W.R.N.L.R. 209, the appellant had been convicted by the Senior Magistrate, Sapele, of stealing a sum of money contrary to section 390(4)(g) of the Criminal Code. The evidence against him was that of a girl under seven years of age that he had first lured her out of her father's house and then proceeded to steal the amount in question from a locked cupboard in the house. The accused appealed on a number of grounds. It was held that the reception of the evidence of a child of tender years is regulated by sections 154 and 182 of the Evidence Act, and that the statement in the trial Magistrate's judgment that after hearing the evidence of the child in the witness box he had come to the conclusion that she was mentally capable of understanding and giving an intelligent account of the case to his satisfaction could not satisfy the statutory condition precedent that before the reception of the child's evidence on oath she should have been examined by the Magistrate as to whether she was aware of the responsibility of speaking the truth and of the obligations of an oath. In *Inspector-General of Police v. Sunmonu* (1957) W.R.N.L.R. 23, the appellant was convicted of indecent assault contrary to section 360 of the Criminal Code. It was held that the evidence of a child is admissible notwithstanding the fact that the child does not understand the nature of an oath, but that before admitting such evidence, it is the duty of the Judge to satisfy himself that the child is sufficiently intelligent to appreciate what he was saying and understands the duty of speakng the truth. See also *Okoye v. The State* (1972) 12 S.C. 115; *The State v. obia* [1974] 4 E.C.S.L.R. 67; *R. v. Uche* (1935) 2 W.A.C.A. 287; *Orosunlemi v. The State* [1967] N.M.L.R. 278.

Accused Person: As Witness for the Prosecution

In *Umole and Others v. Inspector-General of Police* 1957 N.R.N.L.R. 8, a co-accused who pleaded guilty testified as a witness for the prosecution. He had earlier been convicted. Brown, C.J. said at page 10:

> *We have no doubt that at the time when he gave his evidence he was not on trial. When he pleaded guilty he was convicted on his own plea; there was no issue to be tried... (He) was not being tried jointly with the appellants, and he was therefore a competent witness for the prosecution.*

Quaere: Is he not an accomplice in the circumstances? See *R.v. Omisade and Others (supra).*

The Spouse of an Accused Person: As Witness for the Prosecution

It was held in *Ani v. The Queen* (1956-84) 10 S.C.N.D. 165, that under section 160 of the Evidence Act, the wife of a person charged with murder is not competent to give evidence for the prosecution if their marriage is a monogamous one. The onus is on the prosecution to prove the nature of the marriage between the accused husband and the wife. It is submitted that the restriction of the immunity to only spouses of a monogamous marriage is out of tune with the practical realities of a society which predominantly practises polygamy.

In *R.v. Dogbe* (1947) 12 W.A.C.A. 184, the appellant was convicted of muder. The wife gave evidence for the prosecution. There was nothing to show if she were his wife by christain marriage or native custom. Her first name was Emilia, and she was sworn on the Bible. It was held that the natural presumption must be in favour of the appellant that the wife was not a competent witness without the consent of the appellant (which was not sought for or given) and was not in any event compellable. It is submitted that the mere fact that a person answers a christain name and swears on the bible does not make that person invariably a christain. It is an obvious fact that Nigerians, particularly in the days of the case, were very much fond of answering English or christain names. Similarly, it is a matter of experience that a number of persons swear on the bible in court. Some of them do so because of the societal shame to announce themselves as pagans in a crowded court of law. This writer happens to know this. See also *The Queen v. Adesina* (1958) 3 F.S.C. 25, where the Federal Supereme Court arrived at a similar decision. See further *R.v. Ajiyola* (1943) 9 W.A.C.A. 22.

The Parties to a Civil Suit and their Spouses

In *Elias v. Disu and Others* [1962] 1 All N.L.R. 214, the plaintffs brought an action against the defendants to set aside the sale and conveyance of a piece of their family land by the first two defendants to the defendant/appellant. When the defence opened its case, counsel for the first defendant (not the defendant/appellant) applied to call the plaintiff who had given no evidence, as a witness for the defence. No objection was raised by counsel for the plaintiff. The trial Judge ruled that the plaintiff was not a competent witness for the defence and rested his ruling on the absence of any precedent for such a course and on the fact that no subpoena had been issued. It was held that in a civil action, a party is competent to give evidence not only upon his own application, but also upon that of his opponent; and the fact that no subpoena had been issued is immaterial to the question of competency. Brett, F.J. said at page 217:

> *There is nothing in this to indicate that a party in a civil suit is only competent to give evidence upon his own application as is the case under section 159, proviso (a) of the Evidence Ordinance, with a person charged with an offence, and although it is rare for counsel to take the risk of calling an opposing party, I have no doubt that the Judge was wrong in ruling that the plaintiff was not a competent witness for the defence. The fact that no subpoena had been issued was immaterial on the question of competence".*

Counsel: As Witness for the Client

In *Elabanjo v. Tijani* [1986] 5 N.W.L.R. (Pt. 46) 952, the Supreme Court said: Counsel is a competent witness in the case he is conductng on behalf of his client, and can give evidence in that case. Counsel's evidence in a case is admissible in law, whether he continues as counsel after giving such evidence or withdraws as counsel before giving such evidence. It is however desirable to withdraw as counsel before appearing as a witness. The practice requiring counsel to withdraw as counsel before appearing as a witness in the case is a rule of practice designed to ensure a proper administration of justice. There is no irregularity in counsel not observing the rule of practice. In the final analysis, the question whether counsel should withdraw from conducting the case of his client after giving evidence will depend upon the nature of the case of the client and the interest of justice that will be served by such a withdrawal. Where the interest of his client will be adversely affected by his withdrawal, it will not offend against any rules of practice if he continued. If counsel is a competent witness it will be wrong to expunge his evidence from the record as done by the Court of Appeal in this cases.

In *Gachi v. The State* [1965] N.M.L.R. 333, defending counsel gave evidence in support of an alibi on behalf of Agbuku Angula who was acquitted. It was held that although counsel is a competent witness in law, it is highly undesirable that he should give evidence in a case in which he is appearing professionally. If his evidence is thought necessary he should decline to appear as counsel. In *Idowu v. Adekoya* (1960) W.N.L.R. 210, during the trial counsel for the respondent who acted for him throughout the trial gave material evidence on his behalf. Judgment was given for the respondent. Quashie-Idum, C.J. said at page 211:

> *I think case this amply illustrates the importance of adhering to the practice of not allowing counsel to appear both as counsel and as a witness in the same case. It is my view that the procedure adopted in this case is not only contrary to the practice of the courts but it is also an irregularity which has rendered the trial unsatisfactory in that a more competent witness than plaintiff's counsel was not called to give evidence on a very important issue in the case".*

See also *Horn v. Rickard* 1963 N.N.L.R. 67; *Obadara and Others v. The President of Ibadan West District Council Grade 'A' Customary Court* [1965] N.M.L.R. 39; *Administrator-General and Public Trustees v. Ikemefuna and Another* [1974] 4 E.C.S.L.R. 78; *Aladeusi v. Alhaji Dangana* 1975 N.N.L.R. 190; *Akinola v. Solanke* [1985] H.C.N.L.R. 876; *Ambakederemo v. Rivers State*

Utilities Board, Suit No. PHC/370/84 delivered on 16/9/86 (Unreported); *Ceraekie and Another v. Okoye and Another* [1973] 3 E.C.S.L.R. 155.

The rule does not apply to police prosecutors who also took part in the investigation of the case. See *Inspector-General of Police v. Oyiogu and Others* [1961] W.N.L.R. 248; *R.v. Nwachukwu and Another* 1960 L.L.R. 61

Weight of Evidence

In *Nwigboke and Others v. The Queen* (1959) 4 F.S.C. 101, the Federal Supreme Court held that while the practice, introduced by the police, of taking an accused, who had made a confessional statement, before a senior police officer or an administrative officer, in order that his confession may be read over to him, is a wise one, confessional statements, not so treated should not necessarily be viewed with suspicion. Mbanefo, F.J. said at page 103:

> *Where the practice is followed it may add to the weight to be attached to the statement, but failure to observe it does not in our view reduce the weight which normally attaches to any statement proved to have been made voluntrarily.*

In *Agwu and Others v. The State* [1965] N.M.L.R. 18, Onyeama, J. said at page 20:

> *If it appears that a witness had formerly said or written the contrary of what he later swore in evidence (unless the reason of his having done so was satisfactorily accounted for) his evidence should not have much weight with a jury.*

Chapter 20

OFFICIAL AND PRIVILEGED COMMUNICATIONS

Sections 165 to 176 of the Evidence Act.

No judge and, except upon the special order of the High Court of the State, no Magistrate or district judge (in the case of the Northern States) can be compelled to answer any questions as to his own conduct in court as such judge, magistrate or district judge, or as to anything which came to his knowledge in court. However, he may be examined as to other matters, which occurred in his presence whilst he was so acting (S.165). Similarly, no magistrate, police officer or officer employed in or about the business of any branch of the public revenue can be compelled to say how he got information as to the commission of any offence (S. 166).

Subject to any directions of the Minister in any particular case or of the Governor where the records are in the custody of a state, no one shall be permitted to produce any unpublished official records relating to affairs of state, or to give any evidence derived there from, except with the permission of the officer at the head of the department concerned, who shall give or withhold such permission as he thinks fit (S. 167). Similarly, no public officer can be compelled to disclose communications made to him in official confidence, when he considers that the public interests would suffer by the disclosure (S. 168).

A juror may not give evidence as to what passed between the jurymen in the discharge of their duties, as to matters taking place in open court (S. 169). No Legal practitioner shall at any time be permitted, unless with his client's express consent, to disclose any communication made to him in the course and for the purpose of his employment as such legal practitioner by or on behalf of his client, or to state the contents, conditions of any document with which he has become acquainted in the course and for the purpose of his professional employment, or to disclose any advice given by him to his client in the course and for the purpose of such employment. However, the privilege does not extend to (a) any such communication made in furtherance of any illegal purpose; and (b) any fact relating to the commission of any crime or fraud. The privilege continues after the employment (S. 170). The provision of section 170 applies equally to interpreters, and the clerks and agents of legal practitioners (S. 171).

If any party to a suit gives evidence at his own instance or otherwise, he will not be deemed to have consented thereby to such disclosure as is mentioned in section 169. If any party to a suit or proceedings calls any such legal practitioner as a witness, he will be deemed to have consented to such disclosure only if he questions such legal practitioner on matters, which, but for such question, he would not be at liberty to disclose (S. 172). In the same vein, no one can be compelled to disclose to the court any confidential communication which has taken place between him and a legal practitioner consulted by him, unless he offers himself as a witness, in which case he may be compelled to disclose any such communciations as may appear to the court necessary to be known in order to explain any evidence which he has given, but no others (S. 173).

No witness who is not a party to a suit can be compelled to produce title - deeds to any property or any document in virtue of which he holds any property as pledgee, mortgagee, or any document the production of which might tend to incriminate him, unless he has agreed in writing to produce them with the person seeking the production of such deeds or some person through whom he claims (S. 174).

Similarly, no one can be compelled to produce documents in his possession which any other person would be entitled to refuse to produce if they were in his possession, unless such last mentioned person consents to their production (S. 175).

By section 176, no one is bound to answer any question if the answer would, in the opinion of the court, have a tendency to expose the witness, or the spouse of the witness to any criminal charge, penalty or forefeiture which the judge regards as reasonably likely to be preferred or sued for. However,

(a) A person charged with an offence, and being a witness in pursuance of section 160 of the Act is bound to answer questions in cross-examination even when such questions tend to incriminate him.

(b) No one is excused from answering any question only because the answer may establish or tend to establish that he owes a debt or is otherwise liable to any civil suit at the instance of the state or any other persons.

(c) Nothing in section 175 can excuse a witness at any inquiry by direction of the Attorney-General of the Federation or the Attonery-General of a State, under part XLIX of the Criminal Procedure Act from answering any question required to be answered under the provisions of section 458 of that Act. See also s. 220 of the Evidence Act.

Affairs of State

In *Moronu v. Benson and Others* [1966] N.M.L.R. 166, the learned trial Judge ruled that, certain documents relating to an election should not be produced in court by virtue of section 167. Adedipe, J. drew a distinction between sections 167 and 219: "It seems to me that section 167 precludes the court from compelling a public officer to disclose communications made to him in his official confidence when he considers that the public would suffer if such communications were disclosed. This, of course, is quite different from the privilege which a Minister, the Governor of a Region or any person nominated by him may claim in respect of certain documents by virtue of section 219 of the Evidence Act. While the distinction made by the learned trial judge is valid, one is in some confusion whether the documents in the case were excluded under section 167 or 219. If they were excluded under section 167 then the court had the jurisdiction to inspect them but it had no jurisdiction to do so if they were excluded under section 219. It would appear from the judgment that the documents were excluded under section 167 in which case the court ought to have insisted on an inspection before determining on their exclusion. The court also failed to consider the constitutional provision.

In *Maja (Jnr) and Sons Ltd. v. United Africa of Nigeria Ltd.* [1971] N.M.L.R. 157, a writ of subpoena was issued at the instance of the plaintiff compelling the secretary to the Mid-Western State Government to personally attend the court to testify for the plaintiff. State privilege was sought on the ground that "the applicant could not give evidence relating to the subject matter of this suit without causing injury to the Federal Military Government or to the interest of the Mid-Western State". The applicant, the Secretary to the Military Government of the Mid-Western State relied on sections 166, 167 and 219. The court dismissed the application on two grounds. First, the applicant had no *locus standi* to claim privilege on behalf of the Federal Military Government. Second, the learned trial judge was of the opinion that the affidavit evidence before him did not show that the public interest of the Mid-Western State would be affected by the evidence of the applicant. Odesanya, J., after examining the constitutional position, rightly said: "I do not think that it is now a correct view of the law that an affidavit or certificate referred to in the Evidence Act could always automatically take the matter out of the jurisdiction of the court. The present constitutional takes precedence over the Evidence Act".

On the interpretation of section 219, a fairly related section to sections 166 and 167, see *The Queen v. The Administrator, Western Region, Ex parte Bamgbedu* 1962 N.R.N.L.R. 344; *African Press Ltd and Another v. Attorney-General of Western Nigeria* [1965] 1 All N.L.R. 12; *Johnson v. Sarkis* [1969] 2 All N.L.R. 273; and *Apampa and Another v. Balogun,* Suit No. 1/211/65 of 20/10/70 Unreported.

In *Apampa, Aguda, J.* (as he then was) in his usual characteristic forthrightness, did not mince words. He said:

> *In my view, a litigant cannot be said to have had a fair hearing if part of the evidence he requires to establish his case is shut out and he is prevented from leading it. A litigant can only be prevented from leading some evidence (or which amount to the same thing, producing certain documents) only if the leading of such evidence or the production of such documents will be against public interst and such public interest is found by the court to outweigh the public interest in the fair hearing of his case. And in my view the final determination of this issue must be left to the courts which have been created to administer justice between litigants and which both by their very nature and by the training of their personnel are most suitable to perform that function.*

Apampa reminds us of what the United States Supreme Court said in *Dennis v. United States*, 384 U.S. 855:

> *It is especially important that the jury should have the assurance that the doors that may lead to truth have been unlocked. In our adversary system of determining guilt or innocence, it is rarely justifiable for the prosecution to have exclusive access to a storehouse of relevant facts. Exceptions to this are justifiable only by the clearest and most compelling considerations.*

In these days of strong holds of partisan politics with their inbuilt and characterstic idiosyncrasies of victimization, nepotism, favouritism and the like, the court should not only be the final arbiter on claim to privilege in respect of state affairs, but must be firm and fearless in deciding in appropriate cases that the Authority's claim to privilege is outside the requirements of the law. In other words, where the withholding of a document will not work against the public interest, then the court must hold against its non-production.

Legal Practitioners

In *Horn v. Rickard* (supra) Holden J. said: "Every client is entitled to feel safe when making disclosures to his solicitor or counsel, and there are cases establishing firmly that counsel cannot be called to give any evidence which would infringe the client's privilege of secrecy".

Unfortunately, the same privilege does not extend to the relationship between a doctor and his patient. This is certainly an area where the same privilege should be extended. It is submitted that the Act should be amended to reflect the same position as in the case of a legal practitioner and his client in the context of the medical profession. Certainly, it will be most embarrassing in certain instances for a doctor to make public an ailment of his patient.

Statement Without Prejudice

In S.C.O.A. v. Olusoga and Another (1936) 13 N.L.R. 104, the second defendant signed document undertaking to guarantee the fidelity of the first defendant to the plaintiff in whose employment the first defendant was. Although he had duly completed and delivered the document, the second defendant had written at the head of it the words "Without Prejudice". On being sued under the document the second defendant pleaded that the document could not be received in evidence against him because of the words "Without Predudice". It was held that the document in question was a complete and binding contract; that the phrase "Without Prejudice", could have no meaning at all when attached to such a contract; that the phrase must therefore be ignored and that the document was admissible in evidence.

Chapter 21

CORROBORATION

Sections 177 to 179 of the Evidence Act.

No plaintiff in any action for breach of promise of marriage can recover a verdict, unless the testimony is corroborated by some other material evidence in support of such promise. The fact that the defendant did not answer letters affirming that he had promised to marry the plaintiff is not corroboration (S. 177). An accomplice is a competent witness against an accused person, and a conviction is not illegal merely because it proceeds upon the uncorroborated testimony of any accomplice. However, the trial Judge should warn himself that it is unsafe to convict any person upon uncorroborated evidence. Where accused persons are tried jointly and any of them gives evidence on his own behalf which incriminates a co-accused the accused who gives such evidence shall not be considered to be an accomplice (S. 178).

Except as provided in section 179, no particular number of witnesses will be required for the proof of any fact (S. 179(1)).

Treason and Treasonable Offences

No person charged with treason or with any of the felonies mentioned in sections 40, 41 and 42 of the Criminal Code can be convicted, except on his own plea of guilty or on the evidence in open court of two witnesses at least to one overt act of the kind of treason or felony alleged, or the evidence of one witness to one overt act and one other witness to another overt act of the same kind of treason or felony. This provision does not apply to cases in which the overt act of treason alleged in the killing of the sovereign, or a direct attempt to endanger the life or injure the person of the sovereign (S. 179(2)).

Evidence on charge of perjury

A person cannot be convicted of committing perjury or of counselling or procuring the commission of perjury, upon the uncorroborated testimony of one witness, contradicting the oath on which perjury is assigned, unless circumstances are proved which corroborate such witness (S. 179(3)).

Exceeding speed limit

A person charged under the Road Traffic Act with driving at a speed greater than the allowed maximum shall not be convicted solely on the evidence of one witness that in his opinion he was driving at such speed (S. 179)(4)).

Sedition and Sexual Offences.

A person cannot be convicted of the offences mentioned in paragraph (b) of subsection (1) of section 51, sections 218, 211, 223 or 224 of the Criminal Code or section 275, paragraph (e) of subsection (1) section 282 of the Penal Code, upon the uncorroborated testimony of one witness (S. 179(5)). *Note*: The subsection does not provide for the Penal Code provisions.

Nature

In most cases where the question of corroboration arises the question is 'Is there independent testimony which affects the accused by tending to connect him with the crime?' But it is also essential, that there should be some evidence, direct or circumstantial which confirms the evidence given by the accomplice that the crime has been committed... It is of course not necessary that there should be confirmation by independent evidence of everything the accomplice says, but only some independent evidence connecting the accused with the crime: *R. v. Saraki and Others* (1941) 1 W.A.C.A. 10. See also *Saraki v. R.* [1964] N.M.L.R. 28. In considering whether evidence is corroborative, one must take it as a whole; it will not do to say - take this item for instance, it is not corroborated; take this other item, and so forth; one must take all the little items together and consider whether they all add up to corroborate as a whole: *R. v. Omisade and Others* [1964] N.M.L.R. 67 at 77. Corroborative evidence must connect the accused person with the alleged offence: *In Re Ekpata* (1956-84) 10 S.C. N.D. 58; *Re Okpenyi* (1956-84) 10 S.C.N.D. 58; *The Queen v. Ekpata* (1957) 2 R.S.C. 1; *Egede v. The State* (1956-84) 10 S.C.N.D. 61.

Corroborative evidence which shows or tends to show that the story of the accomplice that the accused committed the crime is true, not merely that the crime has been committed, but that it was committed by the accused. The corroboration need not be direct evidence that accused committed the offence; it is sufficient if it is merely circumstantial evidence of his connection with it: *Omisade and Others v. The Queen* [1964] 1 All N.L.R. 236. What amounts to corroboration depends entirely on the circumstances of any case, and the question of corroboration can be sufficiently established where the evidence show element of suspicion against the defender or where the statement made by the defender in rebuttal is proved to be false: *The Republic v. Nwachukwu* [1964] 2 All N.L.R. 184.

Corroboration is evidence which may be direct or circumstantial but in any case it is the duty of the court to ascertain that whatever is being used or regarded as corroboration is independent of the evidence to be corroborated and is such as supports the story of the main evidence to the effect that it renders that story more probable or true and that it implicates the accused person in some material particular: *Okabichi v. The State* (1975) 3 S.C. 135. See also *R. v. Modam* (1938) 4 W.A.C.A. 39. In deciding the issue of the quantum of independent evidence which is required to corroborate the evidence of an accomplice, the court should take all the little items of evidence together and consider whether they all add up to corroboration as a whole: *Elerewe v. The State* (1956-84) 10 S.C.N.D. 66. Corroborative evidence renders more probable the truth of a witness's testimony or a material point: *Eleke v. Olokunboro* (1978) 1 N.C.A.R. 496.

In *Saraki v. The Queen* [1964] N.M.L.R. 28, it was held that the appellant was proved by evidence to have been the person in charge of the trial of which the prosecutrix had written down the number, affords corroboration of her evidence identifying him as one of the men who raped her and the court was not prepared to hold that the finding of the jury was unjustified by the evidence. In *Doka and Others v. The State* [1968] N.M.L.R. 487, it was held that the evidence of the 1st, 2nd and 3rd prosecution witnesses which only went to show that the appellants were on the train, a point they did not deny, could not amount to corroboration of the actual act of bringandage, which was the point in dispute. In *R. v. Falayi* (1949) 12 W.A.C.A. 492, the conduct of the appellant, when on statement by a co-accused deeply implicating him in a revolting crime was read to him, was such as in the opinion of the trial Judge in the opinion of the Court of Appeal, justified, such conduct being treated as corroboration of the evidence of accomplices.

In R. *v. Nweze and Others* (1957) 2 F.S.C. 27, it was held that evidence of mere association of the accused person with some of the other accused persons was not enough corroboration of the offence of robbery. Similarly, in R.*v. Griliopoulos and Others* (1953) 20 N.L.R. 114, it was held that evidence of instances of receiving stolen property; cannot corroborate the act of receiving stolen property; that must he proved *aliuned.* In other words where the crown in a charge of receiving relies mainly on an accomplice or other witness needing corroboration, evidence of other instances of receiving by the accused do not furnish corroboration of the offence charged. But in *Efobi and Another v. Commissioner of Police* 1963 N.N.L.R. 1. the statement of accused persons charged with offering bribe was tape recorded. As a matter of fact, the interview at which the bribe was offered was recorded in the tape which was hidden. It was held that the tape-recording was admissible evidence.

See also R.*v. Kufi* (1960) W.N.L.R. 1; *Inspector-General of Police v. Ogwu 1960* L.L.R. 43; *Idiemo v. Inspector-General of Police* (1959) W.R.N.L.R. 68; *Dabiri v. Inspector-General of Police* 1960 L.L.R. 1; *Okpanefe v. The State* [1969] 1 All N.L.R. 420; *Oke v. The Republic* [1967] N.M.L.R. 69; *Orosunlemi v. The State* [1967] N.M.L.R. 278; *Obot v.* R. (1953) 14 W.A.C.A. 352.

Evidence of Accomplice

In *Nweke v. the Queen* (1955) 15 W.A.C.A. 29, the Court held the view that there is no formal definition of the term 'accomplice' and that the courts are forced to deduce a meaning for the word from the facts and circumstances of each particular case. See also *Wanchi v. The State* (1976) 9-10 S.C. 107; *Akinlenubola v. Police* (1976) 6 S.C. 205. In R. *v. Okoye and Another* (1950) 19 N.L.R. 103 Hallinan, J. said that an accomplice is a person who might on the evidence be convicted of the offence with which the accused person is charged. In *Idahosa and others v.* R. [1965] N.M.L.R. 85, the court adopted the definition in Halsbury's Laws of England as follows: "Persons are accomplice who are *participes criminis* in respect of the actual crime charged whether as principals or accessories before or after the fact in the case of felonies or misdemeanours".

Where two or more persons are accused of a criminal offence and the only proof against them is the evidence of an accomplice, the corroborating evidence against each accused should be carefully distinguished. A conviction is not illegal because it proceeds upon the uncorroborated testimony of an accomplice. If the only proof against an accused is the evidence of an accomplice, uncorroborated in any material particular implicating the accused, the trial Judge shall, in a case tried without a jury, direct himself that it is unsafe to convict any person upon such evidence. Any person who conceals in the commission of the offence, or helps to cover up the offence, is an accomplice and not a victim. In *Queen v. Ezedu* (1962) 1 All N.L.R. 133, it was held that on a charge of obtaining a bribe, a person who voluntarily accedes to a request for money in order to obtain a preference not otherwise open to him is an active participant in the offence, an accomplice, and not a victim. It was further held that the question whether a person is not an accomplice is one of fact to be decided in the circumstances of each case upon the evidence: *Queen v. Ezekpe and Another* (1962) 1 All N.L.R. 637.

Section 177(1) of the Evidence Act imposes a statutory duty on the trial Judge to warn the jury (or himself as the jury) that it is unsafe to convict solely on the uncorroborated evidence of an accomplice. Section 177(2) exempts the Judge from that duty in the case of a defendant who testifying on his behalf in a joint trial incriminates a co-defendant, and does no more, and it is open to the Judge, and may be highly desirable upon the facts of the case, to advise the jury or himself in regard to his evidence as may be fit. Corroboration of the evidence of an accomplice must be independent testimony which affects the accused by connecting or tending to connect him with the offence charged; consequently corroboration must be evidence which implicates an accused person and which confirms in some material particular not only that the crime has been committed but also that the accused person committed it: *Ohuka and Others v. The State* (No. 2) (1988) 4 N.W.L.R. (pt. 86) 36. In a charge of dishonestly using a forged license, an accomplice is a *participes criminis* to the procurement or using of the forged license knowing it to be forged. Evidence of such an accomplice must be corroborated: *Zonkwa v. Commissioner of Police* (1968) N.M.L.R. 11. See further *Queen v. Ezechi* (1962) 1 All N.L.R. 113; *Dada v. The State* 1977 N.N.L.R. 159; *Sigbehim and Others v. The Queen* F.S.C. 219/63.

In *Obi and Others v. Inspector-General of Police* (1959-60) W.N.L.R. 68, the appellant, a police corporal had been convicted and sentenced by a Chief Magistrate for demanding money with menace and with intent to steal contrary to section 406 of the Criminal Code. The prosecution's case was that he had threatened to take to Warri a number of persons who had without authority investigated, a case of murder. When some of the prosecution witnesses later approached him on the matter he demanded and received some money. It was held the witnesses were accomplices.

On accomplice, see further *R. v. Ladipe* (1938) 4 W.A.C.A. 119; *R. v. Dare* (1939) 5 W.A.C.A. 122; *Bassey v. Commissioner of Police* 4 E.R.L.R. 62; *Enahoro v. The Queen* (1965) 1 All N.L.R. 125; *Nwodije v. The Queen* (1956-84) 10 S.C.N.D. 65; *R.v. Modam and Others* (1938) 4 W.A.C.A. 39; *Bello v. The State* (1967) N.M.L.R. 1; *Wahosa v. The Queen* (1965) N.M.L.R. 85; *Ishola v. The State* (1978) 9 S.C. 81; *Uwah v. The State* (1956-84) 10 S.C.N.D. 193; *Ajala v. The State* (1979) 10 C.A. 115; *Ashimiyu and Others v. The State* (1980O C.A. 1; *Badmos v. Police* (1948) 12 W.A.C.A. 361; *R. v. Bakum* (1941) 7 W.A.C.A. 45.

A person who has Mere Knowledge that an offence was to be Committed

In *R. v. Okoye and Another* (supra) the first accused informed a corporal that he and others planned to break into an office strong-room and offered to give a share of the booty if he arranged for the police not to disturb them. Next day the corporal and a sergeant met the two accused persons and another man and said to them they would so arrange, and they learned that the breaking-in would be that night. They later informed a senior officer and the two accused persons were caught red-handed. It was argued that the police witnesses were accomplices as they failed to carry out their duty under section 53 of the Criminal Procedure Ordinance. Hallinan, J. said at page 103; "Putting this argument at its highest, the police could only be convicted of perversely and without lawful excuse omitting to perform a statutory duty contrary to section 198 of the Criminal Code; they could not be convicted of aiding and abetting, counselling or procuring the offence charged in the present information. They are therefore not accomplices".

Agent Provocateur
The Queen v. David and Others
(1960) W.N.L.R. 170

The accused persons arranged to sell a boy to a native doctor. The native doctor was approached to arrange for the sale of the boy. The native doctor agreed. Meanwhile the native doctor had gone to make a report to the police and two officers were detailed to make investigation. One of the police officers introduced himself as a prospective buyer and the other as the cousin of the native doctor. The boy was brought and there was bargain. They agreed for £300. The accused persons were later arrested.

HELD:

> The police officers and the native doctor, the latter acting under police instructions, assumed the role of *agents provocateur* and incited the accused to further their alleged conspiracy of attempting to carry it to completion. The evidence of the witnesses required corroboraton.

In *R. v. Fanugbo*, Case No. AB/7C 63, (Unreported) where the facts were generally similar, Beckley, J. held that where an accused person has manifested a clear intention to commit an offence and the police facilitate the commission of the office by the accused in order that the accused may be caught, the police officers and their aids cannot, and should not, be regarded as *agents provocateurs*, whose evidence requires corroboration. It is submitted that the decision is sound. That is how it should be. The police in the circumstances should not be regarded as *agents provocateurs.* After all the accused person has, by sufficient overt act, manifested his intention to commit the offence.

A person Taking Part in Negotiations Leading to the Commission of an Offence

In *Ereku v.* R. (1959) W.R.N.L.R. 77, it was held that a person who plays the role of an intermediary in the asking and procurement of bribe by a police officer is an accomplice. He is an accomplice both of the giver and the receiver; and as an accomplice, his evidence must be corroborated. See also *Obi v. Inspector-General of Police supra; Ogbu v.* R. 1959 N.R.N.L.R. at 25.

Tainted Witness

It was in the case of *Omisade and Others v. The Queen* (supra) that Mbanefo, Ag J.S.C. (as he then was) developed the concept of tainted witness. The learned Justice said that although Overt Act 4 was proved and it made no difference to the conviction on count 1, in regard to Overt Act 1, the said witness should be regarded as an accomplice or at least a tainted witness in light of section 40 of the Criminal Code on the seriousness of concealment of treason, on whose evidence it would be unsafe to act without corroboration, but he was not corroborated in regard to Overt Act 1. The person the learned Justice described as a tainted witness was one who attended meetings with the conspirators on the treason plan and who swore not to tell the police.

In *Ishola v. The State* (1979) 9-10 S.C. 81, it was held that a tainted witness is one who is either an accomplice or by the evidence he gives may and could be regarded as having some purpose of his own to serve. But in *Mailayi v. The State* [1968] 1 All N.L.R. 116, the court warned that the expression "tainted" is very lose and if its application is not kept within proper bounds a great deal of confusion will be unleashed into an area of evidence which even now is fraught with difficulties.

In *Onuoha v. The State* [1987] 4 N.W.L.R. (Pt. 65) 331, it was held that a tainted witness is a person who may not be strictly an accomplice but a witness with some purpose of his own to serve. The evidence of such a witness ought to be regarded with considerable caution and the trial court should be wary in reaching a verdict of guilt on the uncorroborated evidence of such a witness. The court further held that the evidence of P.W. 10 and P.W. 11 cannot be regarded as evidence of accomplices or tainted witnesses because as lesser officers, they were mere tools in the hands of the accused. It was held in *Ishola v. The State* (1978) 2 L.R.N. 111, that the mere failure of a witness to report to the police a person who designs to commit an offence does not *ipso facto* make him unworthy of credit should he testify at a subsequent trial of the offender, nor does it make him an accomplice were he to testify on behalf of the prosecution in such trial. Further, the term 'tainted witness' should be confined to a person who is either an accomplice by the evidence he gives (either as witness for the prosecution or defence)or may and could be regarded as having some purpose of his own to serve. See also *Azumah and Kehedo v. R.* (1950) 13 W.A.C.A. 87; *Idahosa v. R.* (1965) N.M.L.R. 85; *Sokoto v. The*

State [1968] 1 All N.L.R. 116; *Okosi and Another v. The State* [1989] 1 N.W.L.R. (Pt. 100) 642.

A Person who Witnesses the Commission of an Offence

In *The Queen v. Ukut and Others* (1960) 5 F.S.C. 183, the evidence against the appellants was that of two witnesses, who, hearing shouts in the night, went to the scene and saw the three appellants killing the deceased. The Judge accepted their evidence, and declined to treat them as accomplice. Unsworth, F.J. said at page 185: "It is sufficient for us to say that there is abundant authority for the proposition that a special warning is not required in respect of the evidence of persons who witness a crime in circumstances such as those in the present case. In *Onyikoro v. The Queen* 1959 N.R.N.L.R. 103, the appellants were convicted of the murder of an alleged thief for failing to pay money as earlier agreed by members of a society. The case of the prosecution rested solely on the evidence of a witness who was also a member of the society. He did not participate in the killing but watched the event from outside the house. The next day, the witness was made to pay £5 for his failure to participate in the killing. It was held that the witness not being an accomplice, his evidence needed no corroboration.

Victim of the Offence

In *R. v. Dare* (1939) 5 W.A.C.A. 122, one Dada, in consideration of a loan of some amount was of money advanced by accused, handed over to the accused his son, Musa to remain with him as a pawn until the amount was repaid. It was held that the boy, Musa could not be an accomplice in a crime of which he was a victim but did not commit, and for whose protection the law was enacted. The learned trial Judge was correct in his decision that he was not an accomplice.

In *Okeke v. Commissioner of Police* (1946) 12 W.A.C.A. 363, it was held that a person who pays money in response to an unlawful demand is not an accomplice in the demand. "It is quite untenable in argument that those who met the monetary demand of the appellant were accomplices to the demand. Nor, in meeting the demand, could they be regarded otherwise than as victims of the appellant's rapacity"- Per Abbott, J. at page 365. In *R. v. Pategi and Others* 1957 N.R.N.L.R. 47, persons who were threatened and forced to pay money to an accused person who was a forest guard for alleged offences against the forestry laws, were held not to be accomplices but victims. See also *Osidola v. Commissioner of Police* 1959 N.R.N.L.R. 42. In *Nweke v. The Queen* (1955) 15 W.A.C.A. 29, the appellant, a police sergeant, corruptly asked a sum of money from the complainant on the understanding that if the money was paid he would refrain from arresting the complainant for the offence of unlawful possession of illicit gin. It was held that the complainant was a victim and not a participant in the crime.

Evidence of Co-accused

Evidence of a co-accused giving evidence in his own behalf which inculpates another is not to be regarded as that of an accomplice: *Idahosa and Others v. The Queen* [1965] N.M.L.R. 85. The provisions of section 177(2) of the Evidence Act will not operate to avoid the necessity of corroboration of the evidence of self confessed accomplice. Since there was no independent evidence of someone else against the 5th appellant, the evidence against him being only that of the 1st and 3rd appellants, and since the learned trial Judge did not seem to have considered this aspect of the case the conviction of the 5th appellant on counts 5, 6 and 7 must be quashed and the sentences passed thereon set aside: *Oyediran and Others v. The Republic* [1967] N.M.L.R. 122.

Section 177(2) of the Evidence Act provides that a co-accused's evidence does not require corroboration. However, section 177(2) should be read in conjunction with section 177(1) and where a court has before it the uncorroborated evidence of a co-accused it must exercise caution before convicting solely on such evidence: *Nwachukwu v. Commissioner of Police* (1978) 2 L.R.N. 108. See also *Ukut v. The State* [1966] N.M.L.R. 18; *Oriaku and Another v. Commissioner of Police* (1952) 20 N.L.R. 74; *Yinusa and Another v. The State* (1978) 1 N.C.A.R. 109; *Giwa v. Commissioner of Police* (1980) (2) N.C.R. 308; *R. v. Onuegbe* (1957) 2 F.S.C. 10

In the absence of any other evidence, a trial court should exercise great caution before accepting the evidence of a co-accused. It would need much more than the evidence of a co-accused who may have his own purpose to serve, to infer that the appellant actually took part in the offence: *Adeyeye and Others v. The State* [1968] N.M.L.R. 48. An accused person who gives evidence which incriminates a co-accused is not an accomplice of the co-accused, and though such evidence should be suspiciously regarded and cautiously accepted, it does not require corroboration: *Badmos v. Commissioner of Police* (1946) 12 W.A.C.A. 361; See also Re: Opa (1956-84) 10 S.C.N.D. 66.

In *Inspector-General of Police v. Akinbayode* (1958) W.R.N.L.R. 161, the appellant and another person were jointly charged with stealing, forgery and uttering a forged document. The other accused person gave evidence in his defence which incriminated the appellant. He was convicted on the uncorroborated evidence of that accused. It was held that the evidence of the accused needed corroboration.

Evidence of Children

A trial Judge should satisfy himself that a witness of tender age understands the nature of an oath before he is sworn: *Jaloghe v. The Queen* (1956-84) 10 S.C.N.D. 180; *R.v. Kufi* (1960) W.N.L.R. 1. See also *Ochogwu v. The State* (1956-84) 10 S.C.N.D. 184. The sworn evidence of a child need not as a matter of law be corroborated, but it is a desirable practice to warn the jury not that they must find corroboration, but that there is a risk in acting on the uncorroborated evidence of young boys and girls. The requirement to warn the jury of the risk in acting on the uncorroborated but sworn evidence of a child under fourteen years is observed; it does not follow that the Appeal Court must allow the appeal. It must depend upon all the circumstances of any particular case when in fact, if a Judge does not warn a jury or if sitting alone, does not warn himself of the risk involved in relying solely on the sworn evidence of a child under fourteen years, the court can be satisfied that there has been a miscarriage of justice: *Akpan v. The State* (1967) N.M.L.R. 187. See also *The Queen v. Ekelagu* (1960) 5 F.S.C. 217; *Arebamen v. The State* (1972) 4 S.C. 35; *Olaleye v. The State* [1970] 1 All N.L.R. 300.

In R. *v. Uche* (1935) 2 W.A.C.A. 287, the appellant was convicted on two counts of having defiled a girl of under eleven years, and sentenced to five years imprisonment on each count, such sentences to run concurrently. One of the grounds of appeal was that the trial Judge in his summing up, omitted to warn the jury as to the nature of the evidence of children of tender years. It was held that the misdirection of the jury led to the conviction of the accused since there was no proper warning as to the nature of the evidence of children of tender years. The appeal was upheld.

It is manifest that in order to ground a conviction the unsworn evidence of the complainant, must be corroborated. In every case of where gonorrhea occurs in both the accused and the victim the court must regard this as corroborating evidence implicating the accused. Great care must be taken to isolate individual cases for individual consideration and it is idle to contend that there cannot be cases in which the collateral circumstances can and do make the incidence of veneral infection of the victim a matter of corroboration. Such is the case where the court or the jury is satisfied that the victim was not previously infected and the age of the infection in her, like cause or effect, are reasonably only referrable to the act of the accused complained of: *Olayeye v. The State* [1970] 1 All NLR 300. See also *Akpan v. The State* [1967] N.M.L.R. 185. Unsworn evidence of a child must be corroborated before a conviction can be based on it: *Agiri v. The State* (1956-84) 10 S.C.N.D. 64. See also *Odisu v. Attorney-General* (West) (1956-84) 10 S.C.N.D. 64. Unsworn evidence of a child cannot be corroborated by Unsworn evidence of another child: *The Queen v. Moke* (1956-84) 10 S.C.N. D. 65.

In *The State v. Una* (1966-67) 10 E.N.L.R. 223, it was held that the evidence of the matter of the little girl afforded enough corroboration of the evidence of the little girl showing that she was defiled. The existence of a common condition namely the abnormal presence of pus mixed with spermatic fluid in the girl and the discharging of pus by the accused corroborated the little girl's evidence as to the identity of the accused as the person, who defiled her and was also a strong circumstantial evidence, that it was the accused and no other person, who defiled the girl.

In *Omosivbe v. Commissioner of Police* (1959) W.N.L.R. 209, the appellant had been convicted by a Senior Magistrate, Sapele of stealing a sum of money contrary to section 390(4) (g) of the Criminal Code, Cap 42. The evidence against him was that the girl under seven years of age said that he had lured her out of her father's house and then proceeded to steal the amount in question from a locked cupboard in the house. It was held that the evidence of a child under seven given on oath did not as a matter of law require corroboration although it was not the practice to convict on such uncorroborated evidence except after weighing it in the extreme care.

Treason and Treasonable Offences
Michael Adedapo Omisade and Others v. The Queen
[1964] 1 All N.L.R. 233

The case for the prosecution was that the Action Group having failed to obtain a majority at the Federal Election of December 1959, its leader, Chief Obafemi Awolowo, lost his faith in the ballot box, and proposed to the executive committee of his party in September, 1960, to set up a Tactical Committee whose names he would not announce and who would not submit reports but only recommend to the executive committee the course of action to be taken; and the proposal was accepted. One Dr. Onabamiro testified that he was invited to Awolowo's house, where he met Awolowo, one Ikoku and one Chief Enahoro; that Awolowo said they should capture power by revolution, and assigned duties to each of those present; and that Enahoro was to recruit 200 youths for military training abroad; he also testified that he did not carry out his assignment. He withdraw from the Tactical Committee. The accused persons were charged with treasonable felony and conspiracy. It was held that it is not necessary that a witness must be able to testify to an overt act in its entirety but that it is sufficient if a number of witnesses give evidence of "snippets' which add up to proof of an overt act. See also *Enahoro v. The Queen* [1965] N.M.L.R. 265 at 280. It was further held that an accomplice who is charged with a similar offence but who is not on trial in the case before the court is a competent witness for the prosecution.

Perjury
R.v. Salami Ogunubi
(1932) 11 N.L.R. 91

The accused was charged with perjury under section 119 of the Criminal Code. Only one witness gave evidence of falsity of the perjured statement alleged.

HELD:

By common law in England and Nigeria, corroboration was required as to the falsity of the perjured statement alleged. There was nothing in the terms of section 119 of the Criminal Code to make that rule of common law inapplicable in Nigeria.

Sexual Offences
Inspector-General of Police v. Suara Sunmonu (1957) W.R.N.L.R. 23

The appellant was convicted of indecent assault contrary to section 360 of the Criminal Code. On an appeal on the ground that the learned Magistrate convicted on the uncorroborated evidence of the prosecutrix story, it was held that it is not a rule of law that in sexual offences an accused person should not be convicted on the uncorroborated evidence of a prosecutrix but the proper direction is that it is not safe to convict on the uncorroborated evidence of the prosecutrix; that the jury may, after attention to the warning, nevertheless convict if they are satisfied of the truth of her evidence.

Although in cases of rape and sexual offences against women and girls, a court may convict on the uncorroborated evidence of the prosecution, yet it must warn itself that it is dangerous to do so. A confession properly proved in law needs no corroboration to found a conviction although in practice there is invariably some corroboration: The *State v Adegboye* [1971] 2 All N.L.R. 49. See also *The State v. Ogwudiegwe and Another* [1968] N.M.L.R. 117. By section 178(5) of the Evidence Act, the court cannot convict an accused on a charge or rape without corroboration, and in this regard an early report of the commission of the offence is not tantamount to corroboration: *Okpanefe v. The State* [1969] 1 All N.L.R. 420. On a charge of rape, a doctor's report that injury was consistent with a forceful entrance into the virginia does not amount to corroboration of the evidence of the victim that she was raped: *Alauwku v. The State* (1956-84) 10 S.C.N.D. 62. A trial Judge in a charge of rape should warn himself of the danger of acting on the evidence of the complainant that there was no consent in the absence of corroboration: *Buari v. Attorney-General* (1956-84) 10 S.C.N.D. 62. See also *Ibeakanma v. The Queen* (1956-84) 10 S.C.N.D. 63; *Alankwu v. the State* (1956-84) 10 S.C.N.D. 63; *Yari v. Zaria Native Authority* 1967 N.N.L.R. 85; *Jos Native Authority Police v. Gani* 1967 N.N.L.R. 107; *The State v. Buloo* (1970) 1 R.S.L.R. 35. An accused charged with defilement under section 156 of the Criminal Code of Western Nigeria cannot be convicted on the uncorroborated evidence of one witness: *Odusi v. Attorney-General* (West) (1956-84) 10 S.C.N.D. 64.

Matrimonial Causes

In *Sowande v. Sowande* 1960 L.L.R. 58, Dickson, J. said: "Of course, it is quite plain that a court will not necessarily refrain from pronouncing a decree simply because the evidence is uncorroborated". In *Oshinloye v. Oshinloye* 1960 L.L.R. 38, Dickson, J. said: "In the case of cruelty it is the practice of the court to require corroboration, and not a rule of law; and it has never been decided that the court is not entitled in a proper case where it is not in doubt where the truth lies, to act upon the uncorroborated testimony of the petitioner".

In *Ojo v. Ojo* [1969] 1 All N.L.R. 434, it was held that the evidence of a party alleging cruelty and or desertion must be corroborated but as a matter of practice. Similarly in *Etim v. Etim* [1968] N.M.L.R. 35, it was held that the requirement of corroboration of cruelty in a divorce case is merely a matter of practice and not of law.

On corroboration, see generally *Ndo v. The Queen* (1953) 14 W.A.C.A. 352; *Goe v. The Queen* (1953) 14 W.A.C.A. 277; *R.v. Ajani and Others* (1936) 3 W.A.C.A. 3; *R.v. Adebawole and Others* (1941) 7 W.A.C.A. 142; R.v. Lagos (1941) 7 W.A.C.A. 123; *R.v. Cole* (1942) 8 W.A.C.A. 121; *Boshali v. Allied Commercial Exporters Ltd.* [1961] All N.L.R. 917; *Kadawa v. Kano Native Authority* [1968] N.M.L.R. 318; *Salawu v. The State* [1971] N.M.L.R. 249; *Ukoh v. The State* [1971] N.M.L.R. 140 ; *R.v. Kassi and others* (1939) 5 W.A.C.A. 154; *The State v. Nwokoro* (1956-84) 10 S.C.N.D. 58; *Ugwu v. the Queen* (1956-84) 10 S.C.N.D. 59; *Ofin v. The Queen* (1956-84) 10 S.C.N.D. 61; *Nwodije v. The Queen* (1956-84) 10 S.C.N.D. 65; *Ojo v. the Queen* (1956-84) 10 S.C.N.D. 67; *Chingi v. The Queen* (1956-84) 10 S.C.N.D. 69; *Akinyede and Others v. Commissioner of Police* 1980 (2) N.C.R. 90; *Okon and Others v. The State* [1988] 1 N.W.L.R. (Pt. 69) 172; *Shazali v. The State* [1988] 5 N.W.L.R. (Pt. 93) 164; *Okoro v The State* [1988] 5 N.W.L.R. (Pt. 94) 255. *Mbele R. v. State* [1990] 4 N.W.L.R. (Pt. 145) 484; *Agenu v.* [1992] 7 N.W.L.R. (Pt. 256) 749; *Merotohum v. State* [1992] 7 N.W.L.R. (Pt. 254) 443; *Igboanugo v. State* (1992) 3 N.W.L.R. (Pt. 288) 176; *Oyediran v. Alebiosu* II (1992) 6 N.W.L.R. (Pt. 249) 550; *Ogunleye v. State* [1991] 3 N.W.L.R. (Pt. 177) 1; *Sambo v. State* [1993]6 N.W.L.R. (Pt. 300) 399; *Kanu v. State* [1993] 9 N.W.L.R. (Pt. 317) 304; *Amadi v. State* [1993] 8 N.W.L.R. (Pt. 314) 644; *Ekpe v. State* [1993]6 N.W.L.R. (Pt. 297) 79; *Ajilore v. State* [1993]4 N.W.L.R. (Pt. 289) 572; *Sanni v. State* [1993]6 N.W.L.R. (Pt. 285) 99; *Bassey v. State* [1993] 7 N.W.L.R. (Pt. 306) 469; *Uchegbu v. State* [1993] 8 N.W.L.R. (Pt. 309) 89.

Chapter 22

THE TAKING OF ORAL EVIDENCE AND THE EXAMINATION OF WITNESSES

Sections 180 to 224 of the Evidence Act.

Subject to the provisions of sections 182 and 183 of the Act, all oral evidence given in any proceedings must be given upon oath or affirmation administered in accordance with the provisions of the Oaths and Affirmation Act (S. 180). Where an oath has been duly administered and taken, the fact that the person to whom the same was administered had, at the time of taking such oat, no religious belief, does not for any purpose affect the validity of such oath (S. 181). Section 182 vests in the court the discretionary power to admit evidence not given upon oath, while section 183 deals with unsworn evidence of a child. Section 184 provides for evidence of first and second class chiefs.

The order in which witnesses are produced and examined will be regulated by the law and practice for the time being relating to civil and criminal procedure, and in the absence of any such law, by the discretion of the court (S. 185). By section 186, the court has the discretionary power to decide on the admissibility of evidence. Section 187 provides for the ordering of witnesses out of court and preventing communication with witnesses who are within the court building or its precincts awaiting examination.

The examination of a witness by the party who calls him is called his examination-in-chief. The examination of a witness by a party other than the party who calls him is called his cross-examination. Where a witness has been cross-examined and is then examined by the party who called him, such examination is called re-examination (S. 188). Witnesses shall be first examined-in-chief, then if any other party so desires, cross-examined, then, if the party calling him so desires, re-examined. The examination and cross-examination must relate to relevant facts, but the cross-examination need not be confined to the facts to which the witness testified on his examination-in-chief. The re-examination shall be directed to the explanation of matters referred to in cross-examination; and, if new matter is, by permission of the court, introduced in re-examination, the adverse party may further cross-examine upon that matter (S. 189).

While sections 190 and 191 provide for cross-examination by co-accused person, section 192 and 193 provide for production of documents without giving evidence and the cross-examination of person called to produce a document respectively. Section 194 deals with cross-examination of witnesses as to character and sections 195 to 197 provide for when leading questions are not allowed and when they can be allowed.

Section 198 deals with evidence as to matters in writing while sections 199 and 200 provide for cross-examination as to previous statements in writing and questions lawful in cross-examination. See also section 209 as it relates to section 190.

Section 201 vests in the court the discretionary power to decide whether a particular question shall be asked and when a witness will be compelled to answer it. By section 202, no question can be asked unless the person asking it has reasonable grounds for thinking that the imputation which it conveys is well founded. Section 203 sets out the procedure the court will adopt in case of question being asked without reasonable grounds. By section 204 and 205, the court is empowered to disallow indecent and scandalous questions and questions intended to insult or annoy a witness.

By section 206, the court can exclude evidence designed to contradict answers to questions testing the veracity of a witness. Sections 207 and 208 provide for a hostile witness and how far the party calling him can discredit him by way of cross-examination. Similarly, sections 210 and 212 deal with the impeachment of the credit of a witness, while section 211 deals with the cross-examination of prosecutrix in certain sexual offences. Sections 213 and 214 relate to the admissibility of questions tending to corroborate evidence of relevant fact and the proof of former statements of witness to corroborate later testimony as to same fact, respectively. Section 215 examines what matters may be proved in connection with proved statement relevant under the section.

By section 216, a witness may, while under examination, refresh his memory by referring to any writing made by himself or any other person. An expert may also refresh his memory by reference to professional treatises. Section 217 allows a witness to testify to facts mentioned in section 216 in certain circumstances. By section 218, any writing referred to in sections 126 and 127 must be produced and shown to the adverse party at his request, who has the option to cross-examine on it. While sections 219 and 221 enjoin a witness to produce a document in court, section 220 deals with instances when a document could be excluded on grounds of public interest. By section 222, a party who refuses to produce a document on notice cannot afterwards use the document as evidence without the consent of the other party or the order of the court.

Section 223 provides for the power of the court to put questions to witnesses and ask for the production of any document. Section 227 gives similar power to the jury or assessors as it relates to putting questions to witnesses. There is however no more jury trial in Nigeria.

In *Igwede and Others v.* R. (1959) 4 F.S.C. 104, the court would appear to have in mind the provision of section 184 when the issue arose on the right of the accused to call witnesses and the order of calling such witnesses, Brett, F.J. said at page 104: "There are two further matters, not affecting the merits of the applications, on which we would comment. The first concerns the evidence for the defence of Nwaleke Akpu, who was acquitted. He not only gave evidence himself but called two witnesses, one of them at least was a witness to material facts. But these witnesses gave their evidence before the accused himself, and while there is no statutory rule to prohibit this we think it desirable that the English practice should be followed, under which if an accused person intends both to give evidence himself and to call witnesses as to fact, his evidence is normally taken before that of his witnesses".

On the duty of the prosecutor to call witnesses, see *Okonofua v. The State* (1981) 6-7 S.C. 1; *Udofia v. The State* (1981) 11-12 S.C. 49; *Saidu v. the State* (1992) 4 S.C. 41; *Ereku v. The Queen* (1959) W.N.L.R. 77; *Opayemi v. The State* [1985] 2 N.W.L.R. (Pt. 5) 101; *Peba v. The State* (1979) 1 F.C.A. 185.

The Taking of Oral Evidence: The Oath

In *Chief Nwizuk and Others v. Chief Eneyok and Others* (1953) 14 W.A.C.A. 354, after the evidence the Judge went to inspect the land in dispute in the presence of two plaintiffs as representing the plaintiffs and of a defendant representing the defendants. There the defendant admitted that some of the evidence given for them regarding some at least of the Islands was false. In his judgment dismissing the plaintiffs' claim the

Judge gave an account of his inspection and mentioned the said admission. The plaintiffs appealed, arguing that it was a mistake of law to take into account statements which were not made on oath. It was held that the court did not cease to be a court when on inspection and the statements were as much oral admissions by a party in court as if they had been made in a court-room, and could be taken into account as such.

The Taking of Oral Evidence: Some Special Provisions

In *Aiyewunmi v. Commissioner of Police* (1948) 12 W.A.C.A. 388, in a criminal trial, ten out of the fifteen witnesses gave evidence in the Yoruba and Hausa languages and there was no record of any sworn interpreter. Verity, C.J. said at page 388: "... there is no rule of law in Nigeria, either statutory or at common law, requiring that an interpreter should be sworn, and that, while it is a most salutary rule of practice that interpreters should invariably be sworn, the fact that the interpreter has not been sworn is not itself an illegality involving the quashing of the conviction".

Examination-in-Chief

In *Garba and Another v. The Queen* (1959)4 F.S.C. 162, after suffering an attack which ultimately caused his death, the victim told the person who found him injured that he was going to die, that he had been beaten and that one Momo had instigated the beating. The evidence as to the deceased statement of impending death was extracted by a leading question. No objection to the form of the question was taken until the question had been put and answered. It was held that the trial Judge rightly exercised his discretion in allowing the question to be put, in the particular circumstances, and in those circumstances, in admitting the answer in evidence.

Hostile Witnesses

The deposition (or statement made on oath) at a committal proceedings of a witness who subsequently gives evidence at a criminal trial may be used to discredit his testimony if the trial court allows such a witness to be treated as hostile, but they cannot be substituted for his evidence at the trial: *Jizurumba v. The State* (1976) 3 S.C. 89.

The duty of the prosecution to treat its witness as hostile is discretionary. If the prosecution have information in their possession which shows that the evidence which a witness called for the prosecution has given is in flat contradiction of a previous statement which he has made and so entitles the prosecution to cross-examine they should apply for leave to cross-examine and not leave it to the Judge to do so, because it is counsel's duty to cross-examine in such circumstances. If he has not done so, the Judge has to do it. But that is not right, because it may look as if the Judge is taking sides, but he cannot help intervening in such circumstances, because it is his duty to see that justice is done: *Arehia v. The State* (1982) 4 S.C. 78.

The effect of allowing a party producing a witness to impeach the credit of a hostile witness by showing that the witness made statement inconsistent with the evidence on oath is to make the witness unreliable: *Aderemi v. The State* (1975) 9-11 S.C. 115.

Cross-Examination

The purpose of cross-examination is to demolish an opponent's case and to establish one's own case thereby. Facts elicited in cross-examination go towards the credibility of the witnesses if such facts contradict an earlier statement by the witness cross-examined. Such facts also affect the weight of evidence of the witness: *Adeleke v. Aserifa* [1986] 3 N.W.L.R. (Pt. 30) 575. The aims of cross-examination are either to obtain from one's adversary facts favourable to a party's case or to weaken and dilute the strength of the evidence in-chief: *Ajao Others v. Alao and Others* [1986] 5 N.W.L.R. (Pt. 45) 802. The use of cross-examination is to contradict, destroy or water down the case of an adversary and a party's case is made on his pleading and evidence in-chief, not in cross-examination: *Onwumere v. Agwunendu and Others* [1987] 3 N.W.L.R. (Pt. 62) 673.

When a prosecution witness produces a statement of the accused purporting to show a state of affairs different from that put forward by the defence, it is the duty of counsel for the defence to cross-examine hat witness with a view to showing that the statement was incorrectly recorded. By failing to do so he is, by implication discrediting the defence which he is supposed to be putting forward: *The Queen v. Eguabor* [1962] 1 All N.L.R. 287. It is the duty of the prosecution to cross-examine an accused person if he wants the court to disbelieve his evidence: *Nkwa v. Commissioner of Police* 1977 N.N.L.R. 98.

Where accused person giving evidence had made himself liable to cross-examination as to his character or convictions under exception (section 159(d)(ii) of the Evidence Act) by giving evidence against another person charged with the same offence the Judge had no overriding discretion to allow or disallow such cross-examination and it might be put as a matter of right: *Anyanwu v. The Queen* [1963] 1 All N.L.R. 273.

By the provision of sections 198, 205 and 208 of the Evidence Act, a witness may be cross-examined as to previous statement made by him in writing or reduced into writing by the police or anyone else without such writing shown to him or being produced if the purpose of the cross-examination is to shake the credit of the witness or contradict him. Where the witness admits making the statement, it becomes unnecessary to produce the statement: *Arehia v. The State* (1982) 4 S.C. 78. See also *Locknan v. The State* (1972) 5 S.C. 22; *Akande v. Adike and Another* (1980) 3 C.A. 189; In *Re Bakare* [1969] 1 All N.L.R. 77; *Okwa v. Iwerebor* [1969] 1 All N.L.R. 87.

Power of the Judge, the Jury or Assessors to Put Questions to Witnesses

In *Agbaje v. The Republic* [1964] 1 All N.L.R. 295, it was held that the traditional function of a Jury to decide on the evidence brought out before them by the contesting parties and in the exercise of his discretion to decide that questions are proper the Judge should discourage a Jury from asking questions other than those designed to clarify answers given to questions asked by one of the parties. It is submitted that since Jury trial is no more in vogue in Nigeria, the role earlier played by the Jury is now taken over by the Judge. In *The Queen v. Aderogba* (960) 5 F.S.C. 212, the appellant was on trial with another person who, in the course of the prosecution case, was discharged. When the case for the prosecution was closed, the trial Judge thought, in view of the appellant's statement, that it was necessary to call the person discharged as a witness, and, in spite of the objection of the defence, purporting to act under section 200 of the Criminal Procedure Act, had him examined by counsel for the Crown and cross-examined by counsel for the defence, and later himself put questions to the witness.

HELD:

> The trial Judge erred in calling a witness to help the Crown, and which is not the object of section 200 of the Criminal Procedure Act.

In *Akunfe v. The State* [1988] 3 N.W.L.R. (Pt.85) 729, where the learned trial Judge asked too many probing and searching questions (questions which were in excess of those asked by the prosecuting counsel) which were not confined to the facts which the parties themselves placed before the court, and questions which essentially resulted in the conviction of the accused with murder, the Supreme Court had no difficulty in quashing the conviction. The learned trial Judge was held to be biased. Nnaemeka-Agu, J.S.C., in delivering the lead judgment, said at page 742: "Let me say straightaway that from what I have said above, it cannot be rightly said that the learned Judge did not ask too many questions. He did. Also, as I have stated, those questions were very probing and searching and were not even confined to facts which the parties themselves had placed before the court. They were certainly not limited to questions intended and designed to clear ambiguities or to fill up gaps". Nnamani, J.S.C. also said at page 754: "It seems to me that the learned trial Judge indeed descended into the arena. In our system of criminal adjudication the Judge has to hold the balance between the prosecution and the defence". While Eso, J.S.C. held in the case that a trial Judge is not a dummy, recording evidence without uttering a word, he was of the view that the learned trial Judge took over the entire prosecution of the case. See also *Uso v. Commissioner of Police* (1972) 11 S.C. 37 at 46; *Aermacchi and Others v. A.I.C. Limited* [1986] 2 N.W.L.R. (Pt. 23) 443.

In *R.v. Edem and Others* (1943) 9 W.A.C.A. 25, the appellants were charged with murder. It was alleged for the prosecution that the motive for the murder was the belief that the murdered man had caused the death of another person by means of witchcraft. The trial Judge called a Native Chief, who had been sitting in court, to testify as to his knowledge of native custom on the question thus raised. It was held that the question relating to native custom arose ex improviso, and the trial was correct in calling further evidence.

See further *Evoyona v. Daregba* [1968] 1 All N.L.R. 192; *Omoregbe v. Lawani* (1980) 3-4 S.C. 108; *Ordor v. Nwosu* (1974) 12 S.C. 103; *Tabba v. Lababedi* (1974) 4 S.C. 139; *Ogbodu v. Odogha* [1967] 1All N.L.R. 139; *Elike v. Nwankwoala* (1956-84) 1 S.C.N.D. 174; *Dauda v. Ogbeki* (1956-84) 10

S.C.N.D. 186; *Balla and Another v. Commissioner of Police* [1973] N.M.L.R. 61; *The State v. Amboli* 1972 N.N.L.R. 101; *Bell-Gam v. Bell-Gam* [1965] 1 All N.L.R. 106; *R.v. Kuree* (1941) 7 W.A.C.A. 175.

Impeaching the Credit of a Witness

In *Inspector-General of Police v. Ewekay* 1957 L.L.R. 11, de Comarmand, C.J. said: "I have often had occasion to direct attention to the point that although the production of a previous extra-judicial contradicting statement may destroy or nullify what a witness has said in court, yet it is not evidence of the truth of the facts contained in the extra-judicial statements unless the witness admits that he has tried to mislead the court and then swears to the truth of the facts contained in his previous statements (even where this is done, the court may deem it safer to reject the evidence altogether)".

In *Adisa v. The State* [1964] 1 All N.L.R. 200, it was held that section 205 of the Evidence Act excludes the calling of evidence to contradict the answer given by a witness to questions which are relevant only so far as they tend to shake his credit by injuring his character, but sections 207, 208 and 209(c) clearly and expressly permit the calling of evidence to impeach a witness' credit by proof of former statements inconsistent with any part of his evidence which is liable to be contradicted, as long as the witness has been cross-examined about the statements. Section 198 is to the like effect.

In *Amao v. Oyewale* (1956-84) 10 S.C.N.D. 182, it was held that a party who wishes to impeach the veracity of a witness may refer to a previous statement made by the witness and give him an opportunity of admitting it out of explaining what he meant.

In *Federal Housing Authority v. Asanmer and Other* (1986) 1 N.W.L.R. (Pt. 17) 533, it was held that a party who intends to impeach a witness is bound to give the witness, while in the box, an opportunity of making an explanation to cases in which the witness has not been cross-examined.

Refreshing Memory

In *Amoo and Others v. The Queen* (1956) 4 F.S.C. 113, the trial Judge allowed a witness's memory to be refreshed by the reading to him of his deposition at the preliminary investigation, that deposition having been taken some four months after the incidents to which the witness deposed. It was held that the deposition could not be brought within section 215(1) of the Evidence Act.

In *Nwanyanwu v. The State* (1956-84) 10 S.C.N.D. 183, it was held that a witness cannot refresh his memory by referring to his earlier deposition. And in the *Queen v. Thomas* (1956-84) 10 S.C.N.D. 187, it was held that it is improper for a trial court to allow a witness, when giving his evidence, to refresh his memory from a statement he had previously given to the police.

Production of Documents.

In *Onwuamaka v. Okolie.* (1955-56) W.R.N.L.R. 159, a person who was called by the respondent to produce the record of previous proceedings, which record was required in the suit, went to the witness-box and tendered the record on oath. The learned magistrate refused the appellant the constitutional right to cross-examine him on the ground that he was called merely to produce a document. Rejecting the procedure adopted by the learned trial Magistrate, Onyeama, Ag J. (as he then was) said: "It is to be observed that section 192 of the Evidence Ordinance speaks of 'a person summoned' and not of 'a witness'. I am of the opinion, in view of section 179 of the Evidence Ordinance, that a witness under the Evidence Ordinance is anyone who gives evidence in any proceedings upon oath or affirmation, and by virtue of sections 181 and 182 of the Ordinance. It follows from this that the person who put in the certified copy of the Native Court proceedings, upon being sworn, became a witness for all purposes and was therefore liable to cross-examination.

In *The Queen v. The Administrator, Western Region, Ex parte Bamgbedu* 1962 N.R.N.L.R. 344, the Minster objected to the production of certain documents relating to the appointment of a chief on grounds of state privilege within the meaning of section 219. The learned trial Judge held the view that the claim to privilege was an abuse of the power conferred under section 219, Charles J. said at page 350: "Having looked at these documents, the least about their assertion of the right to exclude them the better. The responsible Minister who signed the certificate for exclusion appears, putting it most favourable to him, to have been the victim of irresponsible advice".

In *African Press Ltd. and Another v. Attorney-General of Western Nigeria* [1965] 1 All N.L.R. 12, the Attorney-General prosecuted the defendants for publishing a seditious article. The article accused the Government of squandermania, misuse of public money and fraudulent diversion of it to private purpose. On a request by the appellants for the production of the official files on industrial projects, the Minster entered a certificate under section 219 of the Evidence Act that their production was contrary to the public interest. The Supreme Court held that the appellants could not, with propriety, demand a wholesome production of the files and were not, on balance, prejudiced by the Minister's refusal to produce. On the wider issue of the right of the accused to fair trial *vis-a-vis* the Minister's right to withhold production of official documents, Brett, J.S.C. said at page 16: "It remains the duty of the court to uphold the right to a fair trial, and if in a criminal case there are reasonable grounds for supposing that the evidence of such a certificate might have prejudiced the accused in making his defence, the court is bound to say that the prosecution has not proved its case beyond reasonable doubt. See *also Moranu v. Benson and Others* [1966] N.M.L.R. 166; *Apampa and Another v. Balogun, supra; Johnson v. Sarkia* [1962] 2 All N.L.R. 273.

Chapter 23

THE SERVICE IN ONE STATE OF WITNESS SUMMONS AND OTHERS PROCESSES ISSUED IN ANOTHER STATE

Section 229 and 230

When a subpoena or summons has been issued by any court in any state or part of the Federation in the exercise of its civil jurisdiction in accordance with any power conferred by law jurisdiction in accordance with any power conferred by law requiring any person to appear and give evidence or to produce books or documents in any proceeding, such subpoena or summons may upon proof that the testimony of such person or the production of such books or documents is necessary in the interest of justice by leave of such court on such terms as the court may impose be served on such person in any other state or part of the Federation (S. 229)1).

If a person upon whom a subpoena or summons has been served in accordance with subsection (1) fails to attend at the time and place mentioned in such subpoena or summons, such court may on proof that the subpoena or summons, was duly served such person and that the sum prescribed by law was tendered to him for his expenses, issue such warrant for the apprehension of such person as such court might have issued if the subpoena or summons had bee served in the state or part of the Federation in which it was issued (S. 229(2). See also S. 229 (3).

Where it appears to any court of a State or part of the Federation that the attendance before the court of a person who is undergoing sentence in any State or part of the Federation is necessary for the purpose of obtaining evidence in any proceeding before the court, the court may issue an order directed to the superintendent of officer in charge of the prison or place where the person is undergoing sentence requiring him to produce the person at the time and place specified in the order (S. 230(1).

Any order made under the section may be served upon the superintendent or offer to whom it is directed in whatever State or part of the Federation he may be and he will thereupon produce in such custody as he thinks fit the person referred to in the order at the time and place specified therein (S. 230). The court before which any person is produced in accordance with an order issued under the section may make such order as to the costs of compliance with the with the order as to the court may seem just (S. 230 (3).

Ben Obi Nwabueze and Another v. Justice Obi Okoye (1988) 4 N.W.L.R. (Pt. 91) 664

The plaintiff commenced the suit against the defendants in the High Court of Anambra State for damages for libel allegedly contained in a book written by the 1st defendant but published and sold by the 2nd defendant within Anambra State, throughout Nigeria and even overseas. The address for service indorsed on the writ are within Lagos State. After the issuance of the writ, the plaintiff by an *ex parte* application obtained leave of the court to serve the defendants with the writ of summons and other processes in the suit by substituted means by sending the documents by registered post to the defendants' addresses as shown on the motion. The 1st defendant's address was then shown to be within Lagos State, while 2nd defendant's address was stated to be within Lagos state and Imo State. The defendants were thereafter accordingly served whereupon they both applied to the High Court to set aside the issue ad service of the writ of summons. The learned trial Judge ruled that the writ of summons was properly issued but that the service of the writ did not comply with section 97 of the Sheriffs and Civil Process Act, 1958.

HELD:

The Service of the writ was null and void as it did not comply with the Sheriff and Civil Process Act. Since there was no valid writ of summons, there was in law nothing to serve, and it was not possible even to comply with the provisions of the Sheriffs and Civil Process Act. See also *Ukoh v. Akatu* (1974) 4 E.C.S.L.R. 202.

www.ingramcontent.com/pod-product-compliance
Lightning Source LLC
Chambersburg PA
CBHW031323230926
51848CB00001B/64